BLACK PROPAGANDA

BLACK PROPAGANDA

IN THE SECOND WORLD WAR

STANLEY NEWCOURT-NOWODWORSKI

First published 2005, this edition published 2020

The History Press
97 St George's Place, Cheltenham,
Gloucestershire, GL50 3QB
www.thehistorypress.co.uk

British Library Cataloguing in Publication Data.
A catalogue record for this book is available from the British Library.

ISBN 978 0 7509 9515 3

Typesetting and origination by The History Press
Printed and bound in Great Britain by TJ International Ltd

Contents

Acknowledgements 6
Preface 7

1 Psychological Warfare Since Sun Tzu 11
2 German Black Propaganda 35
3 British Black Propaganda 74
4 Sefton Delmer Creates a Radically New Concept 99
5 Black Rumours and Black Leaflets 144
6 Polish Operation 'N' – Humble Beginnings 185
7 Operation 'N' – Rise and Fall 208
8 British–Polish Black Cooperation 241
9 Why Did We Achieve So Little? 267

Glossary 317
Notes 324
Bibliography 338
Main Primary Sources 346
Index 348

Acknowledgements

I would like to express my gratitude to the devoted and enthusiastic staff of archives and libraries in Britain as well as in Germany and in Poland, without whose expert assistance my research would have taken much, much longer. My special thanks go to Professor Sir Martin Gilbert for his encouragement, to Dr rer. pol. h. c. Klaus Kirchner of the Ludwig Maximilians University in Munich for pointing my research in the right direction at the very beginning and for reading the first chapters, to Dr K. Stoliński of the Polish Underground Movement Study Trust in London for reading the typescript and for rectifying many errors, to John Montgomery BA, the RUSI Librarian, who was never too busy to help me with my problems and to Radio Stuttgart for information on 'the Traitors of Stuttgart'.

Preface

The poster, about 40 3 20cm, was printed in bold, black letters on red paper. The message, in German, was short: 'The *Gestapo* betrayed the nation and the armed forces. Death to the traitors!' It was signed, 'An old German soldier.'

The boy had a box of drawing pins and pinned the poster to the trunk of a chestnut tree, so that it faced the road. The last pin went in as quickly as he could manage: he could hear a motor vehicle approaching and, since the chances were that it was German, he thought it best to take cover.

The place? Kielce, a town in German-occupied Poland. The date? A day in early summer 1944. The boy? I was the boy, fifteen at the time.

The vehicle was indeed a German army lorry. The only person in the cab was the driver. He stopped opposite the tree, and got out to read the poster. He must have been short-sighted. Then he looked around, read it again and drove away. He did not tear it down.

I was overjoyed: so our propaganda, code-named *Akcja* 'N' (Operation 'N'), which was aimed at the Germans and made to look like a product of a German resistance organisation, was not being rejected. I realised, of course, that a single such event could not be regarded as proof, but surely that soldier was not the only one in the Kielce garrison who had doubts about his country's leadership. There must be more like him.

But what about those who did not have such doubts? Would our posters and leaflets sway them our way? Or were we wasting our efforts preaching to the converted, while the others, the hard core, remained immune to our attempts to make them see the light? What were the practical effects – if any – of Operation 'N'?

These questions remained with me for over fifty years, but it was only after my retirement that I found time to look for the answers. This book is the result.

Displaying the *Gestapo* posters in the summer of 1944 was not my first contribution to anti-German propaganda. My involvement in such operations had begun three months earlier. I was at the time a troop leader in the clandestine Scouts – the *Szare Szeregi*. Clandestine because all youth organisations were banned at the very beginning of the occupation. During the interwar period Polish Scouting followed the original ideals of Baden-Powell: patriotism and service to one's country were the prime duties of a Scout, rather than the post-First World War nebulous service to mankind. These principles were especially relevant under the German occupation. My troop was assigned to Street Propaganda: painting or chalking of anti-German slogans. If caught, the chances of staying alive were negligible.

My father was roughly aware of what I was doing in the Resistance, although, at the time, I had no idea what he was doing. (In fact, as I discovered later, he was in charge of a 'legalisation' cell, which provided false identities to people wanted by the *Gestapo*.) One day, he said to me, 'All these slogans are fine, but our morale does not need boosting. Why don't you target the Jerries for a change? In 1918 there was a very popular slogan among the German troops: *Waffen Nieder!* ['Down arms!'] What about resurrecting it?'

I thought it was a brilliant idea but I was not sure that my superiors would approve. So, in an uncharacteristic surge of insubordination, I spoke to the boys of all three patrols that made up my troop. I explained that the proposed chalking of *Waffen Nieder!* all over our town would be our private venture and that there was no obligation to participate. They all volunteered.

The operation went off without a hitch. The following day I complained forcefully to my commander that somebody was encroaching on my troop's monopoly of street propaganda. A couple of days later he admitted that nobody knew who the perpetrators were, although our intelligence people calculated that between fifteen and twenty people took part. They were right – we were eighteen in number.

A few days later I confessed. The rebuke was relatively mild, with no disciplinary action, although I was reproached for not submitting this idea through proper channels, as it would have been given full support. A week later, all available troops were sent out into the streets of Kielce to cover the walls with *Waffen Nieder!*

Under the conditions of a brutal occupation, when everybody had to face the exceptionally grim reality, children grew up very rapidly. It would be an exaggeration to speak of a direct transition from babyhood to adulthood, but our childhood was certainly shortened by two or three years – perhaps more. At the age of fifteen, my psychological make-up and my sense of responsibilities were those of an adult. After the war, when mortal dangers were no longer lurking round every corner, many of us, consciously or unconsciously, tried to recoup those lost years. At the age of nineteen I was certainly not as serious-minded as I was at fifteen.

I had had a German governess from the age of seven, so by 1939 my German was flawless. In occupied Poland opportunities to learn about the German character as well as the language were plentiful. Needless to say, one could not register many positive aspects of that character. Then, during the last six months of the war, I met Germans of a different type.

In September 1944 I found myself in the Rheinland in a forced labour camp. After two unsuccessful escapes (I was trying to get back to Poland), I managed to convince the *Schupo* (*Schutzpolizei*, the ordinary police) who caught me, that I had come to Germany as a volunteer. I was assigned to work for a gardener and I entered a different world. I lived with his family, I became a member of the household and I participated in their daily life. They were quite different from the Germans I had encountered previously.

So, through these experiences, I came to acquire a certain understanding both of the then *Zeitgeist* and of the German character, which was of considerable help in my research for this book, particularly when visiting German archives, and trying to understand German reactions to Allied propaganda.

I have tried throughout to refrain from making moral or ethical judgements. I leave this to the reader – should he or she be so inclined.

Chapter One

Psychological Warfare Since Sun Tzu

To most people 'propaganda' is – and not without reason – a dirty word. It implies lies, misrepresentation, manipulation. Consequently it evokes negative emotions. 'Information', on the other hand, sounds better: it seems to imply honesty, although it does not follow that it must be objective *per se*. Skilful selection of information can also distort the truth. As Aldous Huxley wrote in *Brave New World*: 'The greatest triumphs of propaganda have been accomplished, not by doing something, but by refraining from doing. By simply not mentioning certain subjects, by lowering … an iron curtain between the masses and such facts or arguments as the local political bosses regard as undesirable, totalitarian propagandists have influenced opinion more effectively than they could have done by the most eloquent denunciations.'[1]

Generally speaking, our enemies – the bad guys – indulge in propaganda. If we are American, we conduct 'Psychological Operations' (PSYOPS*), 'Morale Operations' and 'Psychological Warfare' or, if we are British, 'Political Warfare'.

---

* Term invented in 1945.

Now we also hear of 'Information Operations'. These terms are useful, as they get away from the moral ambiguities inherent in the word 'propaganda', but they are not fully equivalent.

Political warfare, the most comprehensive concept, is the application of propaganda to the needs of total warfare.[2] When this term was first introduced, it did not always present an advantage.[3] Ministers and officials, on whose goodwill the Political Warfare Executive (PWE, responsible for black propaganda) depended, did not appreciate the difference between propaganda and political warfare and assumed that it was a blatant attempt by the propagandists in PWE to inflate their own importance.

According to Bruce Lockhart, the wartime director of PWE, political warfare practises every form of overt and covert non-military attack. It seeks, by special knowledge, to anticipate and forestall the intentions of the enemy; to commit him to military objectives which appeal to the enemy public but which his forces cannot fulfil; to undermine his morale by secret broadcasting stations, allegedly operated by dissatisfied enemy subjects inside his own territory; and by other 'black' operations that can be classified as subversion and deception. Its main purpose is to soften the way and make easier the task of the armed forces, or even to achieve military gains without the use of military force. It begins long before the declaration of war and does not stop with overt hostilities. In addition to propaganda, political warfare includes diplomatic action and economic warfare.[4]

Since this book is not a study of the last two aspects, the term psychological warfare seems more apposite. The credit for coining this term goes to J.F.C. Fuller,* who thought that in the future, traditional means of warfare might be replaced by a purely psychological warfare, wherein instead of using

---

* A distinguished author of books on military history, strategy and tactics.

weapons, the corruption of the human reason, the dimming of the human intellect and the disintegration of the moral and spiritual life of one nation would be accomplished by the influence of the will of another. The aim of psychological warfare could also be defined as to 'create attitudes and behavioural patterns in enemy, friendly or neutral target audiences that will assist in achieving political or military objectives'.[5]

The aim of propaganda is to make others think and act in a particular way. Hans Fritzsche, the top German wartime radio commentator, described it as 'the art to wake up in other people thoughts and feelings that would never come to the surface without such prompting'.[6] His chief, Dr Goebbels, defined propaganda in a more romantic vein as 'the art of listening to the soul of the people',[7] failing to mention that he reserved for himself the right to determine the contents of that soul.

It would be very difficult for propaganda to be effective if, rather than exploiting an existing situation (that does not have to be present in the conscious mind of the target), it tried to create a totally new situation. But it aims at more than this: its ultimate goal is either to force the target into action or to make him stop doing something. This is called 'operational propaganda'. Often, especially in the case of black operations, it has to be preceded by 'preparational propaganda', which aims to produce the right frame of mind in the target. The definition of partisan warfare as 'death by a thousand cuts' could be applied to this process.

A member of the Polish Resistance (who played his part in the P1* team) remembers what he was taught during his training:

---

* A Polish-language black radio station called *Świt*, operated by the Political Warfare Executive.

> When you are engaged in propaganda, you must remember two rules: you must not speak the whole truth and you must not speak what you feel. When we say that you must not speak the whole truth it does not mean that you may lie. You should never tell lies. If you do, you will be inevitably caught out. You must select those parts of the truth which you need to achieve the desired effect. When we say that you must not speak what you feel, it's to prevent you from falling into the delusion that your targets feel the same way as you do. You must concentrate on understanding how your targets think and feel.[8]

There are, generally speaking, three types, or colours, of propaganda – white, black and grey. One should not fall into the trap of thinking that these colours indicate the degree of veracity of the materials being disseminated. Colour – white, grey or black – only indicates the degree to which the identity of the originator is disclosed. In practice, effective propaganda is usually 95 per cent true. The originator hopes that the remaining, vital 5 per cent, hidden by a thick coating of obvious truths, will be swallowed by the addressee. Credibility is a *sine qua non* of propaganda's acceptance.

White propaganda is an open activity where the originator does not disguise his identity: he speaks for his government. Usually he concentrates on the positive aspects of his own side. The safe conduct passes dropped during the Second World War to enemy front-line troops, inviting them to surrender and guaranteeing proper treatment, were a good example of White.

Black propaganda, on the other hand, hides its origin behind false signatures, and usually purports to be produced by clandestine organisations within the enemy country, not necessarily totally opposed to their government. Sometimes it pretends to come from the target audience's own authorities. It concentrates on the failings of the enemy government and, even more, on the failings of the members of the ruling elite. The poster I pinned on the chestnut tree in Kielce in the summer of 1944 was a typical piece of black propaganda.

Grey propaganda is anonymous; it bears no signature and leaves the target guessing its origin. The best-known example is the *Nachrichten für die Truppe* ('News for the Troops') daily newspaper produced by PWE in 1944 and dropped by aircraft to the German troops on the Western Front.

The inherent weakness of white propaganda is the self-evident fact that it is enemy propaganda. It has the daunting task of overcoming the mistrust and suspicions of the target audience, before its message stands a chance of being accepted as credible. The camouflaged or false origins of grey and black propaganda, on the other hand, delay their identification as enemy propaganda, so that the effectiveness of any countermeasures is unavoidably reduced.

The success of black propaganda depends on the complete concealment of its true origin. White propaganda is unable to access and bring out any feelings of resentment towards the authorities that might lurk in the dark recesses of the enemy soldier's mind. This a job for Black. The danger, however, is that detection of the true origin of such propaganda may not only evoke a hatred of the originator for having slyly invaded the target's mind, but will also reduce the effectiveness of any parallel white propaganda.[9] The latter's efforts to convince him of its honesty and truthfulness could now be in vain.

Unfortunately, the term 'black propaganda' carries a double negative charge – *propaganda* plus *black*, as in *black market*. Germans solved this problem by coining the term *getarnte Propaganda* (camouflaged propaganda). They also spoke of *geistige Kriegführung* (intellectual warfare) and *untergrund Propaganda* (underground propaganda). Russians call it *maskirovka*, a word also derived from 'camouflage', but embracing any action aimed at deceiving the enemy. They also invented a related term, 'disinformation'. Perhaps we should call it 'deception propaganda'. Another possibility is offered by the terms 'overt' and 'covert' propaganda, with grey sometimes defined (uncharitably) as 'poorly disguised black'.[10]

Psychological warfare, and especially its black aspects, have always been treated by all governments as State secrets. An impregnable Chinese Wall ensured its total isolation from the departments responsible for internal propaganda, one's own population being denied any knowledge of what was being said to the enemy.

It is difficult to classify some examples of propaganda. For instance, Hitler's *casus belli* for the attack on Poland on 1 September 1939 was an ostensibly Polish armed raid the evening before on a German radio station, close to the Polish border. In fact, it was carried out by SS troops in Polish army uniforms.* Corpses were procured from a nearby concentration camp. Was this political warfare, psychological warfare, black propaganda or, perhaps, 'black warfare'? Or the forged food ration cards dropped over Germany by the RAF? Psychological or economic warfare? Or in 1982, the British broadcasts in Spanish to Argentinian soldiers in the Falklands, just giving them news from home with a devastating effect on their morale?[11] How should we classify this kind of operation?

---

* According to the testimony of General Lahousen (*Abwehr*) at the Nuremberg Trial, the *SS*-men who wore Polish uniforms were 'put out of the way'.

A straitjacket of strict classifications would not be very helpful in discussing black propaganda. Its basic characteristic, in addition to subversive intent, is the false signature. But not always. For instance, the British-based and British-run Polish-language radio station *Świt*, which openly represented the Polish Resistance, was nevertheless regarded as a black station, because its location was disguised. It pretended to broadcast from occupied Poland but was, in fact, situated near Bletchley. So perhaps we should widen the characterisation of black operations by adding to subversiveness not necessarily a false originator, but any attribute calculated to mislead the enemy.

A good introduction to psychological warfare, although this term is not used there, can be found in Hitler's *Mein Kampf*, written while he was imprisoned after the failed *putsch* of 1923. It is certainly not a literary masterpiece; a lot of it is a hotchpotch of ideas that had been cropping up in Germany since the mid-nineteenth century. Hitler did not attempt to conceal his programme; on the contrary, he gave notice of his intentions. One could say that he bared his soul. He devoted an entire chapter to propaganda, especially war propaganda, specifying its rules.[12] He did not claim to have invented these rules; he freely admitted that he had formulated them on the basis of his observation of marxist and British propaganda during the First World War. Propaganda must be a means, he wrote, never an end. It should address itself not to the elites but to the masses. It must appeal to their emotions, rather than to their reason. Its intellectual level must correspond to the lowest mental common denominator of the target public. Propaganda must be confined to a few bare essentials, which should be persistently repeated and, ominously: 'all humane and aesthetic considerations must be set aside'. He quoted von

Moltke,* who wrote that since in war it is essential to bring the matter to a rapid close, the most ruthless methods of fighting are, at the same time, the most humane. According to Hitler, the propagandist must adopt a one-sided attitude towards every problem that he has to deal with, and must never admit that he might be wrong.

Tuning a propaganda campaign to the lowest mental common denominator of the target public, however, does not guarantee that this group will be the most receptive. For instance, after the Second World War communist propaganda made very little headway in the case of simple east European peasants, whose religious beliefs became their near-impenetrable shield. Addressing propaganda to amorphous masses may produce spectacular results, but in the case of black propaganda it is more effective when addressed to relatively small, specific groups, appealing to their common self-interest. BBC broadcasts and RAF leaflets could never do that.

In a pre-war conversation with Sefton Delmer, who became the father of British black propaganda, Hitler said that inside every man lurks a *Schweinehund* ('bastard') who should be propaganda's main target.[13] Delmer based his black propaganda techniques on this principle, and became a worthy heir of Lord Northcliffe, who, during the First World War (ably assisted by H.G. Wells), perfected British psychological warfare first against Austria-Hungary and then against the *Wehrmacht* and the German civilian population.

Hitler rated Northcliffe's psychological warfare very highly, main-taining that Germany was beaten by propaganda, rather than in the field. This theory was first propounded in the

---

* Prolific writer on the theory of warfare and the Chief of the German and Prussian General Staff 1858–88.

early 1920s by Ludendorff* and became the official German line during the inter-war years. In Germany this encouraged a serious study of the theory of propaganda. During those years, twice as many books on propaganda were published in Germany as in Britain, France and the USA combined. It also encouraged many people in Britain to believe that the next war could be won by propaganda alone. They were to be bitterly disappointed. It is now generally acknowledged that propaganda – of any colour – cannot be relied upon to produce miracles on its own; to have a chance of being effective it must be used in conjunction with other weapons.

Since Hitler wrote *Mein Kampf*, the principles of propaganda have been expanded. It is now generally accepted that it should be aimed at both issues and personalities, and that it should be disguised. Rather than create new doubts and controversies, it must take advantage of existing ones, approaching them preferably in an oblique manner. It must be dynamic, responding to developments instantly.[14] It should not use abstracts like 'patriotism', 'freedom' or 'hope'. Its message should be concrete and, ideally, combine social and selfish elements. For example, 'Your cattle have been taken away because Ruritania is enslaved.'[15] It will be more effective if it is addressed to a small specific group rather than to a large amorphous mass, since the self-interest of a small group is easier to identify and invoke.

The importance of psychology in warfare was recognised long before Hitler. The earliest-known military commentator, the Chinese general Sun Tzu, wrote 2,500 years ago: 'Attacking does not merely consist in assaulting walled cities or striking at an army in battle array; it must include the

---

* General Erich Ludendorff, a brilliant tactician, was von Hindenburg's deputy.

art of assailing the enemy's mental equilibrium ... to fight and conquer in all your battles is not supreme excellence; supreme excellence consists in breaking the enemy's resistance without fighting.'[16] One of his main 'force multipliers' were psychological operations aimed at reducing the enemy's will to fight: spreading false rumours and misleading information, corrupting and subverting officials, creating internal discord.

Cicero maintained that there was nothing more glorious than to subjugate people's minds by the power of one's words, making them act according to one's will. Twenty centuries later Lenin was praising 'psychological warfare, wherein weapons are not even used on the battlefield, but instead ... the disintegration of the moral and spiritual fibre of one nation by the will of another is accomplished'.[17] He thought that of all the genres of literature, the most important was propaganda leaflets. He was of the opinion that military operations should be delayed until the morale of the enemy had been so reduced that the final blow could be delivered quickly and decisively. In practice it did not always work that way. During the Second World War Anglo-American propaganda directed at the German soldier began to have an effect, albeit a limited one, only when it became obvious to all that Germany could not possibly win the war. The effect of Soviet propaganda on the German soldier was negligible.

Some of Sun Tzu's ideas were adopted successfully 1,500 years later by Genghis Khan. During his reign, the first two or three cities taken at the beginning of a campaign would be routinely looted and torched and all the inhabitants killed. Then the Mongols made sure that news of what had happened to those who did not surrender on sight preceded their advance, as did rumours of the overwhelming numerical superiority of their forces. Not many cities on their list of targets dared to resist. Ghosts of Genghis Khan and of his hordes still haunt the people of central Europe.

According to the German propaganda expert, Eugen Hadamovsky, propaganda and terror are not opposites, and violence can be an integral part of propaganda.[18] Social-revolutionaries coined the term 'propaganda of the deed', which referred to any violent action aimed at lowering the enemy's morale, be it the assassination of the leader, the torching of a town or the taking of an emotionally significant city. Today we would not regard the laying waste of a city as an act of propaganda. It is a weapon of terror, designed to break the adversary's will to resist. As such it could be, nevertheless, included in the psychological warfare armoury, although its effectiveness cannot be guaranteed. During the Second World War the Germans executed millions of people in occupied countries, but did not manage to break the resistance movements, and air raids on towns carried out by both sides could not break the morale of civilian populations. Opposing psychological factors (patriotism, hate of the oppressor, loyalty to fellow countrymen), reinforced by effective home propaganda, proved stronger than the weapons of terror.

Hitler was probably not familiar – at least not at the time of writing *Mein Kampf* – with the writings of Sun Tzu, but he would not have disagreed with most of his sentiments. Nevertheless, he would probably disapprove of some of Sun Tzu's precepts for breaking the enemy's resistance without fighting, for example, do not make it impossible for the enemy to return home, give a surrounded enemy a chance to escape, show him a way to safety, persuade him that the alternative is certain death. This would not be Hitler's style. He always hankered after the 'mother of all battles', a Clausewitzian* *Hauptschlacht* ('decisive battle'), not on philosophical grounds, not because he considered this to be the best solution dictated by strategic considerations, but because titanic struggles satisfied his lust for Wagnerian high drama. He certainly did not subscribe to the ideas of von Bülow† who thought that war itself was less important than the 'friction' that preceded and caused it, and was convinced that one could solve the problems arising from these 'frictions' by intellectual rather than military means. He suggested that war should be waged in the political rather than the military sphere.[19]

Clausewitz stressed (with some qualifications) that the ultimate object of combat was the physical annihilation of the enemy, but he did not ignore the intangible factors. On the contrary, he thought that 'moral forces' were among the most important factors in war. By 'moral forces' or 'moral powers' he meant more than just the morale of the troops. These concepts embraced 'the talents of the commander, the military virtue of the army, its enthusiasm for the cause'.[20] Nevertheless, he seemed more concerned with preserving the moral powers of his own side, rather than with eroding those of the enemy.

Clausewitz admired Napoleon, among other things for the importance the latter attached to the imponderables and understood the changes in warfare brought about after the French Revolution with the replacement of small, professional or conscript armies by mass armies of patriotic citizens who believed in ideals and were prepared to die for them. Choreographed, set-piece battles were no longer the order of

---

* Carl von Clausewitz, 1780–1831, Prussian general who advocated the concept of total war. His main work, *On War*, has been a major influence on military thinking.

† Prussian aristocrat who published his theories in 1799.

the day, and battlefield casualty rates were rising steeply. The pre-nineteenth-century *condotieri* did not usually become emotionally involved in the causes for which they were paid to fight. Sometimes they could be bought, but because of this absence of emotional involvement they would not readily respond to propaganda. There was no need then to direct propaganda at one's own troops and no point in wasting it on the enemy.

The first propaganda leaflets appeared as soon as Gutenberg invented the printing press in the fifteenth century, and have been in evidence ever since at times of social and political upheaval, for example, the Reformation or the Thirty Years' War.

In 1741, Frederick the Great of Prussia, during one of his wars with Austria, was ambushed and nearly taken prisoner. When he found out that this was the result of a plot hatched by the Vienna court, he became so enraged that he ordered 'this foul deed' to be presented to the European public opinion 'in appropriate colours', in leaflets and newspapers.[21] The Prussian Officer Corps was appalled but the royal will prevailed, achieving the desired propaganda effect.

Two months later Austria retaliated with leaflets, newspaper reports and 'whisper propaganda', telling Europe that during the battle of Mollwitz (which was won by the Prussians), the young king deserted the field of battle at a critical moment. He became known throughout Europe as the 'Runner of Mollwitz'. This was not his only non-complimentary nickname. The other one was 'Frederick the Forger', which he earned for himself having successfully forged and debased the currency of the Kingdom of Poland.[22] He did great things for Prussia but was not necessarily popular elsewhere.

Frederick was ahead of his time but even he did not believe in home propaganda: it was his wish that his subjects should not concern themselves with the wars he was waging. A century later Bismarck's* dictum was that one shot at the enemy with powder and lead, not public opinion, and, early in 1918, German Field Marshal Hindenburg was still rejecting the idea of 'poisoning the soul of his adversary' with propaganda. He changed his mind a few months later.

Conditions suitable for larger-scale psychological warfare did not occur in modern history until the American Revolution. British regular units could be expected to be largely impervious to enemy propaganda, although the rebels/patriots did target the Royal Irish Regiment. The Hessian mercenaries, hired by the British government from German princes, were not professional soldiers; most were press-ganged into service. They were not motivated by professional pride, patriotism or sense of duty. They could be easily influenced by propaganda. Their adversaries, the revolutionary militias, were patriotic and very enthusiastic but mostly undisciplined. Their enthusiasm had to be fed by success. Even a small reverse could demoralise them and make them susceptible to British propaganda.[23]

Both sides kept their printing presses busy throughout the duration of the conflict. Broadsheets, resolutions, counter-resolutions, proclamations, circular letters, pamphlets and manifestos were printed in their thousands, and distributed among the enemy soldiers and civilians by agents and special patrols. Some of the leaflets destined for the Hessians were delivered to their camp as wrapping of packets of tobacco.[24] The main purpose was to suborn the enemy soldier, to persuade him to desert. Material inducements were offered and stories of atrocities tried, although the latter turned out to be

---

* Otto von Bismarck, 1815–98, Prime Minister of Prussia and Chancellor of the German Empire.

largely counterproductive. Whispered propaganda was also widely used. Rumours were spread by agents, sometimes with spectacular results: in 1777, a planted report of an approaching superior rebel force precipitated a panic in a British fort (Stanwix), which was hurriedly abandoned.

This propaganda war was originally targeted at civilians, rather than the military: before the armed confrontation American rebels/patriots did their best to alienate the French Canadians from the British government. At the beginning of 1775, both sides were drawn into a complex propaganda struggle to win over the native Americans. Similar propaganda campaigns were fought over the black population. The revolutionary side printed probably the first ever black leaflet: an appeal to redcoats to surrender, ostensibly signed by a British 'Old Soldier'.[25] Another leaflet tried to subvert British troops by fomenting anti-Catholic feelings. Between 1776 and 1781, George Washington spent about 11 per cent of his budget on intelligence operations, which included psychological warfare.

This psychological warfare was not confined to North America: both sides ran propaganda operations in Europe as well. They both even produced black publications: in Holland the British government published anonymously *Courier de l'Europe*, and the French Foreign Office published *Affaires de l'Angleterre et de l'Amérique* under a fake Antwerp dateline.

In France the situation changed dramatically with the arrival of citizen armies driven by ideals. First they fought in defence of the Revolution, then they wanted to carry their revolutionary ideals to other European nations. For two decades they seemed invincible. Napoleon understood this new phenomenon, estimating that, in war, moral factors outweighed material ones by three to one.[26] Clausewitz's estimate was more cautious: two to one. Napoleon had no doubts about the power of propaganda, and knew how to maintain the enthusiasm of the rank and file by dramatic speeches. And not only by speeches. By 1796, he had ordered a newsletter to be published for his Army of Italy. He used to say that a hostile newspaper represented a greater threat than 1,000 bayonets. Later, as emperor, Napoleon kept a tight rein on the civilian press. His main concern was still the morale of his own side. He firmly believed that moral qualities were the soul of victory.[27]

The French can in fact claim credit for having given the word 'propaganda' its modern meaning. After Pope Gregory XV founded what could be called the world's first 'propaganda agency' – Congregatio de Propaganda Fide – in 1622, the word had been confined to the ecclesiastic vocabulary until the intervention of Citizen Roland whose revolutionary Bureau de Propagande pushed it into the secular world.[28]

The Austrian army was the first army to boast a soldiers' paper printed in the field: in 1814 the Austrian Minister for Foreign Affairs, Metternich, ordered the construction of a mobile printing works, mounted on horse-drawn wagons.[29]

In 1859, during the war with Austria, several newspapers were published in France, devoted mainly to the news from the battlefield. Their main purpose was propaganda. They were not censored and did not have to pay the taxes that were crippling their competitors. This type of publication reappeared in 1870 (*La Guerre Illustrée*), but the rapid collapse of the regime prevented it from becoming a successful propaganda tool. The political importance of the press at the time was enormous, especially that of the numerous revolutionary publications (*La Liberté, Le Combat*, for example), but so far as really effective propaganda was concerned, neither the Second Empire, nor the Government of National Defence, nor the Commune had the will or the means to organise it.[30]

The first delivery of propaganda leaflets by air occurred in September 1870, during the siege of Paris. French balloons were taking off daily from the capital, not only to maintain contact with the provinces, but also to drop proclamations on the Prussians surrounding the city.[31] This was a significant innovation. Until now, leaflets had been mainly a weapon of the revolutionary in targeting the establishment. Now they became an official instrument used by a government. Their use in advertising and electioneering was yet to come.[32]

But the means of delivery then available, balloons and kites, could not cope with mass distribution, neither could they guarantee precision in reaching targets. To satisfy these requirements, Gutenberg's invention had to wait nearly five centuries for the arrival of aircraft.

The planes available to the belligerents at the outbreak of the First World War were few, could not carry significant payloads and had very short ranges. They could be used to drop leaflets over the enemy lines, but objections were raised on all sides, both on moral and legal grounds.

The German General Staff banned leaflet sorties. This was precipitated by the fate of two German airmen, who were ordered by an Austrian commander on the Eastern Front to drop leaflets addressed to Poles conscripted into the Russian army.[33] Their aircraft did not return to base. They were captured, tried and sentenced to death by hanging, but this was commuted to hard labour for life. Presumably they were sentenced under Article 22 of the Hague Convention, according to which, no State may incite the soldiers or citizens of another against their government. The German government consulted legal experts who concurred that the sentences were legal. The German Chief of Staff announced that any enemy aircrew dropping such leaflets would be treated as war criminals. The

RAF stopped all leaflet raids. Leaflets were still despatched by balloons and delivered in artillery shells.

With the passage of time, the opposition against leaflet propaganda began to abate but it never vanished entirely, and gradually, the Western Allies reintroduced leaflet sorties. Germans stopped observing the ban late in 1918, but they had nobody who could match Northcliffe's propaganda skills, and it was by then too late anyway to counter the massive British propaganda effort.

It is worth noting that Article 22 did not prevent German authorities from actively supporting the revolution in Russia: pamphlets advocating the overthrow of the Tsar were widely distributed among Russian prisoners of war in German camps.[34]

There were some instances of black propaganda in the First World War: in 1916, a group of German extreme socialists printed a leaflet deploring food shortages. The French Service de Propagande Aérienne reprinted it, making it even more anti-government and adding a fictitious publisher. These reprints went back to Germany, in the hope that the police there would waste time and effort trying to trace the publisher. They also produced perfect copies of German bread ration cards, which were despatched to Germany by balloons.

The First World War also saw first attempts at radio propaganda. Then there were practically no receivers in private hands, so these efforts were limited to breaking into enemy radio communications and were mainly the result of local initiatives. In May 1917, an enterprising German signals officer set up a primitive broadcasting station, hoping to improve the morale of local troops fighting in northern France. He played popular music records and read newspaper articles. His listeners used, of course, available military equipment. By August, news of his initiative reached higher authorities, who promptly banned this 'misuse of army equipment'.[35]

The totalitarian states were the first to appreciate the propaganda value of broadcasting. Hitler's slogan was: 'Every citizen a radio listener!' To make this possible, he ordered the production of the *Volksempfänger* 301, a simple receiver, which every German family could afford. Although popularly called *Goebbels' Schnautze* (Goebbels's snout), by September 1939, almost 31⁄2 million were sold and 70 per cent of German households had a wireless set. This was the highest percentage in the world. Goebbels wrote in 1935: 'Radio did away with the sharp divisions between town and country, between labourers and intellectuals.' Mussolini agreed: 'Radio is the most powerful instrument ever created by technology, in the hands of the government.' At first, the German propaganda machine's primary targets were their own people, but it was soon expanded to include other countries. In 1933 the German radio foreign service had just a few rooms at the offices of the German Broadcasting Company. By 1941, it occupied two large buildings and employed over a thousand people.

When the Second World War broke out, both sides were better prepared to conduct psychological warfare than they were in 1914 – but not to the same extent. They still had to re-learn their lessons and some propagandists were better at this than others. Britain was fortunate to have Sefton Delmer to run its black operation and to stand up to Goebbels.

Between 1939 and 1945, the British monitoring service identified in the European theatre nearly 200 black stations.[36] Some were on the air only for a few weeks; others functioned for two or even more years.

What made the Second World War different from most previous major conflicts was that it was not just a clash of different states, but also of different ideologies: the democratic Western Allies, the national socialist Germany, the fascist Italy and the communist Soviet Union. The intensity of this clash was comparable to that of the religious conflicts of previous centuries. This made the job easier for propagandists on all sides.

In this context it is interesting to note that although the Fascist Party was banned in Germany, Soviet propaganda kept calling Germans 'fascists'. This was totally counterproductive: the German soldier did not regard himself as a 'fascist', so all the propaganda aimed at 'fascists' was off target. Later, during the Cold War, Soviet propaganda branded a 'fascist' anybody who was anti- or even just non-communist. The roots of this attitude can be traced back to 1943–44 when the Soviet authorities could not or would not believe that Poles could be anti-Nazi and yet not pro-Soviet, the corollary being that anybody who was anti-Soviet had to be pro-Nazi.[37]

Britain's Political Warfare Executive contained only a handful of professional soldiers and civil servants. The rest came from all walks of life; many had an advertising or journalistic background, and those in charge of special operations came mainly from the City: bankers, lawyers and leading businessmen. There were also seemingly incongruous figures, such as fashion designer Hardy Amies and Noel Coward. Admirals, generals and air marshals had suddenly to deal with men, most of whom had never heard a shot fired in anger and who talked about politics, ideologies, psychology and subversion.

Many of the top brass were genuinely horrified. Air Chief Marshal Portal, for instance, when asked to drop into France a team that was to blow up a coach that regularly ferried German pathfinder pilots to and from their base, replied that dropping men in civilian clothes for the purpose of killing members of opposing forces was not an operation with which the Royal Air Force would wish to be associated. Some upright officers deplored the use of any underhand methods, including reading other people's ciphers[38] and training soldiers in unarmed combat.[39] They were of the opinion that a decent soldier should fight only with his weapons and not with a pen or microphone, and that it was impossible to reconcile black activities with being an officer and gentleman. Some German officers shared this view.

It was an opinion held also by a considerable number of people in the British Establishment and in the BBC. The latter was afraid that black propaganda would bring broadcasting in general into disrepute. The 'conscientious objectors' in the Establishment could afford the luxury of occupying the high moral ground because, unlike for instance the Jews and Poles, they were not directly exposed to the harsh realities of total war; they were not facing the prospect of total extermination. When General Grot-Rowecki, the commander of *AK* (*Armia Krajowa*, the main Polish underground army), decided to set up Operation 'N', some of his staff may have had doubts about its cost-effectiveness, but nobody raised any objections on moral grounds. In Poland, unlike in Britain and even in Germany, officers and gentlemen active in black propaganda did not run the risk of their friends refusing to shake hands with them.

Some British officials were prepared to take the notions of fair play to suicidal extremes. For instance, on 25 September 1938, the Air Ministry proposed that after the first German air raid on England leaflets should be dropped over Germany warning the population that, as a countermeasure, the RAF would bomb the Ruhr.[40] This was to be 'on similar lines to that which has been done for many years in the underdeveloped territories of the Empire'. The Air Ministry seems to have disregarded the fact that whereas the 'underdeveloped territories' did not have any anti-aircraft defences, Germany did and the air defence in the threatened region could be rapidly reinforced.

In the event, when war was declared, different leaflets were dropped. They made no impression on the German population, but Poles reacted with incredulity: Germans have been bombing us now for four days, and the best that our British allies can do to help us is to drop leaflets? To give justice where it is due, it should be noted that, at the Cabinet Meeting on 26 September 1939, the Lord Privy Seal questioned the wisdom of dropping leaflets over Germany when Warsaw was being heavily attacked from the air.[41]

Military operations could also be impeded by the British respect for private property. For example, in 1940 in France (near Arras) when a British armoured unit was about to attack a German armoured column, it stopped at a level crossing because the barrier was down. It took some time for the commander to gather enough courage to give the order to break it.

In Britain, black propaganda was regarded generally as a necessary evil, something to be swept under the carpet as soon as possible. Even before the Victory Parade was thought of, records were being destroyed, staff dispersed and a veil of secrecy drawn over achievements. There was no official history or investigation of PWE's effectiveness, no decorations or knighthoods. Despite this, Richard Crossman, who was for a time in charge of PWE, wrote in 1973: 'Subversive operations and black propaganda were the only aspects of war at which we achieved real pre-eminence.'

Professor M.R.D. Foot has noted that black propaganda operations were in fact true to the tradition of English eccentricity, and that Britain has always excelled in the employment of 'special means'. This is perhaps a slightly sinister term, which includes a wide variety of surreptitious, sometimes murderous, always intricate operations.[42] They were carried out to establish the kingdom, then the empire, and ultimately to defend both. In the process, Britain had been outwitting the Spanish, the French and the Dutch for centuries. *Perfide Albion*? Perhaps, but what mattered was success and not that the losers might scream, 'Foul!'

Since the end of the Second World War there has been an orgy of British breast-beating over many subjects: the creation and running of the empire, area bombing, various social inequalities and all the attitudes that transgress the rules of political correctness. The disavowal of the black propaganda achievements seems to have been the first portent of this trend.

Sun Tzu's ideas have maintained their validity for twenty-five centuries. But would they be of any use now? Could they, for instance, help us to formulate an effective response to the current Islamic revenge for the Crusades? It is unlikely that Sun Tzu would have us react with a new crusade. He would most certainly applaud Professor Sir Michael Howard's suggestion to embark upon a 'hearts and minds' campaign.[43] Sir Michael has also said that the qualities needed in a serious campaign against terrorists include 'quiet ruthlessness', and has stressed that covert actions should stay covert.

When Sun Tzu was advocating the softly-softly approach to enemies, he did so not out of the kindness of his heart, but because he believed that this was the most effective way. In fact, he could also be quietly ruthless, envisaging, for instance, the use of expendable 'condemned agents', who would be fed false information and then compromised, so that under torture they could only give information that was misleading to the enemy. No doubt, he would approve the 'quiet ruthlessness'.

Terrorists crave publicity. Their fate should be oblivion rather than obliteration. This would not be an easy task, it would take time. Many terrible things would probably happen before its successful completion. Obviously, it would not be a democratic process, but this method achieved hoped-for results in the past: for instance it saved South America from communism.

British PSYOPS are now, officially, attributable. This means that the British government does not indulge in black or grey propaganda.

Chapter two

German Black Propaganda

As soon as the First World War was over, Germany discontinued its ineffectual attempts at external propaganda. The leadership had to concentrate on internal political and, above all, economic problems. Only when Hitler came to power in 1933, did propaganda – unsurprisingly – come to the fore. One of his first major moves was to create, under Dr Paul Joseph Goebbels, the ponderously named Ministry for National Enlightenment and Propaganda, usually abbreviated to *Promi*.

But Goebbels was not granted a monopoly in this field. The *Reichskriegsministerium* (RKM – War Office) and its successor, the *Oberkommando der Wehrmacht* (OKW – High Command of the Armed Forces) guarded jealously their right to conduct propaganda in military matters. In 1938, they concluded an agreement with Goebbels, allowing them to set up *Propagandatruppen* ('propaganda units'). Until 1943, the main task of these units was to supply the media with suitable material – printed, photographic and film – for the 'Home Front'. Thereafter they became increasingly involved in battlefield propaganda, directed at the enemy soldier.

Waffen-SS (the militarised *SS*) joined the fray in 1940; its propaganda units were steadily expanded and, in 1943, received the status of an independent regiment: *SS-Standarte Kurt Eggers*. By 1944, *Kurt Eggers* took over from the *Propagandatruppen* the initiative in battlefield propaganda.

Sub-section III-D of the *Abwehr* (the military intelligence service), under Major-General Bentivegni, indulged in its own form of black propaganda: its task was to feed false and misleading information to foreign intelligence services, so perhaps it was concerned more with deception than with propaganda.[1] The Foreign Office (*AA – Auswärtiges Amt*) would not dream of letting anybody else dabble in external propaganda.

Otto Dietrich, head of the Reich Press Office and one of Hitler's most trusted collaborators, was responsible for the coordination of the press directives issued by *Promi, AA* and *OKW* and so considered himself to be the senior man.[2] Alfred Rosenberg, in charge of the *Ostministerium* (administration of the occupied territories in the East), would not allow anybody else to participate in his propaganda activities.[3] Goebbels competed and fought with all of them.

This chaotic system, evident also – perhaps even primarily – in the organisation of security, was Hitler's way of minimising the chances of a successful bid for power by one of his courtiers. As long as they were wasting their energies squabbling among themselves about status and areas of responsibility, he was safe from a coup. When he thought that a threat to his authority was real, he would not hesitate to liquidate the prospective challenger, as he did with Röhm, his close friend and the only man with whom he had ever been on first-name terms.

Goebbels did not have any friends among the Nazi elite. He was convinced – not without reason – of his superior intellect, and many of them became sooner or later the butt of his cynical remarks and jokes, but his true hostility was reserved for those with whom he had jurisdictional disputes, such as Dietrich, Rosenberg and the Foreign Minister, von Ribbentrop.[4] These struggles, especially with von Ribbentrop, were far more virulent than those in London between Dr Dalton* and his rivals at the Ministry of Information.[5] With time, Goebbels started gaining the upper hand and he reached the very top just before the end: in his political testament Hitler appointed him as his successor – the new Reich Chancellor. Nevertheless, Hitler, who had always had a keen interest in psychological warfare, decided at the very beginning of the war that the timing and conduct of all major leaflet campaigns must have his consent. A letter from *OKW* to *AA* dated 3 November 1939 states: 'The *Führer* reserves for himself the right to approve all future leaflets.'[6]

Goebbels had the reputation of a brilliant propagandist. The story of the British cruiser allegedly sunk in 1940 off the coast of Norway illustrates how his mind worked. Responding to a summons one day, he found the Führer in a jubilant mood: Hitler had just been told by von Ribbentrop that a British cruiser was sunk off Trondheim. Goebbels had to disabuse him: the story was a fake, planted by *Promi*. He explained that the idea was either to provoke a denial from the British, which might indicate to the German intelligence that there were British cruisers operating off Norway, or an outright statement that there were no British cruisers in the Norwegian waters. In the latter case he would be able to point out to the Norwegians, who were still resisting the German invasion, that the British were, after all, not such a good ally, if they would not even risk a cruiser to come to Norway's assistance.[7]

According to Goebbels, effectiveness rather than truth was the test of permissibility in propaganda. He believed that 'in propaganda, as in love, anything is permissible which is

---

* Minister of Economic Warfare.

successful'.[8] Nevertheless, he described lies as being, in the long run, the most stupid and least effective form of publicity. He said on another occasion that lies should be put out as far as possible through indirect and unofficial channels (i.e. black propaganda), so that, when unmasked by the enemy, they could be disowned. This coincided with the British wartime attitude.

The very character of National Socialism created problems for Germany's external propaganda. It was too German and too totalitarian to be attractive to the majority of Europeans. Hitler himself was of the opinion that Nazism was not for export.[9] German external propaganda extolled Nazi achievements rather than Nazi ideology itself. In the short term, the *Blitzkrieg* did not require any assistance from overt propaganda, and in the long term any attempts at spreading Nazi ideology in occupied countries – especially in the East – would be made to look ridiculous by the actual behaviour of the *Herrenvolk*. It is true that, in June and July 1941, *Wehrmacht* units advancing in the East were often greeted with flowers, but within a few weeks this enthusiasm would evaporate.

Before the Second World War, the Nazi organs of propaganda had their hands full winning the home audience, and Goebbels himself did not show any interest in major campaigns aimed at other countries. Planning and preparations for external operations were nevertheless carried out, and Germans became the pioneers of black propaganda. They even made use of it internally ('whisper propaganda').

The first German black radio station functioned during the Spanish Civil War. It was one of *Promi*'s special operations and it was staffed by *Promi* personnel. It was placed at the disposal of General Franco. Pretending to be a Republican station, it tried to create confusion in the Republican camp.[10] No doubt this was a valuable experience for Goebbels.

Two months into the Second World War, Goebbels instructed Alfred Brendt, the chief of broadcasting at *Promi*, to organise clandestine transmitters (*Geheim Sender*, abbreviated to *GS*). He announced this decision on 30 October 1939 at one of his regular 'Minister Conferences'. The minutes record: 'Herr Brendt shall coordinate with *AA* and *OKW* the necessary preliminary work for the purpose of setting up a black French communist station and a black Irish station.' Black stations are mentioned again in the minutes of the conference on 27 February 1940: 'In the future *Herr* Brauweiler shall involve himself in the work of both French and English *GS*.'

Between the end of October 1939 and the end of February 1940, two black French stations, rather than just one, as mentioned earlier, were set up, and an English *GS* replaced the planned Irish station. It is not quite clear when these stations started operating. Boelcke tells us that 'German clandestine stations commenced operations only from February 1940.'[11] Buchbender and Hauschild contradict: 'Not in February 1940 but already on 16 December 1939 did the new clandestine stations, *Radio Humanité* and *Voix de la Paix*, start transmissions.'[12] Ellic Howe mentions other dates, and gives the two stations slightly different names: '*La Réveil de la Paix* had already been broadcasting since at least 21 December 1939, whereas *La Voix de l'Humanité* was not in action until April.'[13] Buchbender is probably right, since Goebbels wrote in his diary on 3 January 1940: 'The French are giving themselves a headache looking for our *GS*.'

Radio l'Humanité pretended to be the voice of the French Communist Party (FCP), and created the impression that it was broadcasting from France, changing its location at irregular intervals. *L'Humanité* was, before the war, the central organ of the FCP, which faithfully followed the Moscow line of being pro-Nazi and anti-war. Now it calls itself just a 'communist newspaper'. On 26 September the French authorities dissolved the FCP, interned many of its members and suspended publication. The FCP went underground and continued to print its newspaper and leaflets illegally, enthusing: '*Vive Stalin! Vive Hitler*!' It waged an intensive propaganda campaign around the theme that the real enemies of the French people were not the Germans, but the 'infamous 200 families', the cream of France's bourgeoisie, who 'possess all the power and exploit the people'.[14]

La Voix de la Paix tried to appeal to the patriotism and pacifism of a more nationalistically inclined audience. Ostensibly concerned about the future and prosperity of France, it deplored the weakness of the French armaments industry, and criticised the government for neglecting the defence of the country, implying that the results of this neglect would be soon seen at the front. It also pretended to be broadcasting from France. In fact, transmissions of both stations could be beamed from a number of different locations. For instance, in February 1940, *La Voix de la Paix* was broadcasting from occupied Warsaw.[15] The French authorities did not manage to identify positively these stations as black. They were not the only ones to be taken in: the monitoring service of the German III Army Corps classified both stations as French. They must have been good, as were later Sefton Delmer's stations, reported by British Intelligence as voices of a genuine German resistance movement.

Nothing further was heard of the Irish station proposed by Goebbels on 30 October, presumably because there was no one available who could speak as if he was a native of Dublin or Cork. Instead, the New British Broadcasting Station (NBBS) went on the air at the end of February 1940.

At the beginning of the war *Promi* managed to score some successes in its struggle with the BBC. Its technique was to invent false stories or to exaggerate true ones, and to plant them in neutral press agencies or papers. Eventually these stories would reach the BBC, where the rule requiring confirmation from at least two sources was not always observed. *Promi* would then pillory the BBC for inventing or exaggerating stories. *Promi* published a list of 107 such false statements made by the BBC during the winter of 1939/40.[16]

In April 1940 the American magazine *Life* published an article on German subversive radio stations broadcasting in English and French. Its French-language target was Radio Stuttgart. 'The presenters', it wrote, 'of the regular evening programme on medium-wave, Paul Ferdonnet and André Obrecht, are known as "the traitors of Stuttgart".' In fact, Obrecht's name was hardly ever mentioned in France; people talked just of Ferdonnet. What is more, according to the French radio, although Ferdonnet wrote the talks, he never delivered them.[17] In his postwar trial, he maintained he was just a translator. According to Radio Stuttgart, Ferdonnet was a member of a team of three men and one woman, although the French used his name to refer to the whole operation.[18] He was the only member of the team to be caught and executed after the war.

Life made another error. It wrote: 'The Germans employ two Frenchmen, Ferdonnet and Obrecht … to tell France it has been hoodwinked into fighting England's war. … Their words fall on deaf ears. … Frenchmen do not want to be told they are wrong.' In fact, the 'Ferdonnet' station was immensely popular in France. It was regarded by many as a quasi-black station, in spite of every transmission being clearly identified by the German announcer: 'This is *Reichssender Stuttgart*. The time is 19.00 hours. Now follows the news in the French language.' Nevertheless, 'Ferdonnet' purported not to speak on behalf of the German government, claiming to present views of patriotic Frenchmen trying to open the eyes of fellow countrymen to the real dangers, and whose aim was to save France. Naturally, these views were based on the daily directives received from *Promi*, but this was never disclosed to the listeners.

During the winter of 1939/40, the average Frenchman became suspicious of official pronouncements, and stopped believing French propaganda, which was often clumsy and not always truthful. Because of very strict censorship, people were deprived of any information on the military situation. Mothers and wives did not know what was happening to their soldier sons and husbands. On the other hand, the Stuttgart station was providing detailed information on the movements of French units and on the conditions in all parts of France. Ferdonnet seemed to possess a sixth sense for the mood of his audience.[19] He did not invent new doubts, suspicions, misgivings or prejudices. He only widened and deepened the existing ones. He knew the current military jargon, talked with familiarity about the grouses of the *poilu*, about the intrigues in Paris, about the way some people made fortunes out of the war. His prime object was nevertheless to drive a wedge between the French and the British. Most of his transmissions were concluded with the slogan: 'English machines – French lives!' He never tried to make excuses for the Germans, sometimes even referring to them as '*Boches*'. No wonder his French listeners saw him as an antidote to the unconvincing and often untrustworthy efforts of their own propaganda.

From 1940, all German black stations were managed centrally, under the cover name *Concordia*. This organisation was part of the *Reichsrundfunk-Gesellschaft* (something like the BBC), which provided the technical facilities, while *Promi* was responsible for the personnel. The Foreign Director of the *Reichsrundfunk-Gesellschaft* was put in charge of *Concordia*.

He had daily meetings with Goebbels, who would give him detailed instructions on the running of the black stations. Goebbels was in far closer control than his opposite number (or numbers) in London. Minutes of Goebbels's daily conferences from February 1940 reflect his intense personal interest in the propaganda campaign related to the German military operations in the West.

The propaganda onslaught on France was not an ad hoc affair. It had solid foundations constructed painstakingly over a period of several years. Immediately on gaining power, Hitler had ordered psychological operations against France as well as a drive to recruit agents there. They were classified as 'aware', 'unaware' and 'forced'.[20] The last category was made up of refugees, including Jews, who had families in Germany and could be blackmailed. Many French newspaper people accepted retainers in exchange for not pursuing an anti-German line. The USA ambassador reported that in the six months preceding the 1938 Munich crisis, German payments to French newspapers totalled 350 million francs.[21] By 1935 *Promi* could count on the services of 750 active agents and 1,000 sympathisers.

The case of Rudolf Schleier is a good illustration of how this system worked.[22] Schleier, ostensibly a buyer for a German wine merchant, travelled all over France. His orders were substantial and he never haggled over prices. In fact, he was recruiting Germans living in France to become members of the *Promi* propaganda network. But not only Germans. His purchases gave him the opportunity to slip into the ensuing correspondence remarks stressing the prosperity Germany appeared to enjoy under the Nazis. Then came brochures on Europe's future, usually in a very anti-communist tone. After 1940 many of his wine suppliers became members of a network of collaborators. Similar and equally successful campaigns targeted other groups: travel agents, financiers and students, for example.

Hitler was personally directing this campaign, assisted by von Ribbentrop and Göring. The latter specialised in inviting to Germany delegations of French war veterans and invalid organisations. His hospitality was generous and the usual theme was 'we veterans must stick together'. He presented himself as a pacifist, whose main wish was to maintain peace and develop the friendship between the two countries. This campaign may have had unexpectedly long-term effects. Dr Christopher Coker believes that 'in the 1930s, French veterans of the Battle of Verdun began to celebrate the battle not so much as a French victory or as a German defeat but rather as a European disaster. National sentiment was transcended into international reconciliation. It was to be the foundation of the France–German reconciliation, formally attained in the treaty of 1962.'[23] Dr Coker probably exaggerates the importance of this factor but it may have had some influence.

Another black propaganda technique used extensively by Germans was sending subversive material to individuals by post. They despatched considerable quantities of such material through the US mail, both to addresses in America and in Europe. French soldiers manning the Maginot Line were receiving anonymous letters from their home towns, alleging that their wives were committing adultery. This theme was used later in the war by both the British and the Polish black propaganda. The originators realised that some of the letters would be intercepted, and some loyal citizens would surrender them to the authorities. Nevertheless, this was not regarded as a disadvantage: the authorities would expend a lot of effort and resources trying to trace the senders and trying to intercept further letters. Such effects of letters that ended up in the hands of the authorities were considered to be at least equally important as the effects of letters that were received and kept by the addressees.

France was not the only target of German propaganda. Since the German political system had few admirers in other countries, the propaganda had to be disguised, it had to be black. German propagandists used pacifist organisations to keep the democracies from re-arming – a method copied after the war by the Soviet Union. Contacts were established with financial groups to preserve the fiction of normal international relations. Cultural societies were infiltrated and through them was projected an image of a peaceful, culturally minded Germany. They took advantage of any disunity which could weaken a future victim. They tried to set Catholics against communists, communists against democrats, gentiles against Jews, whites against blacks – anyone against anyone, so long as it would lower the country's capacity to resist. They managed to persuade large sections of world opinion that the choice was between communism and Nazism, and once they started their conquests, they succeeded in convincing that opinion that each victim was the last, that they had no further conquests in mind.[24]

In July 1939, the French government appointed the well-known playwright Jean Giraudoux to the newly created post of General Commissioner for Information. As the chief of propaganda he was a total disaster. In his speeches he used a most elaborated and affected style, incomprehensible to the average French soldier or peasant. He never tried to explain what the Nazi ideology was about and what its victory would mean to France. He was also a pacifist. It is thought that the author of *Siegfried et le Limousin* (his best-known book) felt too much respect for Germany to produce strong, effective propaganda against it. What he created was flaccid and aimless. Goebbels thought that the French battle cry '*Ne passerons pas*!' reflected the French passive attitude, and that their passive strategy was doomed to failure. It would seem that in Paris they did not read their Clausewitz, who posed this very pertinent question: 'Can a country which remains on the defensive hope to win a war?'

Rumour had been used as a psychological weapon for thousands of years, but never on the scale employed by Goebbels, and probably never with fellow countrymen also as a target. He organised a countrywide network through which *Promi* could spread information – or disinformation – that was considered unsuitable to be mentioned publicly, or when the government did not wish to appear as the originator. This network was, of course, separate from the party organisation that exercised control over all citizens. Revelations coming from the secretary of a church group would be more readily believed, for example, than from a party official.[25]

Whispered propaganda methods allowed the target audience to be selected geographically or by affinity group. For instance, there was later in the war anxiety over the morale of the wives of the Schweinfurt ball-bearing factory workers. Schweinfurt was one of the favourite targets of the Allied bombers and the workers' families had been evacuated to villages in Bavaria. They were safe there, but the wives could not help worrying about their husbands. So a rumour was floated locally that the men were also safe because revolutionary new camouflage made the plant invisible from the air. Soldiers invalided out of the army were the favourite agents of such propaganda: after all, people in any country respect and trust decorated veterans.[26]

One of the more unusual target groups for whispered propaganda was astrologers who, it was hoped, would in turn suitably influence their followers. *Promi* concocted chain letters, offering celestial proof that Germany would win the war.

They resurrected the prophecies of the sixteenth-century astrologer Nostradamus (incidentally, a Jew) presenting them in a way that implied Germany would be victorious. It is interesting that at the same time identical prophecies became very popular in occupied Poland, but in the Polish version they left no doubt that it was Hitler who would be beaten and then, I quote from memory, 'Four victorious kings will water their mounts in the Vistula'. British black propaganda also dabbled in astrology.

The term 'fifth column' goes back to the Spanish Civil War. When Franco's four columns were marching from different directions to attack the Republican-held Madrid, their commander, General Mola, said that he had in fact under his command five columns, the fifth being the clandestine followers of Franco in Madrid, who would attack the red defenders of the capital at an appropriate moment. Ever since this term has meant subversion, sabotage and hit-and-run attacks by foreign agents, supposedly capable of causing immense damage, but nevertheless remaining invisible.

The fear of the fifth column was an international phenomenon even before the Second World War, and was fuelled by the sensation-hungry press who did Goebbels's spadework, without any cost to him. However, in 1939, a German fifth column in Poland was a reality. It was well armed and well trained. It was made up of members of the German minority who were regularly sent to Germany for training. When the war broke out, Polish forces and police usually managed to contain their activities, unless advancing German forces arrived in time to support them.

But the psychological damage was done. People began to see fifth columnists everywhere – even in central and eastern Poland where the German minority was practically non-existent. To say that there was panic would be an exaggeration, but a wave of fear and suspicion swept the country as hundreds of thousands tried to escape from the advancing *Wehrmacht*. This probably gave Goebbels the idea for his campaign in France. There was no need to have a significant (if one at all) fifth column there, but provided the French could be made to believe through whisper propaganda that a fifth column was active in their midst, the result would be the same: mutual mistrust, fear, panic. He was right. The French campaign gave Goebbels the opportunity to score a double first: the large-scale use of the whisper propaganda and the bogey of the fifth column.

German propaganda directed at the Allies between September 1939 and May 1940 went through three phases.[27] The first two were conducted mainly by white propaganda while black took the lead in the third. The leitmotivs were:

Phase I: Germany does not want a war with France. If the French army does not attack, the *Wehrmacht* will not attack either.

Phase II: The Siegfried Line is immensely strong and it would be futile to try to breach it.

Phase III: The main thrust of the German offensive will be against the Maginot Line.

In addition, during all three phases no effort was spared to drive a wedge between the British and the French.

In September 1939, Hitler's main worry was that France would honour her treaty obligations with regard to Poland, by invading Germany within a fortnight after the outbreak of hostilities. On 3 September he issued the following appeal to the 'Soldiers of the West Front': 'The German nation and your comrades in the East expect from you that you will guard the frontier of the Reich … against any attack, protected by a fortress that is one hundred times stronger than the never-conquered West Front of the Great War'. This message was really intended for the French and the British. Hitler had only thirty-three second-rate divisions guarding his western frontier. The Siegfried Line notwithstanding, the French could have been in Berlin by the end of September. End of war, end of Hitler. So no effort was spared to convince the French that Germany was not a threat to them, but should they become bellicose and attack, they could not possibly win. These ideas did not clash with the feelings of the average Frenchman. There was nothing subtle about them but their success was assured.

To achieve the targets of the third phase, when the German preparations for the invasion of France could no longer be kept secret, more roundabout methods were needed. Von Wedel, who was in charge of the *Wehrmacht* propaganda, wrote after the war: 'False reports of traffic accidents on Schwarzwald [Black Forest] roads involving tanks were printed in the local press. Badly disguised addresses of soldiers participating in request radio concerts indicated troop concentrations in the area of the upper Rhine. Local papers in the Schwarzwald carried an increased number of "posts vacant" advertisements for lumberjacks, road workers, etc.' Everything to create the impression that a major push against the Maginot Line was being prepared.

Once the Germans attacked through Belgium and Holland, and not the Maginot Line, their black propaganda was given a free rein. Goebbels was issuing directives almost daily.[28] The primary aim was to create panic among the French – both military and civilians. And so, early in the second half of May, the black stations announced that the French government was about to abandon Paris. Actually it did not leave for Tours until 11 June. Listeners were warned that as the Germans were occupying French towns, they were seizing all bank deposits. The intended run on the banks did ensue, but not on a scale hoped for by Goebbels. Then it was suggested that all German refugees, including Jews, were in fact members of the German fifth column and should be treated accordingly. There were appeals to stop paying taxes, warnings of cholera and other nasty epidemics, attempts to stir up class hatred, reports of executions carried out by the authorities and of other harsh measures. Invectives were not spared when referring to the government, and its members were threatened with murder. Attempts were made to alienate the front-line troops from their commanders: 'The generals' desks are out of range of the German artillery!' Especially virulent were the attacks on the richest '200 families'. New transmitters were sending an avalanche of meaningless coded messages to non-existing agents and saboteurs supposedly working behind the French lines. The crescendo of the appeals to lay down arms continued to gather strength.

Still, some *Promi* officials thought, not without reason, that many of the broadcasts sounded as if they were written by intellectuals for intellectuals, and so lacked mass appeal. (Later, talks produced by the BBC's German section were similarly criticised by British propaganda experts.) Goebbels agreed and reacted on 2 June by injecting new blood: two real communists, one of whom was extracted from a concentration camp. They became valuable and enthusiastic members of the team – after all, their work did not clash with the Communist Party line.

On 4 June Goebbels intensified the radio campaign by having black programmes transmitted also on medium and long wave by the powerful Cologne and Leipzig stations. Demonstrations 'in favour of peace' were being encouraged and imaginary circles wanting to defend Paris were sharply attacked. In fact, the only person who made such a suggestion to the French government was Churchill. The French were horrified.

Halfway through the hostilities a new theme appeared in German propaganda, proposing moderate contacts with the well-meaning German soldiers. It was suggested that such contacts would not only get round the propaganda of Dr Goebbels, but could even turn the soldiers into anti-Nazis. *La Voix de l'Humanité* could be, when Goebbels thought it advisable, anti-Nazi or even anti-Hitler: it would then describe the *Führer* as a megalomaniac, executioner, scourge and would call him Attila the Hun.

On 18 June, just three days before France's surrender, there was another sea change: a tough line with the French was introduced. The propagandists were instructed to discourage the French from expecting from the Germans a 'kiss and be friends' policy. A menacing tone had been used before to address French listeners, and now it was back.

La Voix de l'Humanité thoroughly confused those French communists who had evaded capture by the security forces and were active in the underground. To add an air of authenticity, German programmes were interspersed with fictitious instructions to carry out certain coded actions, addressed to communist cells in various uncoded localities. Real cells in these localities, which never suspected the station of not being genuinely communist, could not understand what they were supposed to do and felt extremely frustrated.

In his efforts to create hysteria and panic, Goebbels was ably – albeit unwittingly (at least mostly so, one hopes) – assisted by French radio stations. Their broadcasts were full of reports of the activities of the fifth column and of warnings that its members were everywhere. There were also warnings that paratroopers were being dropped disguised as labourers, priests or nuns, or even wearing French or British uniforms. Everybody knew of the successes of the German paratroops in Holland and Belgium, and in this atmosphere of fear they were being endowed with superhuman capabilities. No wonder that 25 per cent of the population – about 11 million people – eventually decided to abandon their homes and flee from the advancing Germans.

The effects of this exodus were catastrophic: a disorganised railway system and clogged-up roads. Reserves and supplies being brought up to the front could not get through, the wounded were dying in immobilised ambulances and retreating units could not reach their new defensive positions and were being taken prisoner as they waited for the roads to clear. In normal conditions some of the French counter-moves would have a chance of success, but in this situation they were doomed to failure, like Weygand's planned counter-strike in the direction of the area between Arras and Bapaume, where the German breakthrough at Sedan and the rapid advance towards the Channel left their left flank open.[29]

When German units approached Paris, *La Voix de l'Humanité* increased the intensity of its exhortations to flee: 'Get away while you can! The capitalists occupy the trains and you, wretched and destitute, are left behind on the station platforms, powerless against the brutal cowardice of the rich. Take your children and flee, because Paris is lost. Soon it will become, just like Warsaw, a pile of smouldering ruins! Save yourselves!' The effect of this appeal was staggering: between 9 and 13 June 1940, out of a population of 2,700,000, at least 2 million left the capital.

The American journalist W.L. Shirer, who was then in Paris, wrote in his diary on 17 June 1940: 'I have the feeling that what we are experiencing here is a total breakdown of the

French society – a collapse of the armed forces, of the government and of the national morale so devastating that one can hardly believe it is happening.'

Most people in authority offered two convenient excuses for the defeat: treason (echoes of Waterloo?) and the fifth column. In fact, there was not much treason in the sense of betraying military secrets – at least not on a scale causing a total defeat – and there was no fifth column in the accepted meaning of this term: the task of the extensive network of German agents was to gather information and to spread disinformation. The French anglophile writer André Maurois believed that in every village there was a member of the fifth column who, as soon as the first bombs fell, would tell the people, 'Leave immediately, while there is time! Our village will soon be destroyed and then the *Gestapo* will come. You know what they are doing to the Poles. Go!'

Maurois credited the German propaganda with another success: driving a wedge between the French and the British. He wrote: 'Since the start of the war … the German propaganda had been telling the French every day that the English forced them into this war, but they themselves were not participating in it … that they were just supplying the equipment while the French were the cannon fodder. By June 1940 the two nations did not just stand apart, there was real enmity between them.'

Those blaming the fifth column were right in a sense, but it was not a real fifth column that was the culprit, merely a phantom, albeit a menacing and fearsome phantom. It was reared by the world media and fattened up by Goebbels's propaganda, an outstanding example of what can be achieved by a perfect coordination of black, white and whispered propaganda and official announcements. But there was another condition that had to be satisfied: success in the field.

Goebbels knew this. In 1943, after the Stalingrad disaster, he said, 'My people at the ministry still cannot grasp the fact that German propaganda depends entirely on the victories of the *Wehrmacht*. On its own it cannot achieve anything.' They probably had not read a book by G. Krause, published in 1940, which stated the obverse: 'The old recipes of Northcliffe, however much effect they had upon a demoralised people tired of war, can only arouse the laughter of a fresh and victorious people.'[30]

Looking at the French side, we see on one hand the official propaganda leaving the people totally unprepared for a defeat and on the other the question lurking in the minds of many, perhaps most Frenchmen: 'To die for Danzig?' The people responsible for maintaining morale at home and for presenting the French case abroad were permanently on the defensive. They concentrated on denying various points made by German propaganda by broadcasting or publishing news items or commentaries starting with, 'It is not true that' or 'It is incorrect to state that'. This only gave wider publicity to the German assertions and was generally counterproductive: feeble denials are soon forgotten but the assertions of propaganda, reinforced by repetition, are remembered.

According to Sun Tzu, the *sine qua non* of a victorious war is that the ruled think in the same way as the rulers. In France of 1940 this condition was not satisfied.

It is strange that in the aftermath of 9/11 American authorities ignored the lessons of May and June 1940. Instead of calming the national mood by explaining how minute were the statistical chances of an individual being caught up in a similar attack, they made statements which only made the panic more acute, just like the French media in 1940. True, this time the fifth column was real enough and the loss of life was tragic beyond comprehension, but the consequential damage need not have been that great. A total breakdown on the French pattern did not ensue but it is taking a long time for the American nation to recover from the trauma. Europeans, not having been directly exposed to the attack and being more resilient psychologically, have been less affected. The scale of the July 2005 terrorist attacks in London cannot be compared to 9/11 and the psychological traumas have been healing rapidly.

After the armistice, several German or German-dominated organisations in France became active in the field of propaganda: the Reich Press Office under Dietrich, the French–German Committee, the French–German Chamber of Commerce, the propaganda department of the *SS*, *AA* represented by Ambassador Abetz and the *Propaganda Abteilung Frankreich* of the *Wehrmacht Propaganda*. *Promi* did have a representative in Paris, but Goebbels was by then not really interested in France. The two main players were the *Propaganda Abteilung* and Abetz, whose mission was 'to guide from the political point of view the press, the radio and the propaganda in the occupied zone'.[31] Although they operated in different ways – the ambassador through personal contacts and lavish entertainment; the *Propaganda Abteilung* by strictly controlling the media – before long, bitter jurisdictional disputes flared up between them, just as in Berlin between Goebbels and von Ribbentrop.

Propaganda Abteilung was probably the only organisation to indulge in a kind of black propaganda. On 2 October 1940 it issued secret instructions on methods to be employed vis-à-vis the French media, so as to generate a wave of anti-British propaganda:

> The German origin of this propaganda must not be revealed … for every propaganda theme one must find a

> French presenter, e.g. the Red Cross, a newspaper, a company, an association … a given propaganda subject must not be treated in the same way by several newspapers – each must preserve its individual style which appeals to its readers … readers must feel that they are being addressed by Frenchmen and therefore one must use exclusively generally known French journalists, writers and illustrators … care must be taken that quotations from French sources are taken from the originals and are not translated back into French from German secondary sources … the real English attitude towards the French nation was revealed at Mers-el-Kebir and Dakar*… food shortages are caused solely by the English blockade … the English will steal the French African colonies, just as they stole the French colonies in America. …[32]

While *Propaganda Abteilung Frankreich* was doing its best to turn the French against Britain, Goebbels – apart from his main task of making sure that the Germans in the Reich toed the line – was expanding his *GS* network. During his *Ministerkonferenz* on 24 July 1940, he set down the rules for the black radio offensive against Britain:

> The secret transmitters must on no account unmask themselves as German. They must therefore, as far as possible, begin each broadcast with attacks on the national socialists. They are to invent political incidents on the Home Front, e.g. in clubs and nightclubs, and protest against these on behalf of the British people. In particular, they must spread horror by presenting British eyewitness reports from

* Royal Navy's successful attacks on the French fleet, which prevented the German navy from using these ships.

> Warsaw, Dunkirk, etc., and they must use every conceivable means to make sure the very first blows against Britain fall on psychologically well-prepared ground. They must conjure up the danger of inflation. They should call on the public to hoard whatever foodstuffs it can, to withdraw money from the banks and buy jewellery and articles of lasting value.

And on the following day: 'It is the particular task of the secret transmitters to arouse alarm and fear among the British people. But since the German propaganda behind this campaign must not be apparent, they must wrap up their real intentions in moral tales and good advice … they should put out expertly prepared ARP [air-raid precautions] instructions … details must be so accurately described that the civilian population is seized with horror.'[33]

This trick was used again later, describing the Dantean scenes that followed the sinking by U-boats of British ships and tankers. (Sefton Delmer reciprocated by describing in painful detail the agony of the U-boat crews that were sunk.)

After the fall of France the two French *GS*s went off the air, but the first English-language *GS*, the New British Broadcasting Station, was soon joined by Caledonia, Workers' Challenge and Christian Peace Movement.

NBBS was described in a secret report dated 26 June 1942 as, 'Nationalistic, Empire-orientated subversive propaganda targeting Churchill's adventurism, with pacifistic undertones. Transmissions about 1hr 30 minutes daily.'[34] The transmissions were concluded with 'God save the King'. Its style was a parody of the BBC.

Caledonia was described as, 'Similar to NBBS but with a clear Scottish Nationalist tendency, tailor-made for Scotland. Transmission time 30 minutes daily.' It appealed to Scotsmen to make a separate peace with Germany. Its signature tune was 'The Bonnie Banks of Loch Lomond' (although Ellic Howe thought that this was the signature tune of the NBBS).[35] The speaker had a pseudo-Scottish accent. It went off the air in July 1942.

Workers' Challenge was broadcasting 'revolutionary worker propaganda, anti-capitalist subversive propaganda aimed at the radically minded British workers, sowing unrest and dissatisfaction. Transmission time about 15 minutes daily.' According to a monitoring report, it used 'material copiously interspersed with foul language to attack capitalists in general and Churchill in particular.' Transmissions continued until May 1944.

Christian Peace Movement, which operated from August 1940 to April 1942, was suggesting that true Christians should refuse to participate in the war effort, thus forcing the government to make peace.

None of these stations managed to acquire large audiences. Most listeners who did tune in did not take them seriously. There were also attempts to broadcast to Wales in a similar vein as to Scotland, but they were not considered satisfactory and were discontinued.

Goebbels spared no effort, employing methods he used against France to create panic in Britain. He had now five *GS*s aimed at Britain, all sending the same message: to avoid further unnecessary bloodshed, get rid of Churchill and make peace. To no avail. Even the threat of an imminent invasion left the British relatively unperturbed. He did have some success with the bogey of the fifth column. Both the authorities and the general public believed that French defences were overwhelmed by paratroopers masquerading as French soldiers, priests or nuns, and could see this happening in Britain, so there was some confusion, disquiet and distrust. The RAF aircraft scanned the countryside looking for suspicious patterns on the ground, which might help German paratroops carrying aircraft and bombers to find their targets.[36] The police, regular forces and Home Guard wasted thousands of hours looking for non-existent fifth columnists, but Goebbels did not achieve his ultimate goal: the overthrow of the British government.[37] It must have been a most disheartening experience for him. During the French campaign he was constantly issuing instructions to his black stations, but during the late summer and autumn of 1940 he had very little to say to them.

Still, German whisper propaganda did have some effect, although, according to an SOE (Special Operations Executive) course script, whereas at the beginning of the war the rumours were quite imaginative, in time they acquired 'an eternal awful-sameness'.[38] The chief dissemination centres were in Madrid, Lisbon, Zurich, Stockholm, Istanbul and the German Legation in Dublin. The lower-class Egyptian and Spanish newspapers were always ready to print whatever sensational material was served to them ('Churchill is drinking himself to death';'General Sikorski was murdered on Churchill's instructions'). Many other papers picked up these stories. One very persistent rumour was connected with William Joyce ('Lord Haw-Haw'), a broadcaster who worked throughout the war for German propaganda. It was said that he would give, from time to time and particularly during the Blitz, notice that a specific British town or even factory would be bombed. He never did, but many factory directors wrote to various government departments asking whether he had mentioned their works as the next victim of German bombers. In the National Archive there are two voluminous files of these letters.[39]

Goebbels's conception of the anti-British propaganda was deeply flawed. It was based on a false picture of the mood of the British people at the beginning of the war, and as time went on it became even more divorced from reality. Churchill was perceived by the British as the embodiment of national unity, the symbol of resistance to aggression. Personal attacks on him – for instance suggestions that he was about to flee to the USA abandoning his countrymen to starvation – were totally counterproductive.

Goebbels could not repeat with Britain the outstanding success he achieved with France not only because he did not have enough sources of information about conditions in Britain – accurate and detailed intelligence from the target country is the lifeblood of propaganda operations of any colour – but also because he could not find enough suitable people to work for him. As it was, he was lucky to have 'Lord Haw-Haw', who was not only a brilliant white propaganda commentator and newsreader – although some authors thought his 'patently assumed upper middle-class accent' was not credible[40] – but also a gifted black propaganda scriptwriter. Having been told the themes for the day, Joyce would dictate fluently for an hour without pause, producing during that hour as much as any other scriptwriter would produce in two days.[41]

The central *Concordia* organisation had not only Britain in its sights. There was the Voice of the Free Arabs, Voice of Free India, For Russia, Radio of Lenin's Old Guard and Free American Radio. There were transmissions in Flemish and Walloon. During the German campaign in the Balkans, *Concordia* operated a Greek-language *GS* called Patris, ostensibly situated in Greece. Its profile was preserved in the archives of the *AA*:

A Cover location: Greek territory
   I. Ostensibly situated in the mountains near Athens
   II. Ostensible parent organisation: a grouping of political clandestine organisations whose members are young, non-party, true patriots; in the hour of need they are

prepared to join an all-party coalition; apparent close links with the Services, Church and some members of the government.

B General ideology: patriotic and European

- I. Internal Politics
  - a) Attitude to government: critical but keeping the door open; offers of cooperation
  - b) Attitude to monarchy: indifferent
  - c) Political programme
    1. Social policy: employment programme for returning soldiers; employment opportunities in Germany; pensions for war disabled
    2. Relief for war victims: widows, orphans; inclusion of reservists in the work programme
    3. Reconstruction: taking advantage of German experience; augmenting the living standard
- II. Foreign Policy: complete reversal – cooperation with Germany is the Greek patriotism's last chance; into Europe with Germany
- III. European perspectives: Germany fights for something much more important than the welfare of a single nation; it fights for Europe; our new tasks correspond to the ideals of Classical Greece; brilliant future for the Greek peasant, for the national economy, for the merchant, for the exports

C Propaganda subjects:

- I. Horror Reports:
  - a) about the British: e.g. do not drink water, they have poisoned the water supply with deadly bacteria
  - b) about the Americans: they plan to throttle the Greek commerce; they are preparing their shops to sell the contents of our museums; they intend to rob our crown jewels

II. Reports creating confusion:
   a) confusing instructions, supposedly issued by ministers to various departments
   b) careful fomenting of misunderstandings between ministers and the royal family
   c) appeals to punish the British by using force.[42]

Sometimes black propaganda was very closely related to military activities. For instance Radio Free India was one of the departments of the *Zentralstelle Freies Indien* ('Free India Centre'), which also included the Department of Military Affairs and Sabotage.[43]

Concordia's output reached its maximum in 1943 with sixteen *GS*s, broadcasting in thirteen languages. But by then the general military situation became irrevocably unfavourable to Germany. The deafening fanfares preceding the 'Special Reports' of spectacular victories of the *Wehrmacht* were only a memory. Defeats on all fronts meant that the waging of a successful black radio war became for Goebbels extremely difficult, and the initiative was lost to the black stations of Sefton Delmer.

Concordia was not the only German black radio organisation. On 1 April 1941, Goebbels set up an enterprise called *Radio Union,* ostensibly to promote German industrial companies abroad. The real intention was to buy up broadcasting stations all over the world and use them for covert propaganda. It was intended that, after the war, they would also advertise German products. Not surprisingly, von Ribbentrop reacted, helped by the *Wehrmacht*, by setting up a rival organisation under the name of *Interradio AG,* whose purpose, according to Goebbels, was identical to that of *Radio Union.*[44] Goebbels was indignant. Eventually, under pressure from above, *Promi* and

AA reached an understanding and, in February 1942, became joint owners of *Interradio AG*. *Radio Union* was dissolved.

Interradio AG had very ambitious plans and moved rapidly to realise them. Soon it was reporting that branch offices were opened in Zurich, Belgrade and Bucharest.[45] Activating and expanding the German Balkan transmitter in Romania cost 9 million Reichsmarks; a German–Spanish broadcasting company was to be assembled, with medium- and short-wave transmitters, in Valencia and Valladolid. The short-wave transmitter would be masquerading as a Spanish station, targeting public opinion in South America. The powerful Andorra transmitter was to be purchased outright, and a majority holding in Radio Monte Carlo would be acquired. *Interradio AG* itself did not produce any programmes, it regulated and guided the work of its subsidiaries and organised programme exchanges between them. Its ambitions were worldwide: the power of the German short-wave transmitter that was set up at the beginning of the war in Shanghai was considerably increased.

The subversive propaganda, spread by the *Interradio AG* transmitters, was well thought out, and adapted to the local conditions. Station Monte Carlo for instance, aimed at Allied military personnel in the Mediterranean theatre, would transmit detailed reports from the fronts, both in the German and in Allied versions, but the latter would be edited, to tone down any anti-German pronouncements. A directive said: 'It is not our task to compete with programmes on politics and strategy emanating from London or New York. We must concentrate on slipping into "News from Home" for Allied soldiers, bits of information of a morale-destroying character, which would suggest that while they are fighting here, conditions at home are getting worse. Programmes should appeal to the infantile sentimentality of the British and the Americans, making them miss their homes and their families even more.'

Nevertheless, interdepartmental wrangles continued. In 1943, territorial disputes between the *Reichsrundfunk* and *Promi* had to be settled, with some difficulty, by a legally binding contract. Again, in 1944, it became necessary to conclude a similar agreement between the *AA*, *Promi* and the Ministry of Postal Services.

The machinations of *Interradio AG* could not escape the notice of the Allied intelligence services for long. Better deals than those offered by Germans were made for the purchase or hire of radio stations. Those that had arrangements with the enemy were blacklisted, reducing sharply their income from advertisements. This happened in October 1942 to the Argentinian station *Prieto*.[46] Its revenue dropped by 80 per cent and it faced ruin. In this case the German embassy came to its rescue and made up the losses. Sometimes more radical methods were used: on 5 August 1942 the Argentinian station *Radio Continental*, whose owner was in German pay, was blown up.

The endless interdepartmental disputes did not deter *AA* and *Promi* from embarking upon another black joint venture. Using the spurious argument that the medium of radio was not being served adequately by existing news agencies, they set up *Radio Mundial*, a news agency to service radio stations exclusively. The real object of the exercise was to supply radio stations in neutral countries with suitably doctored news and features. The project had the support of Schellenberg, the chief of the *Sichercheitsdienst* (*SD* – the intelligence branch of the *SS*).

To enhance the credibility of this agency, it would not confine itself to the provision of German-friendly news. Anti-German items would also be made available. Occasionally it would spread false reports, as antidotes to enemy propaganda and as 'feelers'. It had to ensure that it was regarded as a non-German enterprise.[47]

The company was registered in Lisbon, with sister companies in Stockholm, Vichy and Geneva. Branch offices were established in Madrid, Helsinki, Bucharest, Sofia, Istanbul and Ankara. Soon further offices were set up in China, the USA and South America. There was only one German on the board; others came from Portugal, Brazil, the USA, Mexico, France and Denmark. In theory, only the German member of the board was aware that the show was being run from Berlin. *Radio Mundial* was seriously thinking of sending a correspondent to London.

The usual territorial disputes and squabbles about salaries kept delaying the start of operations, and ensured that anybody who counted in Berlin knew about the project. The chief of the *Reich* Press Office, Dietrich, was dead against the idea, and did his best to torpedo it. He thought it would be penetrated by Allied intelligence services. In the event, after the *Daily Mail* unmasked the whole operation in September 1941, some people connected with *Mundial* were arrested and the organisation was wound up. The article in the *Daily Mail* was filed by its Stockholm correspondent. It is difficult to imagine that he obtained the details of *Radio Mundial*'s plans in Sweden. One cannot help thinking that information was supplied to him by a British intelligence source.

Two more German propaganda flops occurred in occupied Poland. The first campaign followed the discovery in April 1943 of the Katyń Wood murders. In the spring of 1940, nearly 5,000 Polish officers, taken prisoner in September 1939 by the Red Army, were murdered and buried there by the NKVD, the Soviet secret police; the graves of another 20,000 or so have not been located to this day. German propaganda hoped to blunt the activities of the Polish resistance by persuading the Poles that their real enemies were the bolsheviks. It did not work.

They tried again in the spring of 1944, when things were beginning to go really badly for them. They called it Operation Berta, and this time they employed black propaganda techniques as well. This operation had two objectives. Firstly, it was to create a psychological climate in which Poles could be successfully recruited as cannon fodder to fight the Red Army. Secondly, since according to Major-General Bierkamp, the head of the SIPO* in occupied Poland, sufficient resources were not available to crush the Polish Resistance, one should cause its right and left wings to fight each other.[48]

Operation Berta produced a number of publications that pretended to come from the Polish Resistance: *Nowa Polska* ('New Poland'), *Gšos Polski* ('Voice of Poland'), *Gazeta Narodowa* ('National Newspaper'), *Nowy Czas* ('The New Times'), *Wola Ludu* ('The Will of the People') and *Informator*.[49] On four occasions they printed pseudo-illegal copies of an official newspaper called *Goniec Krakowski* ('The Kraków Messenger').[50]

The format of the fake illegal publications was typical of the underground press. They followed its example by appealing to the reader to 'pass it on after reading', and quoted sources such as the BBC, the Anglo-Polish black radio station *Świt*, the Polish government in London, and genuine underground publications. Sometimes they apologised for a delay in publication, 'because the *Gestapo* arrested several members of our editorial team'. They were sharply critical of the Germans and did not even spare Hitler.

---

* *Sicherheitspolizei*; it consisted of the *Gestapo* and the Criminal Police.

The general tenor was that no good could be expected from the Germans, but the bolsheviks would be a hundred times worse, and Poles, in their own interests, should not hinder the German army in its struggle against the hordes from the East. At one stage, Bierkamp considered organising fake Soviet partisan units, which, by mistreating the Polish population, would turn it against the Soviet Union.[51]

Operation Berta also involved white and grey propaganda. At least 12 million brochures and almost 20 million leaflets were printed. It did achieve some success among the Ukrainians in the Galicia region, but it did not work among the Poles. Although the overwhelming majority of Poles were anti-Soviet, the German record of the previous four years made any kind of general collaboration utterly impossible. The Resistance continued its struggle unabated.

It is estimated that around 100 Poles were employed in the German Polish-language propaganda machine. Only a handful of them were pre-war journalists, one of the most patriotic professional bodies. Over 350 were executed or perished in concentration camps.[52]

Operation Berta was probably also the originator of the 'First Revolutionary Order', dated 8 August 1944, signed by the 'Central Executive Committee of the Polish Workers' Party' and addressed to the people of Warsaw.[53] It asserted that General 'Bór' had betrayed the Warsaw Rising and was about to capitulate, so the Central Executive Committee was taking over the leadership of the resistance movement. The instructions that followed were clearly calculated to strengthen the dislike of the Soviet Union shared by all patriotic Poles: do not obey any orders issued by the *Armia Krajowa*, arrest all *AK* officers, replace white and red armbands (worn by all *AK* soldiers in open combat, white and red being the Polish national colours) with red armbands, etc.

There was a warning that the Red Army would treat all wearers of white and red armbands as enemies. It concluded: 'Long live Marshal Stalin!'

Operation Berta had to be confined to the printed word as the possession of a radio receiver by a Pole was a capital offence. Radios had been confiscated at the very beginning of the occupation but many sets – it was estimated nearly 50 per cent – were destroyed by their owners before the new authorities could lay their hands on them. Some German officials thought that depriving themselves of the chance to subject the Poles to their radio propaganda was a mistake.

During the war Germany did have three stations broadcasting in Polish, but they were not addressing Poles in Poland and they were white:

- *Polskie Radio Warszawianka* (*Warszawianka* means a female native of Warsaw; it is also the name of a Polish patriotic song). First heard by the British Monitoring Service on 10 December 1943.[54] It was located near Lübeck.
- *Biašy Orzeš* (White Eagle), addressing Poles in North America. First heard on 6 August 1943; went off the air on 23 April 1945. *AK* monitors picked up its transmissions but did not identify their destination. 'Bór' signalled London on 23 November 1943: 'Germans have set up in Warsaw a short-wave station called the White Eagle, which started recently broadcasting in Polish. The broadcasts are irregular, at various times. … It is probably intended to be heard in most of Poland.'[55]
- *Wanda*, first broadcasting from Rome then from Florence, persisted in trying, without much success, to persuade Polish soldiers of General Anders's Second Corps (British Eighth Army) to change sides (Operation Südstern).

German propaganda carried out black operations also in other occupied countries, but the aims were different. For instance, in Holland, fake copies of underground publications (*Vrij Nederland*, *Trouw*, *De Waarheid* and others) were produced in such a way as to create discord between the various resistance organisations.[56] In March 1944, Seyss-Inquart, the *Reich* Commissioner in occupied Holland, proposed in a letter to Goebbels a wholesale forging of the Dutch underground press. The purpose was to encourage anti-Soviet feelings and to undermine the popularity of the clandestine press. The idea was approved, but had to be abandoned since Allied troops were already approaching Holland.[57]

A different effect was to be achieved by the leaflets dropped by the *Luftwaffe* over occupied Holland and Denmark, purporting to come from the British government, which exhorted the young women of these countries to extend a suitably warm welcome to the thousands of black Allied soldiers who were about to liberate them. In France, on several occasions, fake copies of the communist *L'Humanité* and *the Courrier de l'Air* were distributed, courtesy of the RAF.

It is impossible to ascertain how effective German black versions of a British grey publication were. The *OKW* used to publish weekly, sometimes more frequently, a newspaper for front-line soldiers, *Mitteilungen für die Truppe*. It was delivered very irregularly and the soldiers were hungry for news. This need was ably gratified by daily air deliveries of *Nachrichten für die Truppe*, produced by Sefton Delmer. It was in the style of a German paper but did not give any indication of its origin. Nevertheless, having read it, no German soldier could possibly imagine that it came from his own side. Still, most of them could not wait to lay their hands on it. Goebbels used occasionally to produce his own fake version, calculated to undermine the credibility of the British original.[58] He employed a similar technique trying to persuade German civilians not to avail themselves of millions of near-perfectly forged food ration cards dropped by the RAF. He got his printers to produce some very crude, obvious forgeries of these cards, which were then displayed at Party meetings all over Germany as examples of 'stupid British attempts by which no intelligent German could possibly be deceived', the message being that anybody trying to use the British cards would be unavoidably caught and severely punished.[59]

In most belligerent countries there were scores of people who thought they knew precisely how to conduct propaganda of any colour. On the Allied side they could put their ideas into practice only through appropriate channels. In Germany the situation was different: bodies such as the *Gestapo* could operate in total secrecy, without any fear of interference by other government agencies. And so it came to pass that when British-produced postage stamps with the face of Himmler* instead of Hitler started to appear in Germany (the idea was to suggest that Himmler wanted to take Hitler's place, and so to create bad blood between the two), Himmler was so upset that he decided to take revenge.[60]

Gestapo Department VI-F-4 was one of the most secret departments of that organisation. It was responsible for all-important forgeries, including foreign passports and foreign currency. The printworks were in the Oranienburg-Sachsenhausen concentration camp. The staff – all inmates – were the printing elite of Europe: either leading experts or professional forgers. They enjoyed reasonable living conditions since they were too valuable to lose through mistreatment. Their best-known

---

* *Reichsführer SS* and the head of the Security Service. The most powerful man in Germany after Hitler.

operation was Operation Bernhard, the wholesale production of £5, £10 and £20 banknotes. These notes were going to be dropped over Britain, just as the RAF was going to drop forged German banknotes over Germany, but in both cases, respect for monetary systems prevailed, and both sides desisted from trying to undermine each other's currencies. Just as did the commander of the Polish *AK*, who stopped at the last moment the distribution of forged German 5 Reichsmark notes. The forged sterling notes were used to pay German foreign agents (the Cicero affair in Turkey) and for imports from neutral countries. Their quality was excellent and most of them could be identified as forgeries only after presentation at the Bank of England, where their serial numbers would be checked.

Himmler's revenge was to be a tit-for-tat, by printing and distributing forged British stamps. *Gestapo* Department VI-F-4 was given the job. They came up with several designs. The theme was the same in all of them: Britain is under the domination of Jews and communists. And so the cross on the crown above the head of George VI on the 1⁄2d stamp was replaced by the star of David, which was also superimposed on the rose in the top left-hand corner; the letter 'd' was replaced by a composition of a hammer and sickle, which was placed as well over on the thistle in the top right-hand corner of the stamp. The 'Silver Jubilee' stamp was modified by replacing the King's head with a profile of Stalin, and the words 'Silver Jubilee–Halfpenny' by 'This War is a Jewish War', and the dates '1910–35' by '1939–44', the '1944' being the expected year of Germany's final victory.

The design was excellent: few people could tell at the first glance that something was amiss. Many more similar stamp designs were produced, as well as overprints. In total 9 million of such stamps were printed. Only small quantities were released for distribution by agents in neutral countries. Agents immediately clamoured for more. Again they were sent only small parcels. And then no more: *Gestapo* found out that the agents were making a lot of money by selling these stamps as unrepeatable rarities. Their customers were mainly embassies and Allied intelligence services. It is estimated that 15,000 to 20,000 were sold this way. When reports of this operation eventually reached Goebbels and von Ribbentrop, neither was amused. In the last days of the war the *SS* destroyed nearly the entire remaining stock.

A variation on the black theme was proposed towards the end by Seyss- Inquart.* In a letter dated 14 February 1945 and addressed to Goebbels, he expressed the opinion that the only way to secure victory was to set the Western Allies and the Soviet Union against each other.[61] To achieve this he wanted to transmute the German secret stations into Soviet stations which would start a violent propaganda campaign against the West. He felt that the West could not but reply in kind, provoking in turn a similar reaction from the genuine Soviet stations. He was convinced that this would inevitably lead to an armed conflict, which would give Germany a chance to survive. A scheme like this, to offer the slightest possibility of success, would need much more time than was then available to Germany. Goebbels's reaction is not known.

This pious hope for a disintegration of the coalition had been held by top German echelons for some years, but they were incapable of making it happen. Their propaganda was ineffectual but they persisted to the very end. Even after the surrender, during the 'reign' of the government of *Grossadmiral* Karl Doenitz, which functioned under Allied toleration from 6 to 23 May 1945 in Flensburg, the local radio station

---

* *Reich* Commissioner for the occupied Netherlands, Foreign Minister designate.

continued to stress the differences between the Western Allies and the Soviet Union.[62] Linebarger considers this to be proof that it was under Nazi direction. I think he is wrong. Any decent German who had the fate of East Germany at heart, just as any citizen of the eastern European countries that were gifted by the Western Allies in Teheran and in Yalta to the Soviet Union, saw then the only chance of salvation in an East–West conflict.

The Soviet propaganda succeeded in convincing most Western commentators that anybody who was anti-Soviet was, *ipso facto*, pro-Nazi. It probably did not need to convince Göring, who said during the Nuremberg Trials that it would be illogical to be both anti-Nazi and anti-Soviet.

Chapter Three

British Black Propaganda

Sir Robert Bruce Lockhart, the Deputy Under-Secretary of State in charge of the Political Warfare Executive (PWE) from 1941 to 1945, described in his RUSI lecture in January 1950 the result of an attempt to collaborate with the Soviet Union in the area of anti-German propaganda: 'After months of weary negotiations in Moscow, the Russians at last agreed to co-operate over here, but not in the Soviet Union, and deputed a diplomat and a general to represent them. We at once admitted them to our top Anglo-American committee. They attended three meetings. Then they never came back. ... A little later we learned that they had been recalled to Moscow.'

This was very strange: to give up access to the place where decisions were taken on the direction of Political Warfare according to the general strategic plans seemed foolish in the extreme. But Soviet Intelligence was anything but foolish. Did they have already another, equally highly placed source which made this new source superfluous? True, they had Philby (*et consortes*) who – after a relatively short spell with the SOE where Gubbins* asked him to write the first black propaganda

---

* Then a Brigadier, Director of SOE Operations.

training syllabus and then to lecture on this subject – had managed by then to move to MI6. According to Peter Wright even the British Security Coordination in Washington was penetrated by the Soviet intelligence services.[1] But no intelligence service will give up a source voluntarily, even if it is replicated, and there is no doubt that even if the two Russian delegates were not members of NKVD or GRU, they were reporting to one of the Soviet intelligence services. Why were they recalled after just three meetings? There seems to be only one plausible explanation.

Their first reports almost certainly dealt with the organisation and general set-up of the British propaganda. Having studied these reports, the Moscow controllers could not help reaching the conclusion that they were the target of a deception operation. The reported illogical and chaotic structure of the propaganda organisation had to be the invention of the wily British disinformation experts who were surely planning a fiendishly clever operation against the Soviet Union. Immediate breaking of contact was chosen as the best defence.

There is no proof that this did actually happen, but the Moscow controllers would not have been the first people to be utterly confused by the way that the British propaganda organisation worked, or tried to work, and especially by its black mutation. Perhaps chaos should become a standard defence against penetration by hostile intelligence services.

It is not my intention to describe in detail the evolution and the convolutions of the British propaganda machine. David Garnett in his *Secret History of PWE* needed nearly 500 pages to do that. Apart from a brief description of what preceded the creation of PWE, I propose to concentrate on what British black propaganda was doing rather than dwell on how its organisation was developing. Some aspects of PWE's history will probably remain unexplained for ever. For instance, in the opinion of Professor M.R.D. Foot: 'The confusions between PWE and PID [Political Intelligence Department], a branch of the Foreign Office which PWE used for cover and with which it shared writing paper, will now probably never be sorted out.'[2] Before PWE was formed, one of its constituents, SO1 (Special Operations 1) had also operated under the cover of the non-secret PID. When the PID was closed in 1943, most of its members being moved to a new Foreign Office research department, PWE continued to use its name and initials. Even some of its own staff were confused as to the identity of their employer.[3]

In 1934, the best that the British government could do to counter the superbly run German propaganda was to form the British Council, with the task of improving cultural relations with other countries. The next step was taken in October 1935 when a sub-committee of the Committee on Imperial Defence met for the first time and was given the task to draw up plans for the establishment of a propaganda/information operation.[4] This organisation would come into being only on the outbreak of the war, since the Labour Opposition would never agree to the setting up in peacetime of a department that could be involved in home propaganda.[5] It took nine months for the sub-committee to reach agreement just on the name of the new organisation, which was the Ministry of Information (MoI). Sir Stephen Tallents (Controller of Public Relations at the BBC) was appointed as its Director-General designate, to be replaced later by Lord Perth. When the war broke out, the job actually went to Lord Macmillan, who was replaced in January 1940 by John Reith MP, the Director-General of the BBC 1927–38. Then, in June 1940, came Duff Cooper, who was in turn replaced in July 1941 by Brendan Bracken. He was considered a success in this job, which he held until 1945.

The sub-committee encountered considerable difficulties in agreeing where to place the new body in the governmental structure. Although there was the precedent of MoI during the First World War, it seemed now to be regarded as a neoplasm and it was being rejected by the perhaps ossified but basically still healthy organism of the government. Its apparent advocates seemed to be calculating its usefulness only as a scapegoat in an emergency.

Lord Vansitart thought that the News Department of the Foreign Office should provide the nucleus of the MoI, which would become a part of the Foreign Office. Other members, including John Reith of the BBC, were of the opinion that the Foreign Office was not qualified to look after the Home Front Information function, and that a separate ministry was essential. It was pointed out that MoI should not be just a clearing house for information but also a power house where effective propaganda would be generated.

There was opposition from the Treasury, which was unwilling to loosen its purse strings. The Cabinet meeting on 14 December 1938 was informed that Germany had a propaganda budget of £5 million, Italy £1.5 million and France £1 million. Only £50,000 could be spared for British propaganda.[6]

Six months later[7] it was proposed to strengthen and to expand the News Department of the FO and to explore and give effect to 'other means of conducting publicity abroad'. Presumably, 'other means' were meant to include black activities. As if with some regret, the Cabinet noted that 'it will be necessary to ask Parliament to vote additional funds'.

There were not many people in high places who understood what propaganda was about. Rogerson wrote in 1938: 'It has come as a shock to discuss the subject [of propaganda] with Ministers of the Crown or leading civil servants and to sense by their replies and their reactions that they had little or no idea of what the words I was using were meant to convey.'[8]

Not all members of the Cabinet and people close to them wanted to see British propaganda invigorated. In a minute sent to the Prime Minister in June 1938, his chief adviser, Horace Wilson, asserted that propaganda by governments had poisoned the international atmosphere and was not a substitute for getting on with government business. During the Cabinet meeting on 14 June 1939, the Secretary of State for Air said that 'the less propaganda is under official control the more effective it is'. But then the attitudes of the Air Ministry and of the RAF with regard to propaganda were at times ambiguous: at a meeting a week earlier the same Secretary of State expressed the hope that the propaganda proposals 'would not affect the work at present done by the Air Ministry on propaganda overseas'. At the same time an RAF directive stated: 'The entire responsibility of the Air Ministry is to take over the leaflets at the printing works and to drop them in enemy territory.'[9] Later the Air Ministry claimed the right to reject any leaflet if, in their opinion, its contents might cause the enemy to carry out reprisals on captured air crew, or could undermine air force morale, or on grounds of taste alone.[10] During the 'phoney war' the attitude of the air chiefs to leaflet raids was different.[11] Britain had then neither enough long-range bombers and trained pilots to carry out effective daylight bombing raids on Germany, nor the equipment needed for night-time raids. They did not want to provoke the Germans into an attack which the RAF was not yet ready to repel, and welcomed the leaflet raids as a way of giving their crews training in night-flying over enemy territory. Not surprisingly, they did not admit these reasons to the Cabinet.

Later, when the RAF had the capacity to bomb Germany, 'Bomber' Harris* was of the opinion that only bombs, not leaflets, could win the war, and was loath to make his aircraft available to carry out leaflet raids. He thought that a planeload of bombs would do more harm to the enemy than a planeload of leaflets and that it was not fair to ask his aircrew to risk their lives for the sake of some paper. He was also very critical of all the leaflets being classified as secret, since it followed that they had to be handled according to the complicated and laborious secret documents procedures. On the other hand, he thought also that since these leaflets were, in his opinion, patently idiotic and childish, it was just as well that they were kept from the knowledge of the British public.

The early British leaflets did not impress the neutral countries. According to a memorandum of 9 October 1939 by the Secretary of State for Foreign Affairs, the Dutch General Staff thought that they were doing more harm than good: they created the impression in Germany that Britain was not pursuing the war seriously, and was afraid of reprisals for bombing raids.[12] The Belgian Foreign Office was of the opinion that their effect was opposite to what the British government desired; that unless bombs were also dropped, the Germans would think that Britain and France were afraid to fight. Belgrade could see that the leaflet raids were of no use to the Polish Allies.

According to Duff Cooper,† Churchill did not rate very highly the effects of the war of words.[13] His interest in propaganda was limited to the operational propaganda sort, that

---

* Marshal of the RAF, Sir Arthur Travers Harris, AOC-in-C Bomber Command.

† Minister of Information 1940–1.

is, when the object is not to change enemy attitudes and opinions, but when it is directly related to military operations and is aimed at influencing the enemy's immediate behaviour: persuading for instance, his soldiers to desert or to surrender. In addition, some high-ranking officers had doubts about the cost-effectiveness of propaganda, white or black.

Nevertheless, those involved with propaganda believed that the apparently overwhelming success of the British propaganda in 1918 could be repeated in 1939, and that a few million well-reasoned leaflets, addressed to the 'good Germans', would topple Hitler. It was assumed that these 'good Germans' represented a massive majority, and that they were prepared to listen to the British voice of reason. It was not to be a question of waging political warfare against an enemy but of appealing to people regarded as friends. Sir Campbell Stuart – who made a major contribution to Lord Northcliffe's 1918 propaganda campaign – speaking on 1 November 1939 at a meeting of the Services Consultative Committee of the Department for Publicity in Enemy Countries, said: 'Germany tends to collapse from within, and we may hope that in this war civilian morale will give way even before the enemy forces have sustained a defeat.'[14] Such wishful thinking was encouraged by the numerous German refugees, 'good Germans' all of them. It was believed also that the most effective propaganda medium would be the printed word, since this was the only way it would be possible to present a reasoned argument in a durable form.[15] Goebbels, however, considered broadcasting to be one of the 'great powers', but he was then interested primarily in home propaganda.

Some – but not many – disagreed with the wildly optimistic views on British propaganda's prospects of success. Rogerson, for instance, wrote that 'propaganda is ... only deadly against a tired foe',[16] that British propaganda would stand a chance only when the German population learned of defeats in the field, when they saw their towns turned into ruins, their food running out and their hospitals filled with casualties; but even then, he added, displaying an extraordinary foresight, Germany would be a difficult nut to crack, since its internal propaganda would not lose its grip on the population until the total defeat became obvious to all. Rogerson also realised that conditions were very different from those during the First World War: 'The basis on which the German regime rests has been made much broader. It is now a popular as opposed to a caste regime, and it will have… the support of the bulk of the German masses.'[17] He was convinced also, just like Campbell Stuart, that 'propaganda must always be linked closely to policy and, when possible, precede it. . . . It must come under a central direction which is in the closest touch with those who shape policy in the political, economic and military spheres.'[18] Those in power chose to ignore Rogerson's views.

In spite of the apparently successful defusing of the Munich Crisis in September 1938, not many in Britain believed in 'peace for our time'. Preparations for the war were intensified – also for a propaganda war. Suggestions on how to run propaganda campaigns against Germany were sent to government officials by well-meaning members of the public, and government departments were producing guidelines, often quite detailed. Some contained good ideas, even concerning black propaganda. For instance, a Foreign Office paper under the heading 'Pseudo-Documents' reads:

> If the precedent of the last war is followed, there will come a stage when it is desired to circulate documents which look as if they were of official or at least domestic origin.

> To give these the proper aspect needs a careful study of Nazi methods of presentation and use of symbols. Designs of swastikas, wreathed, tilted and straight, of the eagle-cum-swastika, and of Hitler's personal standard should be ready for blockmaking, and the themes for which each type of design is suitable should be known beforehand. It might also be useful to have actual photographs of Hitler and the other leaders suitable for blockmaking. The badges of different organisations such as the *Hitlerjugend*, in whose name it might be desirable to issue appeals, should also be available. Current leaflets and other publications from German official sources could be scrutinised for printer's imprints, so that these can be copied exactly. The quality and colour of the paper might also be a matter of importance. As it is, the paper used for such purposes in Germany is poorer than ours. This would be still more the case after the war had progressed for some time, and the origin of a document might easily be betrayed by using paper of too good a quality.[19]

The secretary of the MoI sub-committee advised the Stationery Office on 25 January 1939 that, in the event of war, it would be necessary to produce large quantities of pamphlets in the language and types of enemy countries: 'The types should be exactly similar to types widely employed in the countries concerned. The paper should, if possible, not be identifiable as of other than national production. It may further be necessary to imitate the productions of foreign printing firms, and the means for doing so should be available. … The countries generally in view are Germany, Italy, Czechoslovakia, Hungary and Poland.'[20] The intention to indulge in black activities could not be stated more clearly.

Unfortunately, applying the label of 'enemy countries' to all five of the above countries, was regrettable, to say the least.

Not all the suggestions that were put forward were sound. For instance, Tallents, otherwise a most intelligent and clear-headed man, wrote in a memorandum of 7 November 1938 that 'British policy should aim at dealing the German rulers and the German people a blow of the utmost violence'. Nothing wrong with this suggestion but the description of the proposed 'blow of utmost violence' is rather disappointing: 'a) an authoritative definition of the principles on which we have taken our stand, b) a cautious formulation of war aims, envisaging a world order in whose establishment the vanquished as well as the victors will eventually be invited to co-operate, c) a disclaimer of any enmity towards the German people.' Tallents also proposed the printing of black leaflets, made 'to look as if they emanated from official German sources'.

Nevertheless, MoI did not become involved in black operations, which became the preserve mainly of Department EH, although other covert organisations were also interested in subversive propaganda. For the first half of the war all these bodies were interminably involved in disputes concerning both their external control and the division of their responsibilities. Tallents was one of the few forward-looking people in the Civil Service and in the BBC who had argued already during the Munich Crisis that one single body should be made responsible for coordinating all British foreign propaganda. The three most influential civil servants of the day, the Prime Minister's principal adviser, Horace Wilson, the Secretary to the Treasury, Fisher, and the Secretary to the Cabinet, Bridges, were against it. To them propaganda was a dirty word and not only did they think that it should be kept out of sight until the war started, but they could not see any advantages of a single department responsible for all aspects of subversion. It was to be a full three years before such a body – the Political Warfare Executive – was created.

Perhaps one should not be surprised by this lack of enthusiasm and a certain awkwardness with which many people approached the question of active subversion – after all, it does not go well with parliamentary government. The whole concept of secret warfare – embracing espionage, counter-espionage, guerrilla warfare, secret paramilitary and para-naval operations – was anathema to many people. They considered such activities, which involved varying degrees of illegal or unethical methods that violated normal peacetime morality, to be not only improper but even criminal.[21]

The name of Department EH was derived from its location: Electra House on the Victoria Embankment. Following a report on the inadequacies of the MoI that came to light during the Munich Crisis, Prime Minister Neville Chamberlain, using Admiral Sinclair, the head of the SIS, as his emissary, turned to Sir Campbell Stuart with a request to look into the problems of propaganda to enemy countries, and to set up a new clandestine propaganda branch. As a result, in January 1939, Department EH – sometimes called CS after its head (its proper name was Department of Propaganda – or Publicity – in Enemy Countries) – came into being. Electra House was where Campbell Stuart had his office as chairman of the Imperial Communications Advisory Committee, which, for a time, provided cover for the activities of the new secret propaganda operation. For undisclosed reasons the MoI was not informed of this development, and remained unaware of the existence of Department EH until September 1939.

In April 1939, Campbell Stuart set down three guiding principles for British propaganda: it must be related to clearly defined policies, rigorously truthful and never self-contradictory. He made no provision for black propaganda.

These half-hearted efforts to cobble together a viable propaganda organ-isation looked surprisingly menacing through German eyes. German author Bernhard Wittek writes that PWE was created already before the war, and adds that the BBC's war preparations were on a large scale, including the construction of bomb- and gas-proof studios.[22]

There was one small organisation, the D Section, devoted to subversion, which did not wait for the war to begin. Its other name was Section IX, and it was an integral part of the SIS (MI6). Its brief at its inception in April 1938 was to study all possible ways of carrying out sabotage in Germany. This included 'moral sabotage'. To its head, Major Lawrence Grand, who actually was told to write the brief himself, moral sabotage meant whispered and black printed propaganda. He formed a small unit of seven persons, whose task was to produce propaganda material purporting to be of German or of Austrian origin. Apparently some of it reached Germany via neutral countries prior to the outbreak of the war.[23] Eventually the section grew to about fifty officers.

D Section's black activities may have been the cause of this *Gestapo* circular to its branch offices, dated 10 February 1939:

> Illegal writings, which are produced abroad, are now being received here by post. Most of the illegal material is addressed to persons whose addresses are selected at random from directories. These addressees receive as a rule only single copies of the leaflets. These materials are also sent to active Communists, but then the envelopes contain several

> copies ... most of the politically innocent recipients surrender the materials immediately but the Communists bring usually to the police station just one copy of the subversive leaflet and keep the rest for wider dissemination.[24]

Another circular, produced by the Bielefeld *Gestapo* on 10 July 1939, gives more details:

> The intensification of the anti-German propaganda originating from certain circles in France and in England has taken lately the form of considerable quantities of subversive leaflets being sent by post to the Reich. The most noticeable are the leaflets *Tatsachen, Informationsblatt für Deutsche** as well as the subversive leaflets produced by one Stephen King-Hale [*sic*].... According to reliable sources, the enemy propaganda services have at their disposal considerable financial resources, so one must expect an intensification of the subversive propaganda.

The circular goes on to stress the duty of the recipients to surrender immediately the leaflets to the authorities, together with envelopes, and the duty of the police to record full details of the recipients.

On 1 September 1939, Department EH was mobilised. This meant that the planning, editorial and intelligence sections moved to Woburn Abbey, over 40 miles from London, where they were accommodated in the riding school. They were now called 'Country Headquarters' – CHQ. This geographical separation prevented CHQ from establishing satisfactory relations with the political departments that it was to serve and on which it depended for information vital to its work.

Even more serious were the effects of its separation from the BBC. The Department of Propaganda in Enemy Countries had a vague authority over BBC broadcasts in foreign

---

* Facts, Information for Germans.

languages to enemy and enemy-occupied countries, but it soon became obvious that control of broadcasting could not be exercised effectively from a distance. The European Service of the BBC, on its part, resented any interference by a faraway department. Still, throughout the war, both friends and enemies of Britain regarded the BBC as the mouthpiece of HM government.

Sir Campbell Stuart did not join the exodus to Woburn, staying in London with the Military Wing that was responsible for liaison with the Services. Initially Department EH was interested only in Germany, but as more and more countries were occupied, it became interested in them as well. It had also a Neutral Countries section, which had agents at points where intelligence needed by the Department was likely to emerge from Germany, and who could also introduce propaganda material into Germany. Campbell Stuart maintained that he did not intend to set up an intelligence service of his own, but not everybody believed him. This became a source of serious friction with other organisations, especially with D Section.[25]

Winston Churchill was a romantic. He had known and admired Lawrence of Arabia, and was convinced that Lawrence's style of warfare, evolved during the First World War in the Middle Eastern deserts, could be practised successfully in Europe.[26] When he ordered Hugh Dalton* 'to set Europe ablaze', he appeared to believe that subversion could destroy the German morale so that invading Allied forces would encounter very little resistance. Later Churchill's interest in propaganda seemed to wane.

The Chiefs of Staff thought that subversion alone was not enough. In a paper submitted to the War Cabinet they wrote:

---

* The then Minister of Economic Warfare, responsible for the newly created Special Operations Executive.

'Germany might still be defeated by economic pressure, by a combination of air attacks on economic objectives in Germany and of attacks on German morale, and by the creation of widespread revolt in her conquered territories.'[27] In other words: naval blockade, air bombardment *and* subversion. Thus subversion was placed on a level not inferior to other strategic tasks. With heavy demands made on the British manpower by the navy and the RAF it was impossible to muster a force large enough to be victorious without the help of the occupied countries in demoralising and defeating the German forces. This was the prevailing view, until the Soviet Union and then the USA entered the fray.[28]

After the fall of France, it was generally believed that a powerful German fifth column was the decisive factor in the defeat of the Allies, and that Britain could not win the war without a similar organisation. Everybody was in agreement: the existing structure of the subversion function was most unsatisfactory, but full agreement on how to improve it could not be reached. Eventually a compromise emerged and the SOE came into being, nominally subordinate to the new Ministry of Economic Warfare. This was done in a great hurry, since the crisis of the summer of 1940 did not allow enough time for serious planning. On 22 July 1940, the Cabinet approved its charter, containing this directive: 'To co-ordinate all action by way of subversion and sabotage against the enemy overseas.' Dalton's candidature as its head was generally approved since it was thought right and proper that, in a coalition government, Labour should be in charge of at least one secret organisation. Further, many agreed with Dalton's opinion that the resistance movements in occupied Europe would be supported mainly by the Left and would prefer to deal with a British Labour politician. Dalton was given wide powers and almost unlimited objectives.

Campbell Stuart quitted the scene. SOE absorbed Department EH, Section D (the head of the SIS was informed that he had lost it only three weeks later) and a War Office secret outfit called MI(R). The letter 'R' stood for research, and research into all sorts of unconventional devices for what we would call now 'terrorist activities' was one of its specialities, but its main interest lay in organising and supporting guerrilla warfare.

Dalton's first act in office was to split SOE into SO1 – based on the old Department EH – and SO2 – made up chiefly from Section D and MI(R). SO1 was to be responsible for subversive – black – propaganda, and SO2 for sabotage. Right from the start, there was no love lost between these two departments. At the outset there was also SO3, to take care of planning.

In spite of the reorganisation, parallel and overlapping operations, as well as differences of opinion, stemming from interdepartmental wrangling and from Whitehall empire-building, the operation continued just as before. For instance, at the end of 1940, the following bodies were concerned with propaganda in the Middle East:

- The D/H organisation, which dealt with sabotage and propaganda;
- the D/K organisation, which handled subversive propaganda;
- Colonel Thornhill, who represented SO1 and who handled all propaganda for Italy;
- certain independent agencies, operated by the Deputy Director of Military Intelligence, Brigadier Clayton.[29]

A committee set up to examine the propaganda organisations in the Ministry of Economic Warfare reported on 24 July

1941 that nine such separate organisations (including one of the Free French) were active. The report cited examples where two or more bodies were carrying out propaganda to the same people or by the same media without knowing what the others were doing. To quote the historian Andrew Roberts: 'It had not been bureaucratic Britain's finest hour.'[30]

Interdepartmental strife, jealousies, duplication, overlapping and lack of clear direction continued to paralyse British political warfare.[31] Civil servants defending their territories displayed a departmental pride with a ferocity equal to that of the soldiers' regimental pride. Kim Philby wrote of the situation: 'The theme of black propaganda became the toy of a number of government fringe organisations which stumbled about in the dark, bumping into each other. Small wonder that the results were minimal.'[32]

Many ideas on how to resolve the situation were proposed, but none could secure universal support until the emergence of a document that afterwards became known as 'The Political Warfare Executive Charter'. It was eventually agreed by the three ministers concerned on 8 August 1941, and the Prime Minister initialled it a few days later. The strongest opposition to the formation of the new body had been coming from the Foreign Office, but it was overcome when the head of its Political Intelligence Department, Reginald Leeper (who also controlled SO1), was offered a major role in the new Executive.

PWE's effective existence can be regarded as dating from 12 September 1941, when the PM announced in the House its reorganisation. It incorporated the bulk of SO1, parts of the Foreign Publicity Department of the MoI, and the European section of the BBC. This was definitely an improvement, but the operation was still being run jointly by three ministers – the Foreign Secretary (Eden), the Minister of Information (Bracken) and the Minister of Economic Warfare (Dalton) – through an executive committee composed of their representatives.

PWE's deplorable initial performance was highlighted by the cartoonist David Low, by contrasting an efficient-looking German in a modern broadcasting studio with Colonel Blimp playing with a balloon. The caption read: 'The worst cause in the world and the best propaganda, and the best cause in the world and the worst propaganda.'

Dalton's abrasive manner prevented him from being a success as a Minister of Economic Warfare. It did not help when it was found out that he was using SOE's telephone tapping facilities to spy on his colleagues in the Labour Party's National Executive. In February 1942 he was moved to the Board of Trade, and was succeeded by Lord Selborne.[33]

The executive committee disappeared in March 1942 with Lockhart assuming full power as Director-General of political warfare, responsible to Eden and Bracken. A single minister control – by the Foreign Secretary – was not achieved until about a month before VE-Day.

Not all the people in the government who were aware of the black propaganda operation were its enthusiastic supporters. It would seem therefore that the theory of its genesis, propounded by Bernhard Wittek, is not necessarily correct. Wittek wrote that the British government, having been universally condemned for its 'atrocities propaganda' in the First World War, had no choice but to set up a black propaganda department responsible for all kinds of unsavoury propaganda – malicious, atrocity and subversive – and to keep it entirely separate from the overt propaganda produced in its name.[34]

It is worth noting that PWE's black side, which consisted of a number of small and separate groups, operated under extremely tight security, totally apart from Executive's much larger white side. Most of the latter's members were not even aware that their department was engaged in secret black propaganda.

The aims and methods of the British black operation were described in an unsigned and undated paper prepared for the Polish Operation 'N', during the process of setting up cooperation between these two organisations; it would be difficult to provide a better description:

> The aim of black political warfare to Germany is the reduction of Germany to a state of non-combattance. This is the objective of our subversive propaganda in which Germans address Germans seemingly from within Germany, as opposed to the propaganda of the BBC and the leaflets of the RAF, in which Britain addresses Germany from outside.
>
> The limited nature of the channels at our disposal for this inside-Germany work has caused us to concentrate on rumours, the kind of news items which are likely to catch the imagination of the ordinary German and will be passed from mouth to mouth. These rumours should have what we call an 'operational' value, that is to say, they should cause the person believing them to think or act in a way harmful to the German war effort. … We stimulate these rumours by whispers launched by agents operating inside Germany, by broadcasts of clandestine transmitters and by printed material disseminated inside Germany.
>
> This printed material falls into two main groups: leaflets which pretend to be genuine German official documents

or commercial publications, and those which purport to be the product of German (anti-Nazi) clandestine organisations. Each leaflet is so designed as to give authority to a message or a piece of information which we want to get around. Our messages are not intended for particular sections of the German public, they strive to be of interest to all. However, to increase their plausibility and to give them the authority of a good source, we do in many cases make them appear to come from and to be addressed to a certain section of the German public. For instance, our Catholic leaflets, while apparently directed to German Catholics or even to German Catholics in a certain diocese, are in fact intended for anyone who picks them up and reads them. Whether Catholic or not, he will see them as proof that a secret Catholic organisation is capable of printing their own leaflets and he will be inclined to give credence to the received information, e.g. concerning the spread of epidemics from South Eastern Europe into the Reich, because of the authority of the Catholic Church. Our astrological publications, while appealing to the superstitious are so designed as to provide evidence to the non-astrologically inclined reader that his leaders are ardent followers of astrology, and are guided by superstitions rather than by reason.

In the same way our 'official' German documents are intended to provide the reader with evidence of situations undermining the morale which will stimulate demoralising talk even among those who have not actually seen the leaflet, e.g. that foreign workers are spreading venereal diseases among German women, or: 'The British are letting German prisoners of war settle on land in Canada. It's true. The *OKW* themselves say so.' By giving an official format to a subversive leaflet we can accomplish another purpose: we enable its reader, if caught, to plead that he held it in ignorance, mistaking it for the genuine article. This is our method to disguise sabotage instructions, lessons in malingering and the like. All clandestine, allegedly opposition publications, whether they purport to come from middle-class Germans, Communists, Socialists, Trade Unionists, or right-wing army officers opposed to what they call National Bolshevism, or from a doctor alarmed by the effects of bad bread on the public health, have a threefold object. They are to provide evidence of active resistance to the regime, to disseminate subversive information whose alleged authors may be regarded as an authoritative source, and to spread views which will impress Germans as evidence of growing hostility to the National Socialist regime, whether they sympathise with this regime or not.

The disseminated rumours aim chiefly at human self-interest. They are so framed that if a German believes them he will be led into thought or action harmful to the German war effort, regardless of whether he is hostile to the regime or not. While appealing to his individual interest and self-preservation instinct, they play at the same time on his herd instinct by suggesting that 'all those in the know' are doing a certain thing, e.g. hoarding grain against higher prices next year, and it does not matter whether the leaflet attacks the hoarders or praises them: the main thing to get across is: 'those in the know' are hoarding. Our leaflets try to rationalise any stirrings of self-interest, harmful to the war effort, on patriotic or other idealistic grounds, representing them as the emanations of the highest idealism.

Our campaigns are roughly of two types: those addressed to Service personnel at the Front and in the occupied countries, and to the people at home, but to a large extent they dovetail and apply to both. We try to create anxiety among the Forces about conditions at home and alarm people at home about conditions at the Front. At the same time we try to increase defeatism in wide circles of the population. When addressing Service personnel, we stress the exposure of their families at home to air raids, to epidemics and diseases attributable to air raids, to industrial accidents in factories, to general ill-health, loss of good looks, inability to look after their children and their homes due to the call-up and to the obligation to work in war factories. Further there is the unhealthy influence of the foreign worker as a stimulant to infidelity and as a carrier of venereal and other diseases. We stress the victimisation of the soldier by the Party functionaries who stay at home in cushy jobs; the soldiers' businesses are being closed down or taken over by the Party.

We try to give both the Front and the family at home a feeling that they are being deliberately isolated from each other, that their letters are being stopped by Party officials and by military censors and that the only way to combat this is to smuggle letters in food parcels and in other packages. This campaign has the additional result of burdening the postal system with extra mail and the censorship authorities with searching the parcel post. It leads the ordinary German public into clandestine opposition.

Operation 'N' should listen to our station, which reports air raid damage to German residential areas (the BBC reports only damage to industrial targets). According to an order issued by the *OKW*, German soldiers whose homes are bombed or whose families become air raid victims are entitled to home leave. Not all soldiers are informed of this and so, using the above information, we can show them that they are being deliberately prevented from taking the leave due to them. This will create a major cause of discontent and will also help another campaign, aimed at stimulation of desertion.

We encourage desertion by fomenting worries about families at home, by warning the soldier of the dangers and horrors that await him at the Front, by suggesting that there are many successful deserters who the police and security authorities are unable to find because their numbers are insufficient to keep proper order, also because the vast number of foreign workers in Germany provides a good cover for deserters and because, due to the shortage of labour, many employers will take on a good man without asking too many questions. In order to encourage the belief in widespread successful desertions we send to the relatives of soldiers known to be dead or missing information suggesting that the soldier concerned was in fact one of a group of deserters who reached safely a neutral country and who are now waiting for the war to end when their families would be able to join them … We suggest methods of desertion by relating detailed stories of successful desertions.

Similar to the desertion campaign is the campaign to encourage malingering, both in the German Forces and among German workers. Its aim is also to arouse in German doctors a compulsive suspicion of malingering, causing them to diagnose as malingerers men who are genuinely seriously ill. The main tools are booklets of instructions disguised as the kind of handbooks that a German soldier would normally be carrying round with him. They show safe ways of feigning sickness and coach the malingerer in the right replies to the questions of a suspicious doctor.

> On the same psychological basis of the self-preservation lure we give instructions in sabotage, enabling members of the German Armed Forces to avoid duty and to escape danger. For instance we have a handbook for U-boat men on 'How to prevent your U-boat from sailing and how to force its early return'. ... The booklet gives the U-boat man technical advice on how to make his ship unseaworthy and it instructs him how to disguise his sabotage as a genuine accident.
>
> The main line encouraging surrender is that deserting or surrendering to the Allies is both safe and worthwhile. We are letting it be known that German soldiers are being given land and jobs in Canada, United States and Brazil and that they will be allowed to stay there and to keep their jobs after the war and even to have their families join them.[35]

It may seem strange that the above paper makes no mention of the British black radio propaganda, but then it was meant as a guideline for Operation 'N', which did not possess any broadcasting facilities (not until the Warsaw Rising, but even then it was ephemeral). The Joint Planning Sub-committee (meeting on 18 November 1938) thought that 'in a future war, broadcasting would not be adequate as a means of conveying propaganda to an enemy ... Germans are already taking measures for preventing foreign broadcasts from reaching their own people ... it is more likely that aircraft would be employed to an increasing degree for spreading news and propaganda in enemy countries.'

On the other hand, at about the same time, a meeting of ministers discussed the feasibility of setting up 'pirate' stations. It was thought that the most effective way would be to install them onboard ships in the North Sea. In the event, the British black stations – code-name RU for Research Unit – were arguably the most powerful and the most effective of all the black media arrayed against Germany, certainly after the arrival of Sefton Delmer, who became, in June 1944, the director of PWE's Special Operations.

Chapter Four

Sefton Delmer Creates a Radically New Concept

There is no dissent among historians that it was Delmer who laid the foundations of the PWE, and then conducted a most impressive propaganda offensive against the Third *Reich*. In a period of two years he created a new concept of psychological warfare. Until he appeared on the scene in the spring of 1941 nobody had the slightest idea what could be done in the black propaganda department.

Denis Sefton Delmer was born in 1904 in Berlin, where his father, an Australian, was a university lecturer.[1] He attended German primary and secondary schools, acquiring a perfect knowledge of the German language. He could render the exact intonation and phraseology of a Berlin taxi-driver or of a Prussian officer. The Delmer family were deported in 1917 as enemy aliens and he completed his education in England, reading history at Oxford. In 1927 he joined Lord Beaverbrook's *Daily Express* and was in charge of that paper's Berlin bureau from 1928 to 1933.

Delmer was the first British reporter to interview Hitler and became a *persona grata* to the high-ups of the Nazi Party. He was present at many of their gatherings, when they talked about their plans, ambitions, methods and each other. This gave him the opportunity not only to gain a deeper insight into the German psychology, not only to amass interesting information about the top Party leaders, but also to acquire an understanding of the ways their minds worked. It is difficult to say now whether this was his intention at the time, but he had thus obtained one of the essential qualifications for a propagandist – in-depth knowledge of his target. During one of his many meetings with Hitler, he asked the future *Führer* whether it was true that he won his First World War Iron Cross for taking fourteen English soldiers prisoner. 'Certainly not,' was the reply. 'Everybody knows that you cannot take fourteen Englishmen prisoner single-handed. They were French, of course.'

This idyll ended when Delmer published, soon after the event, a list of people murdered during the 'Night of the Long Knives', when Hitler got rid of his competitors in the party. Delmer was given 24 hours to leave Germany. In 1936 he went to Spain, where he reported from both sides of the front (or rather fronts). He went to Czechoslovakia in 1938 as soon as the temperature started rising there, and in August 1939 he was, naturally, in Poland. In May and June 1940 he was in France, at the centre of the action.

After the fall of France Delmer returned to England and continued working for the *Daily Express*. Then he was invited to broadcast for the German section of the BBC. His first job there – and also his debut before a microphone – was to respond to Hitler's peace offer of 19 July 1940.[2] He had just an hour to prepare his broadcast and had to speak live. There was nobody to approve his text, except his section colleagues.

Delmer's response was very emotional and his language was robust, to say the least, not at all in the style of the BBC. It was picked up by the world's media and went round the world.

Churchill confirmed in his memoirs that Delmer's rejection of Hitler's offer was not inspired by HM government.[3] The pacifists in Parliament were outraged, but it was recognised that the contents and tone of Delmer's broadcast were in tune with the thoughts and feelings of the man in the street. It made an impression in Germany, too: Delmer's name was placed at No. 33 in the *Sonderfahndungsliste*, a list of those people who were to be arrested as a priority after the German conquest of Britain.

Delmer's dramatic description of his radio debut on 19 July 1940 does not tally with the minutes of the meetings either of the Foreign Office Planning and Broadcasting Committee or of the BBC Planning Committee. According to the minutes of the meeting of the former on 2 July 1940, 'the BBC representative was authorised to contact Mr Sefton Delmer and to ask him to broadcast again on Friday'.[4]

The meeting of the BBC Committee on 6 July had noted that 'Delmer was excellent at the microphone but his scripts needed more editing' and on 13 July that 'Delmer's style and delivery were excellent'. On 20 July, after Delmer's reply to Hitler, the praise was more cautious: 'Delmer's commentary on the speech last night had made some good points, but … it would have been better as an anonymous expression of British reactions, without the personal touches.'[5] It was probably referring to passages such as, '*Herr Führer* and *Reichskanzler*, we hurl it [the peace offer] right back at you, right in your evil-smelling teeth.' According to the minutes of the Foreign Office Committee meeting on 20 July, referring to Delmer's reply to Hitler, 'Mr Williams and Mr Murray had drawn up a brief which had been telephoned to Mr Sefton Delmer and had been used by him in his commentary'.

There is in Delmer's book at least one more passage that is sheer fantasy, when he writes about his visitors from occupied Europe: 'As I listened to the gay, slim-waisted young Polish aristocrats, who seemed to know the latest and most fashionable London night spots so much better than I did, it seemed incredible to me that only a few days earlier they had been in Kraków helping to publish a German-language newspaper with items monitored from the *Atlantiksender*.'[6] There were no aristocrats among the several score of couriers despatched from Poland during the war. They were selected not because of their alleged familiarity with the London club scene, but because of their special qualities: exceptional memory, languages and the ability to stay in control in any situation. Only one of them had been involved with black propaganda, but in Warsaw, not in Kraków. To reach London they needed anything between several weeks and several months. There were only three Wildhorn operations – specially adapted Dakotas flying from Italy to land in Poland and then flying back – but they were not organised with couriers primarily in mind. For instance, Wildhorn III brought from Poland components of the V2 rocket, secured by the Polish Underground.

In November 1939, Delmer went to Lisbon as a correspondent of the *Daily Express*. Many German refugees found shelter or stayed there while in transit to other places. He found some old friends among them, who introduced him to others. He spoke to as many as he could to glean even the smallest details of life in Germany, of scandals involving Party functionaries of all ranks, any gossip at all. He found that they shared his views on how to shape an effective political warfare against Germany. He wrote at the time: 'For talks, one of the best subjects is corruption of leaders. We should serve up inside dope which is new and true. Talks should strike a tough note, should be rude and robustly abusive.'[7]

While in Lisbon Delmer was summoned to London by SO1. 'An important job awaits you' said the telegram. Ten days later he was back. He resigned from the *Express* and signed up with SO1 for a salary, which was less than a third of what he had been paid as a newspaper reporter. He was given a small office, but nothing to do. He continued with his two or three talks per week for the German Section of the BBC but that was all. He was utterly bored and already considering an offer by his friends in naval intelligence, when he was given the opportunity to organise and to run a new German 'RU'. According to a 'Most Secret' policy document of the time, an RU was:

> a short-wave broadcasting station, which, though situated in Great Britain and controlled by PWE in accordance with the current policy of HMG, purports most frequently, either implicitly or explicitly, to be working in the country which it addresses, in the circumstances of danger and difficulty which such a situation would entail. Its special appeal to and authority with its audience in such cases derive in large part from this fiction. In certain instances the RU may, however, be grey rather than black – that is, it may, for example, give the impression of working from an unspecified neutral territory. In such instances, its authority with the particular group it is addressing will be based in part on its naturally free access to world news and developments.[8]

The special value of an RU was that it could 'speak without apparent regard to the exigencies of High Policy or of diplomatic good taste, and in the same sense and in the idiom in which its listeners would express themselves, were they at liberty to do so'.

Delmer was delighted to accept, and *Gustav Siegfried Eins* (in current signals parlance, 'Golf Sierra One') went on the air for the first time on 23 May 1941.

A few weeks later he was also offered a new assignment with the BBC. The German star propagandist Fritzsche was delivering weekly pep talks on Berlin radio. He was quite popular and had a considerable following. Delmer's job would be to respond an hour and a half later, tearing him to pieces. Luckily, Delmer had known Fritzsche well before the war and knew his weak points. As a result, his responses were truly devastating. According to reports, he could reduce Fritzsche to a state of gibbering rage.[9]

In those days, very few people in Germany, as in other countries, had short-wave receivers. The most widely owned radio receiver in Germany, the *Volksempfänger*, was designed for the almost exclusive reception of the official medium- and long-wave *Deutschlandsender*, the German equivalent of the BBC. Of course, members of armed forces had access to short-wave receivers, and RUs could therefore safely assume that the majority of their listeners would be Service personnel. This proportion did change in 1943 when a 500-kW medium-wave transmitter – the most powerful in Europe, and later upgraded to 600kW – was made available to Delmer.

The year before *Gustav Siegfried Eins* – or *GS1* – was born, the first two German RUs were set up by Department EH (the technical side of the operation was in the hands of the Communications Section of the SIS), but they were 'light grey' rather than black, in that they did not pretend to be operated by oppositionists in Germany.

The first, *Das Wahre Deutschland* ('The True Germany'), of a right-wing character, was run by a former *Reichstag** deputy Dr Spiecker (cover name Mr Turner). When he left for the USA, it was managed by another member of the *Reichstag* but he died, and the station closed down on 15 March 1941.[10]

The second, 'Radio of the European Revolution', was operated by a group of German marxists, who resented any kind of British editorial interference and were left to operate it on their own.[11] They were closely connected with a group of left-wing émigré socialists called *Neubeginn*, who fought all the other émigré groups for the recognition as the official anti-Hitler opposition. Their station – codenames DE and G2, sometimes also called *Neubeginn* – earned high praise from some quarters. According to a contemporary report, their transmissions were 'the best of their kind', and their output 'far superior to the rest of our propaganda to Germany … serious, informative and sometimes very eloquent … Its purpose is to create in Germany the nucleus of future opposition.'[12]

On the other hand, Ellic Howe, who was in charge of black printing, thought that most of the subversive broadcasts during the twelve months following the setting up of the 'Radio of the European Revolution' were a waste both of human effort and of the electricity required to transmit them.[13] This was also Delmer's opinion. He thought 'Radio of the European Revolution' sounded exactly like BBC's German talks, 'like émigrés talking to émigrés, like Maida Vale calling Hampstead, not like London calling Berlin'. The only difference he could find between the two was that the BBC said 'you Germans' and 'Radio of the European Revolution' said 'we Germans'.[14] He was convinced that to the ordinary German listener, both

---

* German parliament.

sounded like enemy propaganda and were too boring to risk the severe penalties for listening to 'enemy stations'. Neither was trying to influence the mass of Germans, who enthusiastically supported Hitler and his war of aggression; they were addressing the very, very few who wanted him to lose it. This was contrary to the cardinal rule of propaganda that you must aim at influencing the multitudes.

Delmer had tried to persuade the BBC to concentrate on building up its reputation in Germany as a reliable provider of news and of talks containing information rather than views, of interpretation of information rather than of comment. However, the BBC would not alter its programme profile. 'Radio of the European Revolution's' style, which was similar, also had its admirers. Delmer had no doubt that the BBC's approach would have a chance of success only when the average German could see that the war was lost and that it would be better to abandon Hitler, rather than continue to fight for him. He came to the conclusion that in order to evoke in the Germans' thoughts and, what was more important, to stimulate them into actions not necessarily hostile to Hitler but certainly harmful to the German war effort, they would have to be tricked.

Now, with *Gustav Siegfried Eins*, he had a chance to put his ideas into practice. This is how Delmer defined the aims of his new station:

> The objective of GS1 is subversive. We want to spread disturbing and disruptive news among the Germans, which will induce them to distrust their government and disobey it, not so much from high-minded political motives as from ordinary human weakness (for which, however, we shall be delighted to supply a high-minded political excuse). We are

> making no attempt to build up a political following in Germany. We are not catering for idealists. Our politics are a stunt. We pretend we have an active following to which we send news and instructions. The purpose of this is to provide ourselves with a platform, from which to put over our stuff. We therefore make no attempt to provide our listeners with a political programme.[15]

The whole operation of *GS1*, code-name *G3*, was based on a gigantic black trick. The object was to undermine Hitler not by opposing but by pretending to support him. The German war machine was to be weakened, not by winning the Germans to the Allied side, but by setting Germans against Germans. By adopting a super-patriotic platform, subversive ideas could be smuggled across under a cover of nationalistic clichés. The desired action would be triggered by Hitler's inner 'bastard';* listeners would be provided with a patriotic reason for doing what they wanted to do all along from self-interest, but did not dare. Using a more refined and also a more effective approach, the precise reason would not be spelled out; listeners would be provided with pertinent facts, suitably selected, not necessarily 100 per cent true, but in such a way that they would inexorably deduce the intended reason themselves.

GS1 would never attempt to order or appeal to the listeners to do anything. It was left to them to ponder the news or the story they had just heard, and then, of their own volition, to do whatever the propagandist had planned that they should do. Delmer called this 'psychological judo', since the impetus of the enemy's ideological teaching was being turned round

---

* See Chapter 1, p. 7.

against him and his followers. This was the blueprint for all black campaigns that followed.

The ultimate object of propaganda is to make the target do or refrain from doing certain things. Whether this happens under the overt pressure of the propagandist's will or as a result of the target's own decision, is of no importance, but the latter can be achieved more easily.

GS1 had other novel features as well. Its broadcasts were not addressed to the general public; they were intended to create the impression that they were meant exclusively for a select and secret audience. The listener would be convinced that he was eavesdropping on the communications of a huge clandestine military organisation, which was sending instructions, some encoded, to its many cells both in Germany and in the occupied countries. The lure of mystery, and of the apparent chance to penetrate this mystery, would be difficult to resist.

The station's call sign itself – *Gustav Siegfried Eins* – helped to form this aura of mystery. Delmer left it to the listeners to decide what *GS* could possibly mean. *Geheim-Sender* ('secret transmitter')? *General-Stab* ('General Staff')? He had no idea, and nor did anyone else. He and his staff enjoyed receiving from Germany, and elsewhere, reports with the most intriguing theories. Number 'one' implied that there were other stations, with different numbers, and in fact the coded messages were addressed to one or more stations numbered two to eighteen.

GS1 did not have a signature tune from the outset. Delmer thought that it was not appropriate for an apparently military transmitter to have one. Nevertheless, he was persuaded that a signature tune was of great help to listeners searching for their favourite station (although the BBC's booming 'V' in Morse code was often criticised for betraying listeners to eavesdropping neighbours and snooping policemen). Delmer's choice of tune was inspired. The signature tune of the *Deutschlandsender* was the first verse of an old folksong, played on the carillon of the Potsdam garrison chapel: '*Üb immer Treu und Redlichkeit*' ('Be always faithful and honest'). Delmer chose for *GS1* the second verse: '*Bis an dein kühles Grab*' ('Until your chilly grave').

Delmer knew from his Fleet Street days that an unfailing way to increase a paper's circulation was to start an anti-vice campaign, describing in detail what was being condemned. Consequently, the language used by *GS1* was the most foul barrack-room slang, often quite graphic in its descriptions. For example, '*Herr Fritzsche*, you can stand on your head and fart into the microphone.' (A mild example.) The alleged sexual practices and malpractices of named – real and fictitious – Party leaders were meticulously presented, culled from medical textbooks. Delmer did not hesitate to use descriptions of extreme indecency. When Sir Stafford Cripps, then the Lord Privy Seal, found out about *GS1*, he asked: 'To what sort of audience could it possibly appeal? Only to the thug section of the Nazi party who are no use to us anyway.' In his opinion RUs should be sending messages of hope and sympathy to the 'good Germans' on whom the Allies could rely to rebuild Germany after the war.[16] Obviously Sir Stafford did not know and did not want to know what black propaganda was about. The situation was saved by Bruce Lockhart, who was then in charge of PWE, by taking the puritan Lord Privy Seal out to lunch. Still, after a while, pressure was put on Delmer by several outraged highly placed people to 'clean up his act'. He held out until he was assured of a steady audience, but even then he only toned down his tirades.

Perhaps not surprisingly, Delmer's book, *Black Boomerang*, does not dwell on the pornographic aspects of *GS1* transmissions. However, in 1972, in an article in *The Times Literary Supplement*, he explained that he did not use pornography to demoralise his audience. He used it for listener appeal, just as some newspapers use salacious stories to increase their circulation. He made sure that the presenter would not appear to enjoy the bawdy details of the sexual excesses of the Party elite; in fact he would sound revolted by the depravity and corruption of Party officials.

Pornography was just the bait to attract listeners in the hope that they would remain tuned to *GS1* to hear details of corruption in high places which followed: black marketing, bribery, cushy jobs far from the front line for called-up Party comrades, extra ration cards for those in safe civilian jobs, immunity from prosecution for cheating when supplying the *Wehrmacht* etc. These revelations – some of them even true – had several purposes.

Apart from the obvious intention to undermine the trust and respect of ordinary Germans for their leadership, they aimed to create a rift between the 'honest, courageous and patriotic soldiers, sailors and airmen' and the Party 'lick-spittles' who only wanted to feather their nests, regardless of the interests of the Fatherland.

At the same time – since there was never any mention of the miscreants being caught and punished – they were tantamount to an encouragement to the listeners, including the rank and file Party members, to look primarily, in a similar fashion, after their own interests, and it was virtually risk-free to boot. Corruption was vehemently denounced but at the same time it was shown how easily and profitably regulations could be evaded.

As a further encouragement, regrets were expressed, with crocodile tears, that police forces were disastrously undermanned and that their records were being destroyed in air raids, rendering the police practically impotent.*

To be convincing, Delmer needed information, a constant flow of intelligence, particularly of the scandalous kind. During the initial period, *GS1* could manage on Delmer's memories of the 1930s and on his notes brought back from Lisbon. But later, current information was required on people and events in Germany. Snippets garnered from German newspapers and from papers published in occupied countries were useful, but this was not enough. Delmer wanted access to the kind of gossip that might be exchanged between officers of the *Wehrmacht* or the *SS* when they thought that nobody else was listening.

He got it when top-secret reports on prisoners of war were made available to him: transcripts of interrogations and of conversations between the POWs, obtained by bugging not only their quarters but even the trees in the gardens where they were allowed to walk. This was also a source of new soldier slang expressions, enabling *GS1* to keep up with the linguistic developments. Equally productive sources were the letters and diaries found on German casualties and POWs, captured mail and censorship intercepts.

For instance, there was an American-born wife of a Cologne industrialist who wrote frequently to her friend in Nevada. She moved in the top local Nazi circles and described in great detail the wonderful parties she went to and the people

---

* This is a fact I can confirm from my own experience. Before my second escape from the forced labour camp in the Rheinland in the autumn of 1944,I obtained details of a volunteer labour camp which had been destroyed, along with its records, in an air raid. When I was caught again, I was able to persuade the *Schutzpolizei* that I had been an inmate of that camp, having come to Germany as a volunteer. This made a considerable difference to my treatment.

she met there. Her letters yielded authentic details on which Delmer could construct many a story. Of course, a piece of intelligence was never used raw. It was always 'improved' and distorted so that the source could not be identified.[17]

Nevertheless, the bulk of the information came from open sources. There was the *Daily Digest* of German broadcasts supplied by the superb BBC monitoring service; there was the DNB (*Deutsches Nachrichten Büro*), the German News Service, whose London office manager left behind in September 1939 his *Hellschreiber*, the latest in teleprinter technology, using wireless communication. Throughout the war, therefore, PWE was receiving all DNB Agency despatches and *Promi* directives at the same time as German newspapers. The importance of the *Hellschreiber* in Delmer's hands cannot be overestimated. His team worked faster, was less inhibited than the journalists in Germany, and was able to broadcast the news items so obtained – suitably modified – before they were seen by newspaper readers in Germany and even before they were broadcast by German radio stations.

There was also the German press, received via Lisbon. It was rumoured at the time that British and German newspaper-carrying aircraft after landing there would park in close proximity to make the exchange of newspaper bundles easier. When it was found that this method was not fast enough, MoI opened a press-reading bureau for PWE in Stockholm. From here items of interest were immediately telegraphed to England. This bureau also interviewed non-Germans who arrived from Germany. Similar but smaller offices were maintained in Bern and in Istanbul.[18]

The Admiralty was the first Service department to realise the importance of Delmer's work, and the resources of the operational propaganda unit of the Naval Intelligence Division (NID) were made available to him. The cooperation between

Delmer and NID developed so successfully that, from 1943 onwards, his organisation could be regarded as practically one of NID's operational outposts.[19] The Air Ministry Intelligence followed enthusiastically. The War Office was last, showing only a cautious and limited interest. These contacts prepared the way for the later close collaboration between British black propaganda and SHAEF (Supreme Headquarters Allied Expeditionary Force).

One of Delmer's most successful ideas came from his contact with the Nazis in the 1930s. He remembered that Hitler's entourage used to refer to him as *der Chef* – the Chief. So, adding a touch of irony, he decided to give this title to the anonymous leader of the mysterious organisation behind *GS1*. According to several publications, Delmer himself played the Chief. This was not so. No doubt he could have done this with success, but his voice was known in Germany and *Gustav Siegfried Eins* would have been identified immediately as a British black station. The part of the Chief was given to the first recruit to join the staff of *GS1*. His name was Peter Seckelmann, a Berlin journalist who also wrote detective stories.

Seckelmann came to Britain in 1937 or 1938 and on the outbreak of the war enlisted in the Pioneer Corps. In 1941 he volunteered to be parachuted to carry out sabotage behind German lines, but it was thought he would be better employed in propaganda so he ended up in *GS1*. Initially he had problems with his microphone voice, but gradually he overcame them and became one of the best radio voices in PWE.

Soon he was joined by Johannes Reiholz, a German journalist, who was to be his announcer and adjutant. It was unthinkable in those days in Germany that *der Chef*, obviously a senior officer, could function, even underground, without an adjutant. Reiholz made a very good one, and gradually took over the writing of the scripts from Delmer. Before long he was joined in this task by Seckelmann, now called Paul Saunders or simply 'the Corporal' (this was his rank in the Pioneer Corps).

The third member of the original team was Max Braun, who was in charge of intelligence. He looked after an extensive card index, started originally by Delmer, containing all sorts of interesting information on tens of thousands of Germans, mainly Party officials. He used to read with great attention all available German newspapers, extracting from them with unmatched skill items of information on people and events that could be used by the unit.

What was the profile of the enigmatic Chief? He was obviously a senior officer of the old Prussian school, who knew his way around and held a senior position in the *Wehrmacht*. He was a man of authority, with inside knowledge, so was worth listening to. He could have been a modest landowner, frugal in his habits and with a distinguished record as a soldier during the First World War. He was a royalist at heart, and would voice caustic and salaciously outspoken views on current events. He was loyal and devoted to the *Führer*, who was making come true his dreams of conquests and expansion, but obscenely contemptuous of the 'Party rabble' that had seized control of the Fatherland in the *Führer*'s name and of the Party functionaries who were motivated by a rapacious self-interest. Naturally, he never criticised Hitler (not, at any rate, while Germany was scoring military successes), neither did he attack the top Nazis such as Göring or Goebbels, unless they were, like Himmler, the top people in the Security Service. Attacking them was left to the white propaganda. He went for the lesser-known local mini-*Führers*. He hated the scoundrels who, safe in jobs far from the front, were dissipating what was paid for by the blood of *Wehrmacht* front-line commanders and soldiers. In fact, he hated practically everybody: the Jews, the British (during his first broadcast ever he referred to Churchill as the 'flat-footed bastard of a drunken old Jew', but this was to counter any suspicions that *GS1* might be a British station), the Russians and the *Parteikommune*, as he called the corrupt higher Party echelons, infected – he asserted – with communism; this was the privileged class whose members seemed to be exempt from normal military service and interfered with the life and liberties of ordinary, decent citizens. Spreading his venom over many targets instead of concentrating it on one selected group was not in accord with rules for effective propaganda, but then only his attacks on the *Parteikommune* were real attacks; the others were meant just to build up his credibility.

His voice was that of patriotic Germans – not to be confused with the 'good Germans'–– who were concerned with the deplorable way their country was being run – without the *Führer* being aware of it – by his underlings in the Party and in the *SS*. He never threatened or criticised the ordinary German civilian or soldier.

The transmissions used to start at 7 minutes to the hour (it seems that after a while the transmission time was extended and they were starting at 12 minutes to the hour), with the adjutant repeating for about 45 seconds the call sign: 'Here is *Gustav Siegfried One*, here is *Gustav Siegfried One. …*' Later this was preceded by the signature tune. Then, for instance: 'Calling *Gustav Siegfried Eighteen*, here is a message for *Gustav Siegfried Eighteen. …*' This was followed by a message in a simple number code which could be easily broken by the German Security Services. It might say, for instance: 'Willy meet Jochen Friday row five stalls second performance Union Cinema.' There were hundreds of Union Cinemas all over Germany and it was hoped that hundreds of *Gestapo* functionaries would be spending that Friday evening trying to apprehend Willy and Jochen. The coded dictation done, the adjutant would announce: '*Jetzt spricht der Chef*' – 'Now will speak the Chief.'

Der Chef would start by answering questions, which, he would say, had been submitted to him after his previous broadcast.[20] Having dealt with these fictitious queries, he would present his views on current events. His first broadcast coincided with Hess's arrival in Britain. For some strange reason, the British official propaganda practically ignored this unique opportunity to gain a tremendous political and propaganda advantage. The embargo did not apply to black propaganda, however, so *der Chef* let rip: 'Hess was a good comrade of ours in the days of the Free Corps,* but like the rest of this clique of cranks, megalomaniacs, string-pullers and parlour bolsheviks who call themselves our leaders, he simply can't keep his nerve in a crisis. As soon as he learns of the darker side of what lies ahead, he loses his head completely and flies off to throw himself and us at the mercy of that flat-footed bastard of a drunken old Jew, Churchill. And he completely overlooks the fact that he is the bearer of the *Reich*'s most precious secrets, all of which the British will now suck out of him as easily as if he was a bottle of Berlin *Weissbier*.'

And so on in this vein. The transmissions were always signed off with: 'That is all for now. I shall be repeating this – all being well – every hour at 7 minutes to the hour.' The Chief's scripts and delivery seemed to improve with every broadcast. Delmer's only regret was that the security regulations did not permit these broadcasts to be live: they all had to be pre-recorded.

---

* Paramilitary units, which, after the defeat of Germany in 1918, became the 'force in being'.

On 6 June 1941, Delmer was summoned to a meeting attended by many eminent people.[21] The chair was the head of the department, Rex Leeper, who revealed a 'most secret' piece of information, namely that Germany was expected to attack Russia on 22 June. Delmer was asked how *der Chef* would react. '*Der Chef*', said Delmer, 'is all for Hitler and his new war against the bolsheviks. *Der Chef* will applaud and support the *Führer*'s decision.' Most of those present, who did not know what Delmer's job was, looked at him in horrified incredulity. He continued: '*Der Chef* will insist that the Führer combines his anti-bolshevik crusade against Soviet Russia with a cleaning-up campaign against the bolsheviks at home, *die Parteikommune*. He has collected a great deal of astonishing material about the *Parteikommune* which he will bring to the attention of the *Führer*.' Now the entire audience roared with laughter.

The Chief was now really in full flight. He ranted against the Russian bolsheviks in Moscow and the Party bolsheviks at home. When things were going badly, he would put the blame on the Party, although he never talked of 'Nazis' since this would sound too much like propaganda. The underlying moral of most of the stories he told was: 'Our brave soldiers are freezing to death in Russia because of the corruption of this *Parteikommune* crowd, who delayed getting the army's winter clothing ready in time since they were out for a bigger profit. These same traitorous swine are having a wonderful time feathering their nests in soft jobs far from danger and privation.'[22] He was also giving the ordinary German a convincing excuse for any dereliction of duty by making him ask himself: 'Why should I put up with this, when these Party swine can wriggle out of it all?' The Chief always revealed in great detail how the Party bigwigs committed their foul deeds, so that his listeners could emulate them without much difficulty. The other, equally important message was: 'The army is against the Party, the army is against the *SS*, the army is against the *Gestapo*.' This legend grew with time until, after the war, it turned – to Delmer's regret – into a 'most dangerous boomerang'.[23]

One of the dangers facing a successful black operation is that it may deceive not only the enemy but also its own side. This did happen to *GS1*. After it had been operating for some weeks, the US embassy in Berlin reported an apparent dramatic increase in the hostility of the army to the Party. The proof seemed clear and convincing: there was a new radio transmitter used by a nameless officer, referred to as *der Chef*, to broadcast violent attacks on certain sections of the Party. His audience was growing rapidly and the authorities were unable to shut down this station. Many German officers, said the report, believe that the *Wehrmacht* secretly supports this station.

Naturally, Delmer and his team were delighted, but this report and several more which followed, created a problem: it was now feared that this alleged manifestation of growing anti-Hitler opposition would encourage the US government to continue to sit on the fence, and to ignore the British efforts to transform the USA from a passive into an active ally. Such American attitude would not be unreasonable: why get involved in the war if the chances are that the Germans will end it by themselves. How could the British tell them the truth without compromising the entire black operation? In the end it was decided that David Bowes-Lyon, the brother of the Queen, should call on President Roosevelt and reveal the secret, on the strict understanding that it was not to go any further. The President was immensely amused, but unfortunately his conception of security was rather lax and within days the story of *Gustav Siegfried Eins* was all over Washington.

It must have reached Berlin, but it did not do any harm to the popularity of *GS1*. We read in a 'most secret' report of that time: 'Interrogations of POWs continue to reveal the ever-widening audience that the station has gained among members of the German armed forces. It is reported that in Vienna young German officers regularly listened with some gusto to *GS1*. German troops in North Africa appear to have listened regularly. One POW, a Bavarian landowner, not only listened himself but also was told by his housekeeper at home that the broadcasts were popular with the local peasants.'[24]

Delmer's initial ruse of heaping invectives upon Churchill did not throw the Germans off the scent for long. Their Radio Direction Finder service soon discovered the true location of *GS1*. It was disclosed by the *Reichsrundfunk* (the main German broadcasting network) but very few of *GS1* listeners would believe it. Rumours were rife as to its real location. Eventually, on 20 July 1943, the Chief himself decided to comment: 'First we were a Russian transmitter, then, when we had not been heard for a week, we had come crashing down on the pavement of the Friedrichstrasse, the RAF being presumably to blame, and broken our collective necks. Then, later, the arseholes located us in a furniture van in Holland and we were simultaneously traced to a ship off the Norwegian coast. Next, according to Dr Goebbels, we were in Scotland. It won't be long before I'm with the flat-footed Jews in American North Africa.'

Gustav Siegfried Eins operated for about thirty months and its audience never waned. Nevertheless, Delmer had more ambitious plans and it was decided to terminate the broadcasts.

A dramatic exit was chosen for the Chief: the noise of a door being broken down, a burst of automatic fire, and a 'Gotcha, you swine!' Unfortunately, there was a breakdown of communications between the editorial and the technical staff, and an hour later the same recording was played again. Fortunately, reception was very poor during the second transmission and the jamming exceptionally strong. There were no questions or complaints. In any case, even if the station had been compromised, it had ceased to exist.

Delmer always wanted to broadcast news bulletins, mixing truth and suitably prepared fiction. He sought to copy the format of the German forces stations, such as those set up in Belgrade, Lwów or Smolensk, and hankered after a livelier style of news writing and news selection. He tried this approach setting up an RU called *Wehrmachtsender Nord*, which targeted German units in Norway and purported to be run by one of these units. This is how he described it:[25]

> Its object is nominally to give news of home to German soldiers in that area … we hope that it will be picked up by curious civilians who want to know what army life and mood are like … the main objectives are to attack the morale of the German army by painting a gloomy picture of conditions inside Germany and to convince civilian listeners that the morale of the army is affected by developments on the Home Front … material for our broadcasts is provided almost entirely by the messages of the DNB which we receive on the *Hellschreiber* before they appear in the German press … by adding a few details or omitting a few qualifying clauses from the German news items, a gloomy picture of conditions in Germany can be presented … by denying rumours we give them publicity … by reporting

court sentences in detail, we show how regulations can be circumvented … a good many of these news items are harmless in themselves and a great deal can be done by implication only. A typical instance of this technique was the issue of a denial that workers imported from North Africa were niggers. They were, we said, only 'dark-skinned French Colonials'. Another constant object is to ridicule and excite the hatred of senior Party officials. Here a great deal is done by juxtaposition of news items with other news items. Thus accounts of unpleasant conditions resulting from British air raids are juxtaposed with news items about the movements and junketings of the local *Gauleiter.**

In another 'most secret' paper we find more detailed instructions on the approach to the Germans in Norway. The news destined for them should suggest:

1. That in their composition, armament and equipment they are inferior to those sent to Fronts of real importance.
2. That they are an army of rejects, troops who were not considered good enough for service on the Eastern Front.
3. That the war in Norway is not a war at all, that it is a phoney war, a *Sitzkrieg*.

We should make them aware of the danger to them resulting from being militarily efficient: soldiers who show themselves efficient are immediately sent to the Eastern Front. They should be made to see their enemy in the German Party high-ups, in the Germans having a better time than themselves, rather than in the Allies whom they are

---

* District leader of the Nazi Party.

> fighting … We should stimulate in them a sense of betrayal by their leaders and superiors, and the desire to desert and/or to surrender.[26]

A similar approach was also used later, when targeting the German troops manning the anti-invasion defences.

A Foreign Office report of September 1942 spoke of 'considerable progress being made with *Wehrmachtsender Nord*', but it was not regarded as a success and after nine months it was taken off the air. Delmer himself was never satisfied with it. He thought that it did not sound right because, in accordance with rules then in force, everything had to be pre-recorded rather than live, and pre-recorded news never sounds like news. Radio news, to sound like news, must be read live. Bulletins must be capable of being updated from hour to hour. Making a new recording for every transmission would have been too complicated, especially as the recording studios were at some distance from the transmitters. There was another overwhelming reason for closing down the station: the transmissions were barely audible in Norway. The Royal Navy even sent a destroyer into Norwegian waters to check the quality of the reception. The resulting report was 100 per cent negative.

Still, the whole enterprise was not a total loss: it gave Delmer and his team invaluable experience of producing suitably doctored news bulletins. What is more, it transpired after the war that German intelligence had carefully monitored all its transmissions. They thought that the fact that the British had a special transmitter beamed on Norway was most significant: it appeared to confirm Hitler's conviction at the time that a major Allied landing would take place there.

Just before Christmas 1942, Delmer was given the opportunity to set up an RU that would broadcast live news bulletins

– *Deutscher Kurzwellensender Atlantik* ('German Short-Wave Station Atlantic'), code name G9. Britain's survival was being then threatened by the German U-boats, and the Admiralty – the most influential of the Services – would support any project that could reduce that threat, including projects targeting the morale of the U-boat crews. Delmer's proposal to set up an RU modelled on German Forces stations, with live news and light music, was approved enthusiastically by both Bruce Lockhart and the Admiralty. With the Navy behind him, Delmer was given the green light to commence live black broadcasting.

The BBC thought that this was deplorable. Black broadcasting was disapproved of by the Corporation from the start, even when it was all pre-recorded. Actually, G9 was not going to be a black but a 'grey' station, which was even worse. Whereas the cover of a black station had to be sufficiently convincing to deceive the listeners into believing that it was situated in the target country, a grey station had only to show that it was worth listening to. BBC considered live news bulletins, interspersed with light music, greetings from home and all the other attractions copied from German forces radio to be a blatant encroachment upon its territory. One of the BBC's executives regretted that 'attention is being focused on the short-term aim of winning the war, instead of the long-term aim of bringing about an ordered civilisation in accordance with British ideas, British values and British needs'.[27] Newsome, the BBC Director of European Broadcasts, stated in a 'Paper of General Guidance' that 'the best political warfare is that waged with the weapons of responsible journalism, not that carried out with the instruments of the clever advertiser'.[28] No doubt the BBC's ire, directed then at PWE, would have been even stronger had they known that Delmer also had plans to obtain the use of 'Aspidistra'.

Aspidistra ('The biggest in the world' – in the words of a popular song; '7980' was another code-name) was the code-name of the 600-kW medium-wave transmitter near Crowborough, the most powerful transmitter in Europe. It was to be a sort of a 'counter-battery'. It could drown the voice of any enemy station and impose on it its own voice. It was imported from the USA (where it was deemed too powerful to be granted a broadcasting licence) by PWE who made it available temporarily to the BBC. Inevitably, after a while, the BBC came to regard it as its own property. But that conflict was yet to come.

A practical reason – in addition to the reasons of principle – why Delmer could not have his live broadcasting had been a shortage of broadcasting studios. Now he was given brand-new, purpose-built studios at Milton Bryan near Woburn. All the equipment was the best available. He was to start with six half-hour night-time broadcasts, but this was to be extended as soon as he and his team had gained sufficient confidence and proficiency. His ambition was to provide continuous, all-night broadcasts. Obviously he needed more staff, and premises to accommodate that staff. Additional prefab huts were constructed around the studios. The whole compound, of about 5 acres, was surrounded by a 12-ft-high mesh-wire fence. Armed police – rifles and tommy-guns – patrolled the area at night.[29]

Like *GS1*, but unlike the BBC,* *Atlantik* would have no English journalists to write news and talks in English, to be then translated into German; everything would be written from the start in German by Germans. Delmer introduced a new kind of radio language, which was to make listening

---

* Eventually some German BBC programmes were written and presented by German POWs; their proportion increased after the invasion.

easier for German listeners. He banned the long sentences of classical German with the verb invariably at the end. He wanted the sentences to be short, colloquial and easily understood. It was to be like the language and idiom of the German soldier. Such style was anathema to his Germans who, although soldiers themselves, had been brought up to believe that anything simple and colloquial was ungrammatical and 'bad German', but Delmer persevered and his ideas prevailed.

While organising *GS1* he had experienced difficulties in finding suitable German staff. Now the situation was much easier: promising recruits were being found among the increasingly numerous POWs and deserters. All three services of the *Wehrmacht* were represented among Delmer's German personnel, but the strongest contingent came from the navy. This is not surprising, as the German navy and especially the U-boat crews were *Atlantik*'s original and prime targets.

Atlantik posed as a station run for their entertainment. In time it encompassed in its target audience the other two Services. Since it was pretending to be a *Wehrmacht*-run station, it could not use pornography to attract listeners. Instead, Delmer decided to broadcast music that would captivate and retain an appreciative following. As American jazz was banned in Germany, Delmer assumed – correctly – that many young Germans, especially those in uniform, would want to listen to it. To make it even more attractive, he introduced 'American jazz with a German flavour'. Not only did he have American hits re-recorded with German lyrics but he also had a German band to perform them. One of the top German bands, under Henry Zeisel, was touring Rommel's units in North Africa when they were captured by the Eighth Army. In due course they were brought to Britain and were delighted to be given, by Delmer, an opportunity to continue their professional activities, even playing for the same audience, the *Wehrmacht*. Another purveyor of music was the band of the Royal Marines.[30] One of the tunes they recorded was a popular Berlin music-hall song called '*Es war in Schöneberg im Monat Mai*' ('It happened in Schöneberg in the month of May'). It was a favourite with U-boat crews who made up new, rather bawdy verses, and Delmer decided to use the new lyrics. The vocalist was a nephew of the former German Chief of Staff, General von Fritzsche. The first line went 'I was in a cathouse in St Nazaire …' 'Fortunately', wrote Delmer, 'the bandmaster colonel conducting the marines did not ask me to translate the rest of the words.' So it would seem that the *GS1* style did reappear occasionally in *Atlantik*.

In many cases the music was recorded by dance bands and German singers in the USA, always carefully chosen to be attractive to German servicemen. German lyrics were especially written for new songs being launched there and were often sung by such famous artistes as Marlene Dietrich. (Actually, Dietrich was led to believe that she was recording for the Voice of America. She did not learn the truth until after the war when she visited her native Berlin where right-wing extremists, who regarded her as a traitor, greeted her with a barrage of rotten tomatoes.) The latest German hits were also broadcast, the records having been obtained routinely via Stockholm and flown over to England by Mosquito.

In a 'most secret' paper prepared in October 1943, probably for the Foreign Office, the *modus operandi* of the station was described:

> *Atlantik* is on the air without intermission from 18.30 to 08.00 hours BST … it plays recorded dance music continually, with short interruptions for news flashes and longer ones, lasting 15–20 minutes for full news bulletins and features.

News bulletins consist of reports from the Front, from inside Germany and from Germany's allies together with items of special interest to service men, and they include information taken straight from the official German news agencies as well as material slightly 'doctored' for subversive purposes and items which are out-and-out, but nevertheless plausible, inventions. In addition to straight news a number of human interest stories as well as expertly written sports bulletins are constantly introduced for cover purposes.

Useful cover has also been obtained by pretending to hook up … with the *Soldatensender Mittelmeer*, an official German station broadcasting from the Balkans. Every item used is given as a plain statement of fact without comment, and no view-point is expressed except in the special naval talks in which the attitude of the speaker is merely that of a man defending the interests of the ordinary seaman. Regular features include talks warning U-boat crews against certain reckless and incompetent commanders, greetings supposedly from their families and reports of air raid damage, street by street. … These are always followed by reference to the German High Command order entitling members of armed forces to compassionate leave if they have received news that their homes had been bombed … The entire programme is broadcast live, even during the night and this enables the station to offer its listeners an up-to-the-minute news service which often scoops the official *Reich* Radio …

[The object is] to undermine the morale of the German armed forces in Western Europe – particularly of the U-boat crews operating in the Atlantic – by creating alarm in their minds regarding conditions at home, by unsettling their faith in their arms and equipment and in their leaders, by rationalising bad discipline and

> performance of military duty, and wherever possible by encouraging actual desertion. The general line is to win the confidence and the interest of the German Services listeners by presenting them with informative news of current events and with pleasant entertainment in the form of good dance music – such as they are no longer given by the *Reich* Radio.[31]

The musical entertainment provided by *Atlantik* was first class. Listeners, unless they were exceptionally serious-minded, preferred it both to the BBC and to genuine German stations. Eventually *Promi* felt obliged to provide an imitation entertainment programme but it was not a success and *Atlantik* remained the German forces' favourite.[32]

Atlantik's music served not only as a lure but also as weapon to attack the morale of U-boat crews. When U-boats were leaving their bases on operations, Navy Intelligence was often alerted by its agents, or, especially in the case of bases in Germany, they could deduce it sometimes by analysing other information. *Atlantik* would then send out greetings and play records dedicated to named U-boats and even to individual crew members. Delmer's German index was being continually expanded, the sources being the German press, DNB bulletins, interrogation of POWs and their correspondence with their families, so that the greetings could include personal and family details. This index made it also possible to send out birthday greetings and congratulations on wedding anniversaries. The effect of these broadcasts was devastating. In the words of a German petty officer, when taken prisoner: 'We had sailed under the usual secrecy, strict radio silence and all that, but we had not been at sea for more than two days when *Atlantik* calls us up and plays some special music. It's a mighty unpleasant sensation, I can tell you, to feel that you're being watched like that. And that the enemy knows exactly where you are.'[33]

The 'enemy', of course, did not know the U-boat's position.

Deducing the enemy's plans and intentions by analysing available data – including, for instance, trends in German propaganda – became a highly specialised and important intelligence activity. Exact methods employed have never been made public. Perhaps they were akin to the methods of Operational Research which were invented to optimise the characteristics of transatlantic convoys. But bullseyes could be scored with the help of common sense – plus a bit of luck. For example, Navy Intelligence discovered that a number of German armed merchant vessels and a *Kriegsmarine* ship were lying upstream in the Gironde estuary, with steam up. It was assumed that this flotilla intended to break through the British naval cordon and sail for Japan. The crews were addressed by the velvet-voiced *Atlantik* announcer Vicky: 'And now, by special request of the comrade blockade runners who are getting awfully bored in the Gironde estuary while they await orders to sail, I am going to play a little selection of music from our brave allies in the East!' Then followed a most awful pot-pourri of Japanese records. It was repeated the following day, with a talk on the difficulties the *Luftwaffe* would have providing air cover during the break-out. Soon after, the commander of the *Luftwaffe* in the Bay of Biscay area was taken prisoner. Even before the first question was put to him by the interrogators, he said: 'No good my attempting to keep anything secret from you fellows. You know it all anyhow. *Atlantik* even broadcast a verbatim report of my top-secret conference with the Navy onboard a blockade breaker in the Gironde estuary. Incredible!'

To conduct a successful psychological warfare campaign against U-boat crews it was imperative to be familiar with every aspect of their life at sea and during their rest periods on land. Much of this knowledge was gained from the increasingly skilful interrogation of U-boat men taken prisoner. Usually, when they realised how much was already known about their equipment, operational tactics, colleagues and especially their officers, they would talk quite freely, adding further details to Delmer's data bank.

About ten former U-boat men were recruited to join the *Atlantik* team. The most valuable of them was a man called Mander. His technical knowledge, especially in the area of signals, his many friends and acquaintances in the navy and his proficiency in lower-deck slang were most useful. He was also brilliant at thinking up ways of delaying the departures of U-boats by untraceable acts of sabotage. Royal Navy experts admitted that they could not beat him in this field. Of course, it would not do for *Atlantik* to incite sabotage; it would only describe minutely, as news items, the unattributable acts of deplorable sabotage that resulted in delayed departures. It was meant to appeal to the submariners' self-preservation instinct by suggesting how they could improve their life expectancy. Mander also helped the Royal Navy to lure two U-boats into a trap. After the war he returned to Germany, where he soon died – most probably at the hands of vengeful Nazis.[34]

Sometimes German regulations offered unmissable propaganda opportunities. For instance, if a soldier started divorce proceedings on grounds of adultery, but was killed before the hearing, then the widow was still entitled to all the normal benefits, receiving a pension and inheriting his estate. This was considered to be a scandal by many, including Hitler, who issued an order that such divorces should be carried through to the end, as if the soldier was still alive. What was more, divorce proceedings were now to be instituted by the Party authorities in those cases where the dead soldier would probably have started proceedings had he lived. In addition, the Party was given the authority to start proceedings even in the cases where the soldier was not aware of his wife's infidelity. This order obviously presented Party officials with an opportunity to use pressure, and blackmail the unfortunate widows. *Atlantik* did not spare airtime to describe how the Party high-ups were taking advantage of these opportunities to profit from the misfortunes of heroic soldiers' families.

Delmer did everything he could to maintain the cover of a German station. He went so far as using Goebbels's jargon: raids by the RAF and US Air Force were referred to as 'terror raids' and the crews were 'terror flyers'. The Allies were 'the enemy', characterised with whatever pejorative epithets were in vogue in Germany at the time. The speeches of Hitler and Goebbels were re-transmitted live. Delmer realised that, in spite of this camouflage, listeners of even average intelligence would eventually see through it or would be disabused by their own propaganda or by their superiors. This did not worry him unduly. He was convinced – and he was proven right – that they would not desert his station because they liked its patriotic and nationalistic viewpoint, its music and its news, which was never stale. 'Enemy' station or not, it spelled out the fears, doubts and suspicions they did not dare to mention to their subordinates, peers or superiors, frequently not even to their families.

One of Delmer's rules was: 'Accuracy first. We must never lie by accident, or through slovenliness, only deliberately!'[35] This rule was applied rigorously, especially to the news from the battlefields. Very often *Atlantik* would be first with such news, beating all German stations. This ensured a good following, especially as all the military details were always 100 per cent correct. Delmer expected that the listener, suitably impressed by the presentation of the battlefield news, would receive with equal trust the items in the bulletin that followed, which would contain both true and invented facts concerning domestic, economic and political events. It does not follow that there was a great divide between the battlefield news and the rest, the former offering nothing but the truth and the latter nothing but lies. The latter also contained a proportion of uncontroversial and inconsequential items to build up the station's credibility, such as: 'This afternoon in Lorient the Seventh U-Boat Flotilla beat the Second Flotilla by three goals to two. The two teams are now celebrating at the Café Réunion …' Such information would be supplied by a local Navy Intelligence agent.

A regular service provided by *Atlantik*, which also had to be 100 per cent correct, was reports of bomb damage to residential areas. Using air reconnaissance photographs and town street plans, a specially trained team was able to pinpoint individual houses that had been destroyed or badly damaged. Their addresses were then broadcast. Obviously, every soldier with a family in a bombed town was eager to listen. The reports were so accurate and so prompt that the *Gestapo* was convinced *Atlantik* had agents all over Germany who were sending messages even during the air raids. They wasted much effort trying to catch them.

Atlantik broadcasts were used also for deception purposes. For instance, when the Germans came up with a new anti-radar device called 'Aphrodite' – a balloon tethered to a surfaced U-boat, which was supposed to protect it from British radar – the navy asked for a vigorous 'anti-Aphrodite' campaign. It was hoped that Germans would conclude that the Admiralty was seriously worried about Aphrodite, and would continue to use this device which was, in fact, totally ineffective. The bluff worked. The Germans stopped looking for other countermeasures and continued to use the ludicrous balloon for a long time.

Delmer had now more sources of intelligence and more gifted propagandists working for him. In broadcast after broadcast examples were given of 'inequality of sacrifice' between ordinary men and the privileged Party functionaries. Listeners were reminded that functionaries were exempted from front-line military service (there really was a decree exempting officials of the propaganda ministry from military service). If they did get called up it was only for a token period. The wives and daughters of Party high-ups, maintained *Atlantik*, were exempt from the call-up for women, including work in industry, and they did not have to provide accommodation in their homes for evacuees or bombed-out families, as ordinary Germans were compelled to do. Examples were given of defeatism among the higher Party echelons, who were selling the businesses they had acquired in occupied countries, realising that they would have to leave before long, and were smuggling their ill-gotten gains to Switzerland and South America.

The credibility and the attractiveness of the station did not depend on its ability to convince the listener that it was a German station, but on proving that it knew what it was talking about, that the information it provided was reliable and up to date, that its stories were at least broadly based on truth. It was equally important that these stories were presented by men who were obviously the listeners' comrades-in-arms who shared their feelings and anxieties and expressed themselves in their idiom. Had the BBC tried this approach, it would have lost its credibility, which depended on reporting the truth and nothing but the truth, separating it rigorously from rumour and speculation. That it did not always report all the truth was not known at the time and so did not harm its reputation.

RUs, like all other media, observed the government policy directives for the countries to which they related, but they did so from the standpoint of their listeners. Occasionally they were allowed to diverge from the official line, but at all times they had to avoid overlapping or clashing with white propaganda. They were not expensive to run. The costs of operating short-wave transmitters were low and the average number of staff was only six: a British housemaster who was responsible for ensuring that policy directives were followed, for the control of scripts and for the discipline within his team, four scriptwriters and speakers, and a housekeeper. Each team was accommodated in its own, separate detached house in Woburn. Contacts with other teams were banned, as were contacts with the locals. The reason for the isolation from other RU teams was to prevent any exchange of ideas on programme form and contents: similarities between the outputs of individual RUs would betray their common origins.

On 21 July 1943, Delmer fired his first shot in the battle for Aspidistra. Soon the battle was joined by the principal departments, the Combined Chiefs of Staff and, of course, by the BBC. Many memoranda were exchanged, many arguments – often spurious – presented, and many strings pulled. It took five months for common sense to prevail and, at 8 p.m. on 14 November 1943, the first medium-wave grey station went on the air with the announcement: 'Here is the *Soldatensender Calais* broadcasting on wavelengths of 360, 410 and 492 metres, linked with the German short-wave transmitter *Atlantik* broadcasting on short-wave bands of 30.7 and 48.3 metres. We bring music and news for our comrades in the Command Areas West and Norway.'

The programme was common to both stations. To start, *Calais* was given only 3 hours daily, but this was gradually increased until in 1945 it was broadcasting practically round the clock. After D-Day its name was changed to *Soldatensender West*.

After the invasion the German army communications were in total disarray. Many *Wehrmacht* commanders were reduced to relying on *West*'s situation reports to update their staff maps.

Aspidistra did not always transmit on the same medium wavelengths. It could switch its wavelengths with ease and this facility was put to a good use: to defend British bombers against attacks by German night-fighters.[36] When the German radar network reached the stage in its development that it could successfully direct the night-fighters to their targets, the instructions were transmitted on short wave. British jammers soon put an end to this and the system was transferred to medium wave. The instructions were now in a coded form, hidden in normal programmes. When this was eventually discovered, it was decided to use Aspidistra to jam these programmes, using recordings of suitable noises. Soon it was realised that normal *Calais* programmes could fulfil this function just as well. This operation, code-named Dartboard, was a resounding success. The chief of Bomber Command calculated that it was saving six or seven bombers a night.

Aspidistra's full capabilities were not used until the final months of the war, when Allied troops were already fighting on German soil. Originally SHAEF (Supreme Headquarters Allied Expeditionary Force) did not want the civilian population to flee from the fighting, assuming that crowds of refugees clogging up the roads would be just as great a hindrance to the advancing Allies as to the retreating Germans. All the official Allied radio stations were telling them to stay put. When Churchill found out about it he did not like it at all, and persuaded Eisenhower that the reverse would be much more appropriate. Germans were to be panicked out of their cellars onto the roads. But neither the BBC nor the Voice of America could go back on their previous appeals without losing authority and goodwill. It was a job for Aspidistra, Delmer's 'Big Bertha'. Delmer's team had been training for a long time to carry out 'intrusion' operations of this kind. They were especially well prepared to impersonate the Cologne radio station.

When British bombers were flying in the general direction of a major German town, the local radio station would always go off the air, so as not to act as a navigational beacon. The German anti-aircraft defence did not know that the RAF never made such use of German stations. Other stations would continue transmitting the national programme on their usual frequencies. Research into the behaviour of German broadcasting stations in relation to the approach of enemy aircraft had been carried out over a considerable period and the Big Bertha team was ready for action.[37] That evening their luck held: RAF bombers would be flying towards Cologne. At 2120hr Cologne stopped transmitting and Aspidistra seamlessly took its place, re-transmitting on its frequency the national programme, picked up from another German station. After a few minutes this programme was interrupted for an 'important local announcement'. Delmer had two announcers – a man and a woman – who could imitate perfectly a similar Radio Cologne team. The 'important announcement' was supposedly an order issued by the local *Gauleiter*. It was very urgent: enemy armoured units were approaching rapidly and women and children were to leave their homes immediately, taking with them only the most essential belongings – not more than 15kg. To make this easier, they should use any available handcarts, perambulators or bicycles. Their Party leaders would form them into columns and take them to assembly points, where evacuation trains would be waiting to take them to safe areas in Bavaria. The men should stay behind, joining the *Volksturm*, to defend their villages. There was, in fact, a German contingency plan to evacuate the area, and Delmer was in possession of documents related to it, so he could include some genuine instructions and use appropriate code-names. This announcement, whose authenticity was difficult to question, was repeated several times, returning to the national programme in between. Eventually 'Cologne' went off the air. On the following nights this performance was repeated with similar visits to Frankfurt and Leipzig radio stations.

German authorities did not react immediately and some people followed the instructions. Others decided to obey the previous Allied white instructions, and stayed in their cellars. When the authorities did react, unmasking the instructions as enemy propaganda, the Big Bertha team replied with counterclaims, as to which instructions were emanating from real German authorities. In the end nobody could be sure which broadcasts were genuine and which counterfeit.

Aspidistra made similar forays during the Rhein crossings.[38] In the end, facing total chaos, German authorities gave up using the medium wave for issuing orders to the population. They limited themselves to the long wave and the *Drahtfunk*, a wired diffusion network on which Delmer could not intrude, but whose scope was very restricted.[39] Anticipating the use of *Drahtfunk* and pre-empting this move, Delmer's team warned the population that the enemy was using undamaged telephone lines between occupied and unoccupied areas to send misleading instructions. More confusion. Aspidistra finally went off the air on 1 May 1945, when the collapse of Germany's resistance was evident and further black propaganda operations were considered to be superfluous.

There were other German-language RUs, bringing the total to nine, but none could boast an audience even approaching the numbers of the aficionados of *Gustav Siegfried Eins*, *Atlantik*, *Calais* or *West*.

The purpose of G8, the 'German Workers' Station', was not clear. It operated from July 1942 to March 1943. According to a memorandum dated 11 October 1942, its atmosphere was 'conspiratorial'.[40] Its first programmes, with 'Lili Marleen' as the signature tune, were to build in the minds of the audience an idea of a well-developed opposition organisation within Germany. It provided, almost exclusively, news from Germany and represented workers' opposition in general, without allegiance to any party. According to Delmer, the underlying idea of the station was that it was run by anti-Nazi engineers working in some large concern, like Siemens, that was building radio transmitters. They were supposed to be using these transmitters for their broadcasts, on the pretence of testing them. They offered information on conditions and grievances in various factories, as well as detailed instructions on factory sabotage, go-slow techniques and methods of malingering. On the other hand, Howe writes, quoting a paper by Reginald Leeper, that the true purpose of this left-wing station was known to very few people in PWE: 'By an agreement made with General Sikorski, Polish agents operating inside Poland, and even inside Germany, will take down news transmitted through this station for insertion in a pseudo-German clandestine press. The Poles already produce and distribute in Germany such newspapers.'[41] This information is repeated in Cruikshank's *The Fourth Arm*.[42]

Perhaps Leeper confused G8 with Polish language RUs P1 and P2. P1 (*Świt,* active from November 1942 to November

1944) was the station set up under an agreement with Sikorski, but supplying news copy to the Polish Resistance was not its function. This was the purpose of P2 ('The Voice of Polish Women'), which did not start operations until October 1943. On the other hand, Major Thurston wrote to Major Dziewanowski of the VI Bureau of the Polish General Staff on 23 December 1942: 'I should be very interested to know… whether you have yet received any reports from Poland of the reception of our left-wing transmitter.' Dziewanowski replied: 'I telegraphed asking about the reception of the left-wing transmitter, on 14 December, but I have received no answer yet.'[43] Howe quotes also a report by the US Foreign Broadcast Intelligence Service that this station also broadcast 'special messages to foreign workers, in French and Italian'. G8's operations are rather confusing.

G7, the 'German Priest' station (in operation from September 1942 to April 1945), was black in so far as it purported to be located in southern Germany, but it did not indulge in Delmer-style subversive offerings. Father Andreas, who was both the scriptwriter and presenter, was a young Austrian Roman Catholic priest who had received his church authorities' permission to join Delmer's team. He was on the air five or six days a week, twice in the morning on 49 metres and twice in the evening on 31 metres.[44] Each broadcast opened with organ music or Gregorian chants (which served as the station identification signal) followed by a short quotation from the Bible and a sermon of 6 to 9 minutes. The prayer with which the broadcast ended served as a summary of the main points of the sermon, as well as an invocation. One of the priest's main themes was to contrast 'Christ the King' with 'Hitler the *Führer*' and to stress the chasm between the idea of Christian charity and the narrow and selfish conception of the Nazi 'people's community'. He told his listeners about some of the infamous things that were being done in their name to the Jews, the Slavs and their own people – such as the euthanasia programme and the *SS Lebensborn* programme under which single girls were to bear children sired by *SS* men to produce a master race – and about the Party's contempt for human and moral laws. He described the horrors of Auschwitz and Mauthausen. His talks were factual and accurate. They contained no inventions, no rumours. Several of his scripts were issued as leaflets.

Not long after Father Andreas started his broadcasts, Delmer asked his friends in SOE and OSS (Office of Strategic Services, the US counterpart of SOE) to have their rumour agents in neutral capitals spread it around that the 'German Priest' radio was a Vatican black station. This rumour caught on remarkably well.[45]

In Delmer's virtual German world a place was found even for an opposition movement within the *Waffen-SS*. Two RUs were set up: G10, called *Kampfgruppe Yorck Waffen-SS* (in operation from December 1943 to April 1945), and U1, *Hagedorn* (from January to April 1945). Very little information is available about these two stations. It seems that the man who made it possible for these stations to operate in a credible manner was one Zech-Nenntwich (Nentwig?), cover name Nansen, a genuine officer deserter of the *Waffen-SS*. He claimed to be the second-in-command of a resistance group led by Brigadier Hermann Fegelein, brother-in-law of Hitler's mistress Eva Braun (this did not stop Hitler from having him shot for treason in the last days of the war). He claimed also to have co-operated with the Polish *AK*, selling them arms and ammunition, and helping their couriers to reach Sweden; when he was arrested by the security service, Poles in turn helped him to get away, and smuggled him to Sweden. Delmer checked this story with his Polish friends and it was confirmed. Nevertheless, he never fully trusted the only *SS* man in his team.[46]

The main theme of both stations was that the patriotic ideals of the noble knights of the *Waffen-SS* had been betrayed by the unworthy *Führer* who forced upon them as comrades-in-arms the worst scum of murderers, sadists and other criminals, thereby soiling their good name throughout the world; the small but powerful opposition group, it was said, intended to curb the nefarious excesses of the *Gestapo*, the security services and of the Party.

The complete list of German-language RUs contains one called *Astrologie und Okkultismus* but it never became operational. The idea was to have in the studio an alleged medium who would be receiving messages from soldiers killed in action, for transmission to their families. However, the actress impersonating the medium could not help giggling and only a few programmes were recorded. None were broadcast.

There were also Italian-language RUs, numbered W1 to W6, the 'W' standing for 'Wop'. The first one, *Radio Italia*, was started in November 1940 and the second, *Radio Libertá*, seven months later. According to all sources, their broadcasts were 'spasmodic, unplanned and amateurish'. *Libertá* was closed down after five months, but *Italia* survived for eighteen months. In 1943 four new Italian RUs were started. Probably the most important, although the shortest lived, was *Radio Livorno* (W3), which helped to bring about the surrender of the Italian navy. It pretended to operate on behalf of a navy resistance organisation from a cabin of an Italian warship lying in the Livorno base. Night after night it warned other Italian warships to be on guard against the Germans, especially against German attempts to seize their ships. It also told them not to make any moves without orders from itself. Then gradually it became clearer and clearer that *Livorno* was negotiating with the Allies the 'liberation' of the Italian navy. Its commanders must have realised that *Livorno* was in fact the voice of the British Admiralty. When at last, on 10 September 1943, *Livorno* gave the order to sail to Malta, the Italian ships did so without hesitation and surrendered there to Admiral Cunningham. The whole operation was carried out under the Admiralty's close control.

W6 was set up for one purpose only: to intrude upon the transmissions of the 'Fascist Republican Radio'. After being rescued from his anti-fascist captors in a spectacular operation by German paratroopers,* Mussolini set up a new Fascist Republican government in northern Italy. Goebbels put at his disposal a short-wave transmitter in Munich. It broadcast on two frequencies, in half-hourly periods. Each period was divided into three parts, separated by military and patriotic music. W6 would re-transmit on its own frequency the first part of the programme, then come in with its own musical intermission and news or a talk replacing the second part, and return to re-transmitting for the last part. It was hoped that listeners twiddling the dial looking for the Duce's programme would come across the counterfeit programme and stay with it.

After a few days, Munich was indignantly denying that they had said the appalling things that monitors all over the world reported them as saying. Denials and counter-denials created an impossible situation and Goebbels gave up the short wave, transferring the programme to the medium wave. This antagonised the Bavarians, who were deprived of their radio

---

* Contrary to generally held view, Colonel of the *Waffen-SS* Skorzeny was not in charge of this operation. (*British Army Review*, No. 70, April 1982)

entertainment. The overall effect of this intrusion was perhaps not great but Delmer and his team gained invaluable experience of intrusion operations, which was put to good use later with Big Bertha.

There were RUs broadcasting in other languages as well: French, Roumanian, Norwegian, Danish, Czech, Serb and Croat, Flemish, Dutch, Slovene, Bulgarian, Hungarian and Slovak. It is amazing how much Delmer had achieved since 23 May 1941 when *Gustav Siegfried Eins* was first heard and the Corporal was his only assistant.

Chapter Five

Black Rumours and Black Leaflets

Before the arrival of mass media people had to rely for their news on word-of-mouth dissemination. It is thought that rumours had almost as great an influence on public opinion as the radio or press, and that only the arrival of television drastically reduced the importance of the whispered rumour as an effective channel of propaganda. In the United States, within weeks of Pearl Harbor, nearly a thousand malicious rumours were recorded by researchers. They promoted anti-Semitism and distrust of the armed forces, tried to stimulate evasion of military service and opposition to the purchase of War Bonds – anything that would weaken the war effort. President Roosevelt had to repudiate them in a special 'fireside chat'.[1]

'Made in Britain' wartime propaganda rumours were called 'sibs', from Latin *sibillare* – to whisper. Some of them could be classified as black but most were grey. Rumours, like any other instrument of propaganda, are produced for definite and specific purposes, for example to make the enemy move his troops, to undermine his morale, to destroy his faith in his leaders or to confuse and mislead neutrals friendly to the enemy.[2] A rumour may be based on truth, but by the time it starts to circulate it will have shed most of the elements of that truth.

Rumours as weapons must not be created in a haphazard fashion. They have to be part of a strategic or political plan designed to achieve a specific result. Unrelated rumours can do more harm than good. They should also be short. Verbose rumours lose their padding while being passed, while lean sibs become more elaborate. They must be directed at a well-defined target and they must not breach unwittingly your own security. If they are about enemy leaders, salacious details will enhance their effectiveness.

Sibs were fabricated at CHQ by the Underground Propaganda Committee (UPC), which was also receiving suggestions from other sources. Sibs of a military nature were then submitted for approval to the Inter-Service Security Board (ISSB) and to the Joint Intelligence Committee (JIC). At first, non-military rumours were not submitted to any authority, but later all needed the Foreign Office's approval. After the formation of PWE, UPC became a sub-committee of the Executive Committee. Surprisingly, Delmer was never a member of UPC; he had his own rumour manufactory.

It seems that, at the outset, the rumourmongers were going for quantity rather than quality. SIS complained that they did not have enough agents to handle all the material supplied. Dalton issued orders to cut the production by one-third. According to some opinions, British sibbing suffered from the absence of a whole-time professional endowed with a gift of a scientific approach combined with a brilliant imagination, and consequently the majority of the sibs were feeble and often childish.[3] There was, for example, the 1940 sib, attacked in the *Daily Mail*, that the British government had imported from

Australia 200 man-eating sharks and let them loose in the Channel as an anti-invasion measure. Another said that von Ribbentrop had instructed Cardinal Innitzer ofVienna to ask the Pope to canonise Hitler's mother.

On the other hand, a short sib put out at about the same time became one of the most successful of the whole war: 'The English have invented a method of setting the sea on fire.' It was disseminated using several channels and soon there were eyewitness reports of charred bodies, the casualties of an unsuccessful invasion. According to *Wehrmacht* barrack-room gossip, hospitals equipped to deal with burns were being set up all along the Channel coast. What is more, the German navy started to test fireproofed invasion craft and asbestos suits for their crews. The story stuck. As late as Christmas 1944 (I was working then for the gardener in the Rheinland)I heard from a young *Waffen-SS* man that, according to a veteran in his unit, a trial Operation Seelöwe (invasion of Britain) was repulsed by the dastardly Brits who had set the Channel on fire. Another sib that was accepted as truth by many soldiers, and probably by even more numerous German civilians – undoubtedly because they wanted to believe it – was that top Nazi leaders, like the Minister of Labour, Ley, were not subject to normal food rationing and that they received most generous 'diplomat rations'.

A typical indirect approach was exemplified in a 'report' about the alleged high mortality rate in camps set up to accommodate children evacuated from bombed-out areas:'Dr Conti, the *Reichsführer* for Physicians, has congratulated the medical officers at the KLV *[Kinderlandverschickungslager* – Evacuation Camp for Children] camps in the Gau Wartheland* for the selfless devotion with which they are fighting the diphtheria

---

* The Polish Poznań district, annexed to the *Reich*.

epidemic among the children in their care. He has expressed satisfaction at their success in overcoming the tragic lack of medicaments, and reducing deaths by an average of sixty a week.'[4]

Another medical sib concerned allegedly contaminated blood supplies in military hospitals. The story was that blood had been taken from Russian POWs to be given to German wounded, and that most of this blood was infected with venereal disease and other bacteria. To give an appearance of authenticity, names of members of military transfusion teams were used, culled from propaganda articles in the German press praising the achievements of the transfusion service.

Most sibs were quite simple, for example:

- 'You do not see any seagulls over the Mediterranean – they have all been killed by oil from sunken German tankers which tried to supply Rommel.'
- 'British flame-throwing aircraft are patrolling the Libyan coast.'
- 'Britain has now an "invisible searchlight" that illuminates an aircraft without the crew being aware of it.'
- 'Women in war factories are losing their good looks, their skins go yellow and they lose their capacity to bear children.'
- 'Badly wounded soldiers are given mercy injections to prevent them being a burden to the State.'
- 'The engines of the new He 177 aircraft tend to burst into flames in the air.' (Actually, there were problems with the He 177 engines.)
- 'Ships arriving in Denmark from the Eastern Baltic brought back a pig disease, which can affect humans who eat pork.'
- 'Typhus is sweeping westward from the destroyed cities of Poland.'

- 'Inflation and financial collapse are just round the corner.'
- 'Hitler has given instructions to Goebbels that no more references are to be made to his having been a corporal.'

And during the last phase of the war:

- '*SS* men are forcing regular soldiers to exchange uniforms and IDs with them.'
- 'Only those officers who are sure of execution as war criminals are to command last-stand defences.'
- 'Foreign workers in Germany are organised into efficient military battalions led by British and American paratroop officers. They are cutting railways and roads in the rear of German troops.'

The construction of some sibs was more complex. For instance, after the 1943 successful bombing by the RAF of the Ruhr dams ('The Dambusters'), it was put out that their destruction was attributed to a secret organisation of foreign workers in Germany; the RAF raids were just a camouflage to enable the saboteurs to do their job. The idea was to make the *Gestapo* waste time and resources on looking for a non-existent underground organisation of foreign workers. For good measure it was also asserted that the resulting floods contaminated vegetable crops and grain; the population must be ready for an epidemic of dysentery, followed by typhoid.

A deeper plot surrounded the bombing of HMS *Ark Royal*. Early in the war the *Ark Royal* was bombed, and a German pilot was decorated for sinking the ship, which, however, had only been damaged. Later, the *Ark Royal* was actually sunk. *Promi* was in a dilemma: to ignore a success or to repeat its claim. A PWE sib seemed to solve this problem: it claimed that both sinkings were true, the explanation being that Britain had broken the Anglo-German naval convention and had built two *Ark Royals*. The unpleasant – for the Germans – corollary was that if there were two *Ark Royals*, there might be two of every other capital ship as well.[5]

There is no record of the total number of produced sibs but it is estimated that *Atlantik* alone broadcast about 10,000.

Few people can resist the temptation to pass on bad news; even more love to know and to pass on spicy details of the lives of their local or national leaders, and practically everybody can be seduced by the prospect of acquiring some pieces of secret or restricted information and, once in possession, to enhance his status by passing them on. These traits of human nature are the basis of whispered propaganda. The agent who drops a well-constructed rumour will have, in a matter of days, hundreds of sub-agents working unwittingly for him. Of course, a successful rumour must be alarming or scandalous enough to be passed on, and credible enough to conceal the fact that it is a concoction.

There were many rumour dissemination channels, apart from the RUs. Occasionally black leaflets would be dropped by the RAF or by special leaflet balloons. This was not done very frequently, since, in most cases, leaflets dropping from the sky could hardly pretend to be black. They were more convincing when received in envelopes posted in Germany. Addressees were provided by Delmer's index, and the agent networks had no problems smuggling them into Germany for despatch. There was the SOE agent network and the SIS network, but the latter could be used only subject to the assurance that the same sibs would not be propagated by other means. There were also agents at ports and airports who would talk to seamen and passengers about to embark, agents connected with neutral seamen's hostels and clubs, agents in touch with neutral journalists and diplomats, with persons suspected of being in communication with the enemy and, before 1941, with communists.[6] Reports were planted in the British and American press, letters were written by people in England to friends abroad and passed by special arrangement with the censorship. Members of British embassies and legations abroad, as well as military attachés, also did their bit.

And, of course, there were bars in Lisbon, Stockholm, Ankara and other neutral capitals frequented by neutral and enemy journalists and agents, who were doing the same thing – trying to plant their rumours. While doing so they were also picking up gossip fabricated by PWE.

Channels for the transmission of particular sibs had to be selected with some care. The same rumour arriving simultaneously from several sources could be regarded as suspect. For instance, should the *AA* (the German Foreign Office) receive the same information from, say, Madrid, Buenos Aires and Stockholm, it could conclude that it was inspired by a common source. Therefore, channels had to be selected very judiciously. Propaganda of a deceptive nature is a very dangerous game to play.[7] It is of the utmost importance that the parallel, straight propaganda is so worded as not to permit inferences being drawn from it by the enemy which would compromise the deception plans. Weekly meetings were arranged between PWE and the London Controlling Section (LCS)* at which the weekly propaganda directives to be issued by PWE were carefully studied and altered, if necessary. It was equally important that the misinformation passed to the enemy by SIS's own

---

* An organisation under the Chiefs of Staff, responsible for the overall planning and implementation of deception plans and for the coordination of deception plans in the various theatres.

channels should not be compromised by low-level rumours or obvious propaganda; close similarity would ring alarm bells at the *Abwehr*.

Before the war a number of people considered the possibility of black printing but it seems that only Section D produced some materials. This work, and the work done during the SO1 period, consisted of typewritten circulars and of matter purporting to have been produced by an anti-Nazi opposition. Many technical and linguistic errors were committed and the chances of deceiving the enemy for long were nil. High-grade forged material, which could survive an expert examination, was not produced until after November 1941, when Ellic Howe (cover name Armin Hull) joined PWE. His fakes and forgery unit became really productive in the spring of 1942.

Howe was a printer whose pre-war hobby was collecting specimens of German printing: newspapers, stationery (both commercial and private), forms, posters, tickets, anything he could lay his hands on. He made a special study of German typography and printing techniques. He was also familiar with the British printing industry and knew precisely where to go to satisfy any printing requirement. He had a first-class knowledge of the papermaking industry and was able to arrange on numerous occasions the perfect counterfeiting of German papers and watermarks by British mills. He could also arrange the forging of handwriting and of signatures. As he explained to Delmer: 'I asked a friend at Scotland Yard whether he knew a good forger who would like to serve his King and Country, and he put me on to an artist doing time for forgery in Wormwood Scrubs, and there you are!'[8]

Howe was a perfectionist, and it is difficult to imagine how Delmer could have produced the convincing black prints without his help. Even his intentionally imperfect prints were faultless in their authenticity, such as prints that had to look as if they had been produced by underground amateurs in a dark cellar. He maintained that no professional printer was capable of doing such work badly enough, and so he installed a tiny printing press in his office, often spending his evenings printing short runs of authentic-looking underground leaflets.

Large print runs, often of millions of pages, were executed by commercial printing firms. A total of seventeen such firms worked for Howe. During its existence, with a total establishment of 3 or 4, 'Mr Howe's Unit' dealt with about 2,000 separate orders, ranging from 5 million German food ration cards to a single forged letter. Jobs were also done for the Free French and for the Americans.[9]

Black leaflets, owing to the relative slowness of the channels through which they were disseminated, had to be non-topical, practically timeless. Acute political and military questions could not be tackled. The German recipient had to be approached from a general human-interest angle, while his sense of self-interest was being exploited, to make him think and act in a way contrary to the interests of the German war effort.

The main topics of the black leaflets – not necessarily in the order of importance – were:

- Self-interest: promoting it both among Service personnel and civilians.
- Dissatisfaction: encouraging this in the ranks with references to irregular pay, officers who were much better off and soldiers who were being spied upon by the *Gestapo*.
- Anxiety: references to soldiers' homes bombed by the RAF, their wives and girlfriends having to yield to *SS* men – who are on the spot by virtue of their safe jobs far away from the front – and to foreign workers.

- Loneliness: isolation from home, infrequent and very slow field post.
- Deprivation: poor food, lack of vitamins and no winter clothing.
- Sex: only officers have decent brothels.
- Terror: front-line casualties; if in an occupied country – lethal attacks by the local resistance; fear of being liquidated by own side when becoming a serious casualty.[10]

During 1942–3, the principal aims of black leaflet campaigns were:

- To encourage dereliction of duty in the armed forces (malingering, desertion, sabotage).
- To stimulate despondency and anxiety concerning the Home Front (air raids), the course of the war, their own future after the war, foreign workers (the fidelity of wives and girlfriends).
- To provide evidence of a split in the leadership and to promote doubts about the leadership.
- To provide evidence of left-wing and Roman Catholic opposition, and to give rise to misgivings about the justification for the war.[11]

The most highly decorated soldier of the Third *Reich*, the fighter ace Colonel Werner Mölders (14 kills in the Spanish Civil War and 115 in the Second World War) was a national hero. He was also a devout Catholic and was known to be critical of the Nazi regime. He had the bad luck of falling victim to 'blue on blue': in November 1941 he was shot down by German flak, although, according to some sources, it was a flying accident in bad weather. It was to be expected that the death of one of the most popular fighter pilots would be widely discussed in Germany, and Delmer decided to exploit it.

On *GS1 der Chef* denounced Himmler's henchmen who, conforming with the Party's anti-religious campaign, 'had murdered the shining light of German manhood'.[12] Then followed the leaflets, which became widely known as the 'Mölders letter'.

The letter purported to have been written by Mölders to an old friend, a parish priest at Stettin (now Szczecin), called Johst. At the first glance the letter seemed quite innocuous but it was subtly drawing attention to the Party's anti-religious attitude. It was also defeatist, and although it did not overtly preach rebellion against the Party, the reader, on reflection, could not help experiencing rebellious sentiments. It did not name those responsible – it was left to the reader to deduce who they were. This is the most effective kind of propaganda, where the target is subtly steered to reach himself the intended conclusions. Some people saw in the letter indications that there existed a Catholic opposition – the *Gestapo* certainly did. The text was typewritten and roneoed on forged *Luftwaffe* signals message forms. It was preceded by a few introductory remarks, allegedly written by a friend, also a fighter pilot, explaining that the letter was written by Mölders shortly before his death. The leaflets were dropped at night by two RAF Mosquitoes, over an area where several squadrons of German night-fighters were based, the idea being that one of their pilots would be blamed for the drop. It was the first of the very few black leaflet drops by the RAF.

The letter struck a chord not only with Catholics, but also with Protestants. In church circles it was accepted as genuine, and was read from many pulpits. Church leaders encouraged people to send copies of the letter to their friends, and it became known all over Germany. This worried Goebbels, who mentioned it several times in his diaries. He was convinced that it was a forgery, perpetrated by Catholic circles. The only prominent person called Johst that could be traced turned out to be a Nazi playwright who put into the mouth of one of his characters the saying (usually attributed to Göring): 'When I hear the word "culture", I reach for my revolver.'[13] The *Gestapo* offered a reward of 100,000 Reichsmarks for help in tracing the author of the leaflet, and announced that disseminators would be locked up in concentration camps.[14] Parish premises were searched and typewriters and duplicating machines were requisitioned. To no avail – the more the authorities condemned the letter and its unknown author, the more the people were convinced that it was genuine. Only after the war did the Germans learn the true origins of the 'Mölders letter', and Delmer – the extent of its success.

During the First World War Germany started suffering food shortages barely one year into the war. These escalated rapidly and thousands died of starvation. Two decades later many people could still remember vividly the hunger they suffered then. German authorities were aware of this and were determined not to let it happen again. They introduced food rationing well before they started the war, so that reserves could be built up. But it seems that not only generals always fight the previous war; propagandists can also fall into this trap.

From mid-1940, British propaganda – both white and black – assumed that food ration cuts in Germany were unavoidable and imminent, on the First World War pattern, and proceeded accordingly. In the event, cuts were not needed until Germany started losing the territories she had conquered and had been exploiting mercilessly. Before this happened, Delmer devised two strategies that belonged to economic rather than psychological warfare: to cause runs (by planting rumours) on articles that were still unrationed, and to flood Germany with forged food ration cards. Both were successful to a degree.

Runs did happen in some areas on certain textile articles, and air-dropped food ration cards were used by finders, but to what extent nobody knows. Howe printed nearly sixty different types of food ration cards, some runs going into millions. Most were coupons for travellers and for soldiers on leave, although the first ration cards were printed for SOE agents who were not legally resident in Germany and therefore had no cards. Whereas the central parts of some of the cards could be identified as forgeries, the surrounding coupons – which had to be cut or torn off, if perforated, by the supplier or restaurant owner (coupons had to be surrendered in a restaurant for a meat course) – were indistinguishable from the originals. How many were used by not-so-patriotic Germans, will never be known. But whatever their number, they did not cause a noticeable supply crisis. Some clothing coupons were dropped early in 1941 in the Hamburg area, with unknown effect.[15]

The dropping of the forged ration cards precipitated an unexpected reaction from Warsaw. On 12 May 1943, the commander of *AK* signalled London: 'I understand that the RAF are dropping ration cards over Germany. The resulting tighter controls create problems for our operatives in the *Reich*, who are using ration cards printed by ourselves. Please cause the RAF to stop these airdrops.'

Some of Delmer's campaigns, especially on the German Front, were of considerable duration, such as the one aimed at U-boat crews, and others encouraging malingering, desertion and surrender. This is how he described the methods of encouraging desertion in a paper of December 1943:

> Black has for some time run a special campaign with the object of stimulating attempts at desertion, thereby

undermining general morale among the enemy. We have tried to stimulate desertion in two directions:

1. Desertion to neutral countries.
2. Absence without leave at home and in occupied territories. We have not yet tried to stimulate desertion to a United Nations territory. By a special operation … we probably could stimulate desertion to Britain of German Naval and Air Force personnel.

Desertion to Sweden, Switzerland and Spain has been fostered by the dissemination of leaflets through clandestine channels and by balloon, advising on the best methods for desertion to these countries, giving advice on what to say to the police on arrival, and explaining that the deserter need not fear retribution against his family in Germany since the German authorities have no means of telling whether a man is missing because he has deserted or because he has been killed or captured; further, the neutral countries keep their identity secret, and, in any case, there is no need for them to reveal their true identity.

By leaflet, radio and rumours we strive to create an atmosphere favourable to desertion by both stimulating the desire for desertion and suggesting that many soldiers are deserting and finding useful employment in occupied territories and in neutral countries. Our campaign, suggesting the breakdown of police efficiency and the impossibility of control, supports this operation.[16]

The remainder of the paper deals with a proposal to set up a 'German Air Force Deserter Reception Zone' to encourage pilots to fly over in their aircraft. Delmer goes on to say, that the main benefit of such a scheme would be a tightening up of the supervision of German pilots by their security, which would inevitably affect adversely their morale.

A good example of the black approach was a poster addressed to German soldiers in Norway, allegedly signed by General von Falkenhorst, commander of the German troops in that country. It starts by condemning desertion in no uncertain terms, but then it offers the valuable information that Sweden will grant asylum to anybody wearing civilian clothing, who has stayed on Swedish territory for a minimum of 24 hours. It concludes by making it a duty of all members of the *Wehrmacht* to eradicate this 'growing evil'.

A poster like this, or any document issued in the name of the *OKW*, denouncing vehemently desertion, but at the same time implying that it is neither difficult nor risky, would be more effective than a white leaflet describing a deserters' paradise in Sweden or elsewhere. The soldier would be much more impressed if he thought that he deduced the facts himself and that the conclusions were his own.

The basic ideas and principles of black propaganda encouraging desertion retained their validity throughout the war. Their practical application was gradually expanded and embellished. *Atlantik* might assert that, after the war, POWs would have an advantage over those who kept on fighting: in the prison camps they could attend excellent training courses, learning new trades and professions, while others were working outside the camps, earning good wages and would eventually return home with significant savings.

One of Delmer's schemes, concocted to add substance to these assertions, would now be considered rather cruel. Anybody could send food parcels to addresses in Germany through specialist companies in Switzerland and Sweden. Sumptuous parcels were being sent by PWE to home addresses of German soldiers killed or missing in action (easily obtainable from the obituary notices in the German press), to show their families that they were in fact alive and were doing well. It was hoped that the families would boast to everybody around that their sons and husbands enjoyed excellent conditions in captivity and were not short of money, thus encouraging more soldiers to desert.

Arguably, the most successful campaign was that which encouraged malingering, by showing German workers and soldiers, and workers of other nationalities, how to trick their doctors into granting them a spell of sick leave. By July 1944, captured documents indicated that the extent of malingering had reached higher levels than expected, and was causing considerable concern in the medical branch of the *Wehrmacht*; all commands were required to submit regularly 'returns of malingerers acting on instructions distributed by the enemy'.[17]

The campaign was based on an instruction booklet, widely disseminated all over Europe. The first edition had 64 pages but it was gradually expanded to 104 pages. The original title was *Krankheit rettet* ('Illness Saves') but soon it was being disguised as a German publication – for example, a German navy handbook on sport, a railway timetable, a German–French dictionary. In total there were more than twenty different editions. The cover and the first few pages were copies of the publications used as camouflage. One edition was disguised as packets of a well-known make of German cigarette paper. The printed text was hidden under a layer of genuine cigarette papers. The instructions did not only explain how to fake certain symptoms – sometimes with the help of drugs or chemicals – but also how to behave before the examining medical officer: 'The malingerer must give the physician the impression that here is a patriotic citizen, dedicated to his duty, who has the misfortune to be ill … [he] must never tell the doctor that he is ill, that he is suffering from some specific disease, or volunteer symptoms. One single symptom … which the doctor has discovered by his own questions, is worth ten which the patient has volunteered.'[18] The object of the campaign was not only to encourage malingering, but also to cause German doctors, who would be warned about the British handbook, to suspect malingering where there was none. It was hoped that they would also be sending back to duty the genuinely sick, possibly spreading infections and certainly fomenting discontent.

An extreme option for soldiers was the self-inflicted wound. The supposed author of the booklet, a Dr Wohltat (Dr Welldone), gave advice on how to do it without leaving the tell-tale powder-burns (fire the shot through a loaf of bread). Judging from the numerous *Wehrmacht* reports and orders on this subject, malingering, and especially self-mutilation, was quite a problem in some units, in spite of an automatic death penalty for the latter.

An unexpected compliment from the enemy was an English translation of the booklet, which *Wehrmacht Propaganda* sent over to the Allied side in special artillery shells. There was a demand for Dr Wohltat's *opus* even after the war: both in Britain and in Germany social security scroungers became its avid readers.

One of Delmer's campaigns that was not only not very effective but also basically flawed was intended to turn both ordinary Germans and the police authorities against the millions of foreign workers and prisoners who worked in German agriculture and industry. Its cost – increased persecution – was to be borne by them. Delmer probably had a bad conscience and in his book tried to justify this campaign: 'I did not believe that the majority of foreign workers were "press-ganged into slave labour". I looked on them as willing collaborators, attracted to Germany by the good pay and good rations the astute Minister of Munitions, Speer, was giving them.'[19] What utter nonsense! Delmer goes on to say that after the war he was able to obtain a confirmation of this view. And what was the source of this confirmation? Speer's right-hand man, Willy Schlieker. Delmer also described us, the foreign labour force, as 'loyal and devoted'!

In Polish villages there had been an old tradition among smallholders to do seasonal farm work in Germany. Not surprisingly, during the initial period of the occupation quite a few people volunteered to work there. Later, when it became known how the majority of them were being treated, the trains bringing the badly needed labour were carrying rounded-up forced labourers, rather than volunteers. There were still some volunteers: those who could not make ends meet and those who by this method tried to avoid the clutches of the *Gestapo*. As far as their 'loyalty and devotion' are concerned, a German author, van Ishoven, disagrees: 'The hundreds of thousands of foreign workers were a threat to the German armament industry, and the *Gestapo* was kept busy investigating cases of sabotage and espionage.'[20]

Delmer's campaign started with airdrops of small incendiary devices, cover name 'Braddocks'. They had 15-minute time fuses and could be used by anybody to set fire to buildings, vehicles, haystacks, etc. They came with instructions in several languages. Delmer did not expect (correctly) that many would be used. His RUs would suitably exaggerate the scale and the effects of Braddocks, causing – he hoped – administrative confusion and panic action both by individuals and by the authorities. According to a top-secret memorandum of the time, the intended effect would be achieved 'by ordering and encouraging the collection of Braddocks, to make the German authorities believe that many foreign workers were keeping them hidden for future use. By tricking German civilians and members of the defence forces into action against foreign workers, to give the latter an opportunity and incentive to desert their factories, to go underground, and to give the police authorities the maximum trouble to keep them under control.'[21]

The campaign was flawed, because farm workers were widely dispersed and obviously could not be organised to carry out any significant sabotage. They might find some Braddocks but they were too intimidated to risk setting their bosses' farms on fire, and those who were treated well would not want to do this. Industrial workers lived in camps, under guard, and the chances of Braddocks being dropped into these camps were very slim. The same applied to concentration camp inmates, and their chances of breaking out were practically non-existent. And how did Delmer imagine them going 'underground' in a hostile country? Quite impossible. Incidentally, Braddocks turned out to be most unreliable and burst into flames only rarely.

An equally unscrupulous operation was directed at Poles who were conscripted into the *Wehrmacht* and were serving in Italy. In some units the proportion of non-Germans (Poles, Ukrainians, Russians) was as high as 20 per cent. Delmer wanted to make the German soldiers treat their comrades of other nationalities as enemies, who could not be trusted and had to be watched all the time. He hoped that deteriorating relations within the units would force the non-Germans, especially the Poles, to desert.[22]

Another mutation of this campaign – cover name Periwig – tried to create the impression that the Allies were in touch with a German resistance movement inside Germany, which was willing to cooperate with them: 'The plan was to dispatch stores and agents, to send code messages and to make open appeals to its alleged members. It was obvious that *Gestapo* would monitor the messages and a proportion of the stores and agents would fall into its hands. This might convince it that there existed a widespread resistance movement and wholesale arrests would follow. … The main objective was to divert the energy of the police system into a wasteful activity … Volunteers were asked for among anti-Nazi prisoners of war … [they] were deluded into believing that the German resistance movement did exist.'[23] Echoes of Sun Tzu's 'condemned agents'?

SIS opposed Periwig, fearing that by provoking wholesale arrests, it might endanger their own agents. It was realised also that, should this blatant exploitation of genuine German anti-Nazis become known, it would create a wave of indignation not only in Germany, but also in Britain and in America. Nevertheless, it went ahead. It did not produce any tangible results. Fortunately, and miraculously, all four Germans parachuted into Germany survived.

A campaign that misfired, and one on which Delmer did not 'look back with pride and satisfaction', was another attempt to sow discord among the Nazi leadership. Its main theme was that Himmler was plotting to take Hitler's place. It culminated in the dissemination of a postage stamp with Himmler's face instead of that of Hitler. Howe had plenty of practice forging normal German stamps for the use of British agents in Germany and his Himmler stamp looked so genuine, so normal, that nobody paid any attention to it. It was used by SOE operatives in Germany, also in Sweden and in Switzerland (Howe supplied the necessary equipment for cancelling them, so that the envelopes containing propaganda materials, which were dropped into private letterboxes, looked as if they were posted in Germany). In the end desperate SOE agents, hoping by this to attract attention to them, were offering covers with the Himmler stamp to stamp dealers. Now this stamp is quite valuable (there are reports of forgeries!) but at the time it did not have the effect hoped for by Delmer.

A very different operation was *Nachrichten für die Truppe* – the daily newspaper destined primarily for German soldiers in the West. It appeared from 25 April 1944 to 4 May 1945. It was not black, but light grey, or perhaps even just off-white, and was openly dropped by Allied aircraft. It did not try to fool anybody as to its origin, although it refrained from mentioning its provenance. Unlike the *Soldatensender* it did not refer to the Allies as 'the enemy'. They were called 'the Anglo-American forces' or 'the Russians'. The Germans were '*die Deutsche Truppen*' and Germany was '*die Heimat*'.* The print volumes were of an entirely different order, too: they started with 500,000 2-page sheets, increasing rapidly to a daily average of 2 million 4-page sheets. It was clearly linked to the *Soldatensender*. It was also a joint British–American venture: a team of first-class American editors and news writers was placed under Delmer's orders to reinforce his own team. News and talks were supplied by the *Soldatensender* but had to be rewritten to make them suitable for printing. Without the Americans, the intended scale of the operation could not have been attained. Neither could the dissemination be carried out without the help of the American Air Force: a squadron of night-flying B-17s (Flying Fortresses) was put at Delmer's disposal.

Nachrichten tried to be as 'newsy' as possible. It combined punctiliously accurate military news with international and German home news. Such complete news coverage was not available to German soldiers from any other source. The *Wehrmacht*'s own troop newspaper, the *Frontkurier*, was being delivered to the front line most irregularly and usually

* German troops' and 'the Fatherland'.

several days late. *Nachrichten* filled this void. German soldiers were hungry for news and they were eagerly reading the *Nachrichten*, notwithstanding the threat of severe punishment. The true news stories were on the front page and served to gain readers' confidence and trust. The propaganda sting was concealed in the news from Germany, prepared in such a way as to undermine the reader's faith in his leaders and to convince him of the inevitability of defeat.

In detail, the paper was made up as follows: on the front page, and in some columns on the back page, were news stories from all fronts on which German troops were fighting, the Western Front being covered in greater detail than the others. These stories were written in such a way as to encourage the German soldier in the West to look over his shoulder. It was emphasised that the Party and High Command only took the Russian Front seriously, and that consequently the Western Front was a useless sacrifice and diversion of strength. On page two was the daily topical commentary expressing a critical and indignant attitude to the conduct of the war, both at the front and at home. On page three the German soldier found startling and worrying news from home, describing, for instance, the flagrant inequality of sacrifice by the man in the front line and the officials at home, by ordinary civilians and by Party members. He learned about the scandals of reserved occupations, of the overworking of women, of conditions in children's evacuation camps, of black marketing in high quarters and of the insincere and bombastic appeals for sacrifices by bosses and by wire-pullers hundreds of miles behind the front. Attention was paid to the failures of Germany's satellites and allies. Sports news and pin-ups assured that this page did not have a purely propaganda content.

Some of the *Nachrichten* propaganda tricks now seem too far-fetched. For example, on page two of the 31 August 1944 issue we find the description of a British invention that was supposed to ensure that an Allied fighter would shoot down every German plane it attacked: the pilot just sets the type of the German plane on a dial and presses a button. The gadget, called Automatic Sight Mk 11D, then takes over: it flies the plane, assumes the firing position and opens fire, guaranteeing a kill at any deflection. In 1944, when rumours of new, wonderful weapons were coming thick and fast from all directions, this would not have been lightly shrugged off.[24] In fact, a few months earlier a new sight, called the *Giro Gunsight*, was made available to both RAF and US fighters. It calculated its own rate of turn and helped the pilot to estimate correctly the angle of deflection. It did not take over the flying of the aircraft, but it increased by 50 per cent the chances of a kill.

Delmer wrote that of all the enterprises he launched during the war, this newspaper was the one of which he was proudest.[25] The German historian, Buchbender, agrees: 'With a circulation of 2 million, and because of the quality of its textual and graphic presentation, *Nachrichten für die Truppe* was the most significant and the most influential of all the leaflet-newspapers produced during the Second World War by the Allied combat propaganda.'[26] On the other hand, Howe thought that 'such success that it could claim was due more to the sheer inefficiency of the news service provided by the Germans for their troops than the actual merits of *Nachrichten*'.[27] Similarly, an officer who interrogated German POWs did not think much of the *Nachrichten* grey approach: a high proportion were irritated or merely amused by it; he thought that white or black propaganda were more effective.[28]

After D-Day, *OKW* decided to counter the massive Allied propaganda onslaught on the morale of the *Wehrmacht* in a novel way: by being honest and truthful – to a degree. The *Waffen-SS* propaganda unit *Kurt Eggers* was given this job. The operation was called *Skorpion West* (its predecessor was *Skorpion Ost*, on the Russian Front). A series of leaflets was published under a scorpion logo and the banner: 'If you want to know the truth, Comrade, ask the *Skorpion*!' The format was that of short questions and reasonably frank answers, and the language that of a typical private, quite different from the products of *Promi*. The main object was to neutralise the demoralising effect on the German soldier of the invariably lost battles and of the never-ending retreat. The leaflets, dropped by the *Luftwaffe*, were well received by the troops.

This presented an opportunity that Delmer could not miss. Within a few weeks, millions of false *Skorpion* leaflets floated down on German lines and behind them. The paper, founts and style were identical, but the message was different. For instance, the question 'Why do we go on fighting?' was answered in a way that did nothing to remove the question mark: 'We go on fighting because we must prove ourselves to be worthy of the idealism of the *Führer* and of the National-Socialist ideas, even when this will lead to the destruction of ourselves, of our Fatherland and of the future generations. We must show that we are worthy of the trust bestowed upon the fighting soldiers by the *Führer* and by other great National Socialists who are at his side.' Other counterfeit *Skorpions* informed obliquely that desertion had become easier, that soldiers and NCOs were shooting unpopular officers and getting away with it, that it was High Command's intention to scorch every foot of German soil.

When one of these leaflets was shown to the Army West commander, Field Marshal Model, he could not believe his eyes. He summoned the head of the *Skorpion West* operation, who explained that the issue in Model's hands was a forgery. Model was furious and wanted to abort the operation there and then, but was persuaded to let it continue. When a few days later he was shown another forged copy, he decided to stop the dissemination by air; soldiers were ordered to read only copies distributed by hand. But the harm was already done: *Skorpion*'s credibility plummeted and the operation was cancelled.

Above, left: Viscount Northcliffe, who successfully directed British anti-German propaganda in 1918. (*Getty Images*)

Above, right: Sir Campbell Stuart, deputy director of Propaganda in Enemy Countries 1918. Before the outbreak of the Second World War he was asked to set up a clandestine propaganda department which became known as Department EH. (*Getty Images*)

Sir Stephen Tallents, Controller of BBC Public Relations 1935–40 and of the Overseas Broadcasts 1940–1. He was an early advocate of a propaganda organisation on the lines of the Political Warfare Executive. (*Getty Images*)

Above, left: Sir Robert Bruce Lockhart, Deputy Under Secretary of State in charge of the Political Warfare Executive 1941–5. (*Getty Images*)

Above, right: Major General Sir Colin Gubbins, head of Special Operations Executive from September 1943.

Hugh Dalton, President of the Polish Government in Exile W. Raczkiewicz, General Sikorski and Major General Sir Colin Gubbins, 1940.

Sefton Delmer, journalist, born in Berlin of Australian parents. He conducted a brilliant Black propaganda operation from 1941. (*Getty Images*)

Below, left: General Wšadyššaw Sikorski, Commander in Chief of Polish Forces under British command and Prime Minister of the Polish Government in Exile. He died in 1943 in an aircrash in Gibraltar, which has never been fully explained.

Below, right: General Stefan 'Grot'-Rowecki, Commander of the Polish *Armia Krajowa* or Home Army. He was arrested by *Gestapo* in 1943 and executed in 1944.

Deutsche Soldaten

Anf jedem Schritt seid Ihr durch Eure Führer belogen. Die Mehrzahl von ihnen glaubt nicht an das, was man Euch glauben machen will. Nur sehr wenige verblendete Parteigenomen rechnen mit einem Sieg. Der Rest gibt sich den Anschein das Glaubens.

Die „Genialität" Hitlers, eines Unteroffiziers der Landwehr, kann Euch vor der Niederlage nicht erretten. Ein Dummer könnte das nicht einmal glauben. Eure „Erfolge" sind nur das Ergebnis einer planvollen Aktion der polnischen Heeresleitung. Je weiter Ihr vordringen werdet, unso grösser wird Eure Niederlage.

Wisst Ihr, dass Eure Städte durch französiche, englische und polnische Flugzenge bombardiert werden?!!

Wisst Ihr, dass Eure Panzertruppen, die bis vor Warszawa vorgedrungen sind, durch das polnische Heer umzingeltsind und durch Mangel an Kraftstoff lahmgelegt sind?!

Wisst Ihr, dass das ganze Saargebiet in französischen Händen ist und dass die französiche Offensive Eure Siegfriedslinie, an der sich Eure Machthaber bereichert haben, zerschmettert?!

Wisst Ihr, dass Danzig im Besitz von englischen Truppen ist, die dort die englische Flotte an Land gesetzt hat.

Wisst Ihr, dass die ganze Wel gegen Euch rüstet, dass die Völker, die noch neutral sind, mobilisieren, um zur gegebenen Stunde Euch ein Stück Landes abzuschneiden.

Wisst Ihr, dass im Reiche Gestapo wütet und hunderte von Euren Angehörigen hinrichtet, die sich den Anordnungen widersetzen, die sie dem Hungertode aussetzen?

Wisst Ihr, dass man vor dem Palast des Führers in Berlin zu den hungernden Manifestanten schiesst?

Nein, Ihr wisst es nicht. Diese Nachrichten werden Euch durch die Agenten der Gestapo und Eure Führer geheimgehalten!

Verlangt von ihnen eine Beantwortung dieser Fragen!

Deutsche Soldaten! verlangt Beendigung des Krieges!

Tretet auf allen Fronten mit der Waffe in der Hand über und ergebet Euch, dann ist das Ende des Krieges nahe.

Weg mit dem verblendeten wahnsinnigen Hitler!

Es lebe das von Tyrannen freie Deutsche Reich.

Deutsche in Polen.

Above: '*Deutsche Soldaten*' – according to German sources these leaflets were dropped in September 1939 by Polish aircraft.

Opposite, above left: Tadeusz Żenczykowski, appointed by General 'Grot'-Rowecki in 1940 to head Operation 'N', and continued in this capacity until the Warsaw Rising in 1944.

Opposite, above right: Dr Joseph Goebbels and Adolf Hitler. (*Bundesarchiv*)

Opposite, left: Hans Fritzsche, top German radio journalist and radio propaganda chief in the Ministry for Public Enlightment and Propaganda (*Promi*), during the Nuremberg Trial (he was found not guilty). (*Getty Images*)

DEUTSCHER SOLDAT!

DIE schimpfliche Zunahme der Fälle, in denen Mannschaften und sogar Offiziere der mir unterstellten Einheiten und Dienststellen sich ihrer Wehrverpflichtung durch Übertritt auf spanisches Gebiet entzogen haben, gibt mir Veranlassung, an das Ehr- und Pflichtbewußtsein aller deutschen Wehrmachtangehörigen in meinem Befehlsbereich zu appellieren.

Bedauerlicherweise gewährt die spanische Regierung unter Berufung auf weltfremde Bestimmungen des Völkerrechts fahnenflüchtigen deutschen Wehrmachtangehörigen in Spanien Asylrecht, wenn sie die spanische Grenze in Zivil und ohne Papiere überschreiten und sich als Elsässer oder Lothringer ausgeben.

Ich verlasse mich darauf, daß dieses schwer erklärbare Verhalten der spanischen Regierung für ehrliebende deutsche Soldaten keine Verlockung zu dem schimpflichen Verbrechen der Fahnenflucht bedeuten wird.

In diesem kritischen Augenblick höchster Bereitschaft kommt es auf jeden Einzelnen an.

Der Militärbefehlshaber in Frankreich
(gez.) von Rundstedt
Generalfeldmarschall
Oberbefehlshaber West.

Paris, den 4. 9. 1943.

'*Deutscher Soldat*' – such leaflets and posters appeared in France in 1943. The text reads: The disgraceful increase in the number of soldiers and officers … who negate their military duty by going over to the Spanish territory, makes it necessary for me to appeal to the honour and to the sense of duty of all *Wehrmacht* members under my command. Regretfully, the Spanish government … grants German deserters asylum, when they cross the frontier as civilians without any documents, purporting to be Alsatians or Lorrainers. I hope that this attitude of the Spanish government will not be regarded by honourable German soldiers as an enticement to desertion. At this critical time … every man counts. Signed – Field Marshal von Rundstedt.

Deutsche Volksgenossen! Angehörige der Wehrmacht!

Der Führer ist in Gefahr!

Die Reaktion will den Führer beseitigen, und das Reich einer Militärdiktatur unterwerfen, die gegen den Willen des Volks sofortige Friedensverhandlungen einleiten soll.

Gewisse Kreise, die den geheiligten Namen des Preußentums im Munde führen, aber in ihrer Haltung nichts vom Heldengeist des Siebenjährigen Krieges zeigen, streuten Zweckgerüchte aus, der Führer sei wegen seiner geschwächten Gesundheit nicht mehr den Bürden seines Amtes gewachsen.

Mit diesen Gerüchten bereitet die Reaktion einen Putsch vor, der den Führer aus seiner Stellung als Oberbefehlshaber der Wehrmacht verdrängen soll. An seine Stelle ein eidbrüchiger General treten.

Der Führer hat es bisher in seiner Großmütigkeit abgelehnt, drastische Schritte gegen die Verräter zu unternehmen, um nicht in dieser kritischen Stunde das Heer seiner Führer zu berauben. Daher ist es unserer Aller Pflicht, zusammenzustehen im Kampf gegen die Reaktion.

Ich habe selbst kürzlich die Ehre gehabt, den Führer in seinem Hauptquartier zu besuchen. Aus seinem Auge strahlte die Gewißheit des Sieges, in seinem Händedruck durfte ich die ganze, gesunde Kraft des von keinem Schicksalschlag gebrochenen Mannes spüren, der Deutschlands Schicksal ist und bleiben muß.

Wer uns den Führer rauben will, stürzt Deutschland in den Bürgerkrieg!

Wir stehen zu unserem Führer, dem wir den Treueid geleistet haben.

Das Deutsche Volk will nicht den Frieden — das Deutsche Volk will den Sieg, koste er, was er wolle.

Volksgenossen! Haltet die Augen und Ohren offen! Erkennt die Gefahr!

Meldet jeden verdächtigen Vorfall, jedes Gerücht, jede getarnte, verleumderische Äußerung über den Führer sofort bei der nächsten Dienststelle der Partei, der Polizei oder der SS.

Es lebe der Führer!

'*Der Führer ist in Gefahr*!' – similar leaflets were produced in several occupied countries. Their purpose was to create among Germans a feeling of uncertainty and the impression that 'reactionary forces' intend to remove Hitler. They warned of the dangers of a civil war, encouraging denunciations and informing on anybody suspicious.

Steckbrief

10 000 Mark Belohnung!

Gesucht wird wegen Fahnenflucht in Verbindung mit Unterschlagung und Vermögensflucht der nachstehend abgebildete

SS Standartenführer Karl Vollmeyer

Personalien :	Zuletzt wohnhaft: Bremen, Altenwall 24.
Geboren: 25. Juni 1887.	Beruf: Kaufmann.
Geburtsort: Nienburg a.d. Weser.	Besondere Kennzeichen: keine.

SS Standartenführer Karl Vollmeyer wird seit dem 10. Dezember 1944 vermißt. Nachforschungen, die in Verbindung mit seinem Verschwinden durch das Fahndungskommando des Finanzamts Bremen angestellt wurden, ergaben schwere Verfehlungen gegen die Steuer- und Vermögensfluchtgesetze. Der Gesuchte mißbrauchte sein Amt als Mitglied der Gauwirtschaftskammer Weser-Ems, um im Rahmen von Transaktionen seiner Firma A. Held, Bremen, schwere Veruntreuungen an staatlichen Vermögenswerten zu begehen. Es besteht Verdacht, daß der Gesuchte, der den Rang eines SS Standartenführers bekleidete und seit dem 10. Dezember verschwunden ist, ins neutrale Ausland, vermutlich über die schweizer Grenze, zu entkommen versucht. Sämtliche Parteidienststellen sind angewiesen, den Vollmeyer dingfest zu machen. Haftbefehl ist ergangen. Die Bevölkerung wird gebeten, an der Auffindung und Festsetzung des Gesuchten mitzuhelfen.

Zweckdienliche Mitteilungen sind zu den Akten J III 824/44 an die unterzeichnete Behörde zu machen.

Für Angaben, die zur Verhaftung des Gesuchten führen, ist die obenstehende Belohnung ausgesetzt.

Der Polizeipräsident
Schroers,
Generalmajor d. Polizei.

Bremen, den 20. Dez. 1944
Kriminalpolizei, Am Wall 1.

In this leaflet, in the form of a 'Wanted' poster, the reward of 10,000 Reichsmarks was offered to encourage people to apprehend anybody even remotely resembling the mythical criminal Karl Vollmeyer. More work for the police authorities, more disruption, more distrust.

The 20-*grosh* stamp with the face of the governor of occupied Poland Frank instead of Hitler was printed in London and used on letters sent from Poland to Germany.

British stamps made in Germany. The Jewish and communist symbols were to imply that Britain was ruled by Jews and communists.

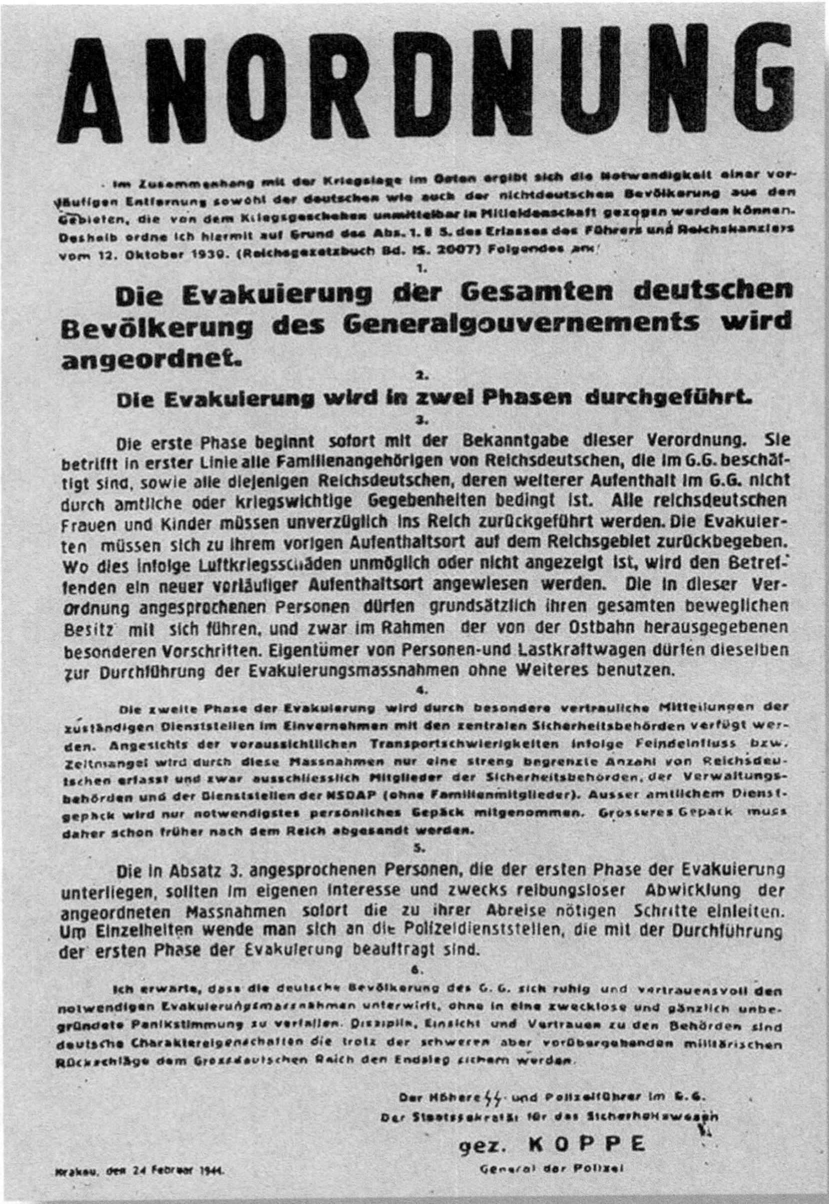

ANORDNUNG

Im Zusammenhang mit der Kriegslage im Osten ergibt sich die Notwendigkeit einer vorläufigen Entfernung sowohl der deutschen wie auch der nichtdeutschen Bevölkerung aus den Gebieten, die von dem Kriegsgeschehen unmittelbar in Mitleidenschaft gezogen werden können. Deshalb ordne ich hiermit auf Grund des Abs. 1. § 5. des Erlasses des Führers und Reichskanzlers vom 12. Oktober 1939. (Reichsgesetzbuch Bd. I S. 2007) Folgendes an:

1.

Die Evakuierung der Gesamten deutschen Bevölkerung des Generalgouvernements wird angeordnet.

2.

Die Evakuierung wird in zwei Phasen durchgeführt.

3.

Die erste Phase beginnt sofort mit der Bekanntgabe dieser Verordnung. Sie betrifft in erster Linie alle Familienangehörigen von Reichsdeutschen, die im G.G. beschäftigt sind, sowie alle diejenigen Reichsdeutschen, deren weiterer Aufenthalt im G.G. nicht durch amtliche oder kriegswichtige Gegebenheiten bedingt ist. Alle reichsdeutschen Frauen und Kinder müssen unverzüglich ins Reich zurückgeführt werden. Die Evakuierten müssen sich zu ihrem vorigen Aufenthaltsort auf dem Reichsgebiet zurückbegeben. Wo dies infolge Luftkriegsschäden unmöglich oder nicht angezeigt ist, wird den Betreffenden ein neuer vorläufiger Aufenthaltsort angewiesen werden. Die in dieser Verordnung angesprochenen Personen dürfen grundsätzlich ihren gesamten beweglichen Besitz mit sich führen, und zwar im Rahmen der von der Ostbahn herausgegebenen besonderen Vorschriften. Eigentümer von Personen-und Lastkraftwagen dürfen dieselben zur Durchführung der Evakuierungsmassnahmen ohne Weiteres benutzen.

4.

Die zweite Phase der Evakuierung wird durch besondere vertrauliche Mitteilungen der zuständigen Dienststellen im Einvernehmen mit den zentralen Sicherheitsbehörden verfügt werden. Angesichts der voraussichtlichen Transportschwierigkeiten infolge Feindeinfluss bzw. Zeitmangel wird durch diese Massnahmen nur eine streng begrenzte Anzahl von Reichsdeutschen erfasst und zwar ausschliesslich Mitglieder der Sicherheitsbehörden, der Verwaltungsbehörden und der Dienststellen der NSDAP (ohne Familienmitglieder). Ausser amtlichem Dienstgepäck wird nur notwendigstes persönliches Gepäck mitgenommen. Grosseres Gepack muss daher schon früher nach dem Reich abgesandt werden.

5.

Die in Absatz 3. angesprochenen Personen, die der ersten Phase der Evakuierung unterliegen, sollten im eigenen Interesse und zwecks reibungsloser Abwicklung der angeordneten Massnahmen sofort die zu ihrer Abreise nötigen Schritte einleiten. Um Einzelheiten wende man sich an die Polizeidienststellen, die mit der Durchführung der ersten Phase der Evakuierung beauftragt sind.

6.

Ich erwarte, dass die deutsche Bevölkerung des G.G. sich ruhig und vertrauensvoll den notwendigen Evakuierungsmassnahmen unterwirft, ohne in eine zwecklose und gänzlich unbegründete Panikstimmung zu verfallen. Disziplin, Einsicht und Vertrauen zu den Behörden sind deutsche Charaktereigenschaften die trotz der schweren aber vorübergehenden militärischen Rückschläge dem Grossdeutschen Reich den Endsieg sichern werden.

Der Höhere SS- und Polizeiführer im G.G.
Der Staatssekretär für das Sicherheitswesen

gez. KOPPE

General der Polizei

Krakau, den 24 Februar 1944.

The 'Koppe' postear.

According to the beliefs of German sailors, *Klabautermann* was a shipboard spirit that used to appear as a harbinger of disasters. It was an apt name for a Black satirical publication. Page 1 of its January 1943 issue depicts an allegory of the Third *Reich* and that of October 1942 is full of bitter irony: 'Oh *Führer*, we praise thee …'.

A selection of Black titles, reproduced from an *Oberkommando der Wehrmacht* publication.

Der Hammer
24 November 1941

Nummer 9 DER SOLDAT 28.X.19

HITLERSGESCHWÄTZ
Betrachtungen zur letzten Führerrede

Oberkommando der Wehrmacht

Bilder für die Truppe
(Zur Weitergabe in zwei Ausfertigungen bis zu den ... Für Belehrung und Aushang bestimmt)

Flugblätter zur Kriegslage —

UND FRAUEN DEUTSCHLANDS!

Der Klabautermann
Nummer 3. (13). Januar 1943

DAS DRITTE R

Der WINDMACHER
Ich bin der erste Muskieter

Another selection of Black titles. *Der Windmacher* (The Wind Maker) was an Operation 'N' anti-Hitler pamphlet disguised as an anti-Churchill one. A copy was despatched by courier to London and was presented to the Prime Minister. He was highly amused.

Examples of stickers used for example in German railway carriages and on German vehicles.

Wer weiterkämpft – kämpft gegen UNSERE KINDER

a

b

Weiter Hitlerkrieg bedeutet weiter Luftkrieg, bedeutet Vernichtung unserer Industrieen, bedeutet Arbeitslosigkeit OHNE ENDE –

KEHRT UM DIE FLINTEN DER FEIND STEHT HINTEN

c

e

SCHEISSE

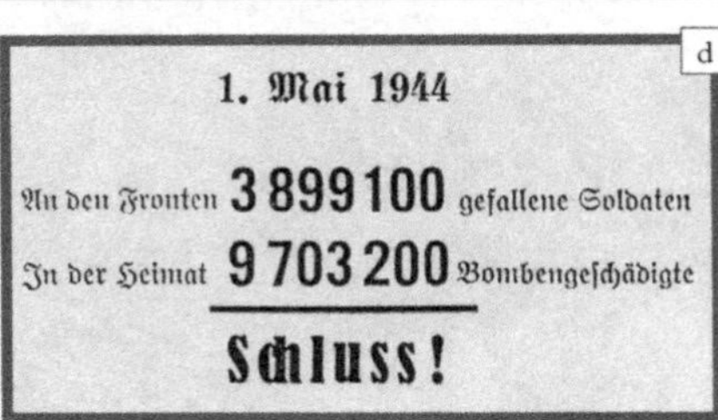

d

1. Mai 1944

An den Fronten 3 899 100 gefallene Soldaten

In der Heimat 9 703 200 Bombengeschädigte

Schluss!

a. Who continues the fight, fights against our children.

b. Continuing Hitler's war means the destruction of our industry and endless unemployment.

c. Turn your guns the other way – the enemy is behind you.

d.

At the front	3,899,100	fallen soldiers
In the Fatherland	9,703,200	bombed out
	ENOUGH!	

e. SCHEI**SS**E.

Opposite:

Top, left: The author, summer 1944.

Top, right: The 'Green Card' that gave a four-week exemption from having to dig trenches. It was totally counterfeit, but good enough to pass several police inspections.

Centre: The author's medical certificate, 100 per cent authentic. For 2kg of butter the official German Medical Officer diagnosed an organic defect of the heart valves and a tubercular pulmonary condition. Verdict: incapable of any physical work. A good document but it did not help when caught up in a razzia: the *Schupos* (German policemen) just would not read it.

Bottom: The author's identity card. The blank card was genuine – it was stolen – but the official stamps and signatures were forged.

ARBEITSAMT KIELCE

Kielce, den 9.8. 1944

Der die Nowodworski Stanisław
geb. 26.10.28 wohnhaft in Kielce
Strasse Urzędnicza 15 wird auf Grund der erfolgten Überprüfung von der allgemeinen Arbeitspflicht für die Dauer von 4 Wochen freigestellt.

Im Auftrage

GENERALGOUVERNEMENT
DER KREISHAUPTMANN
ARBEITSAMT KIELCE

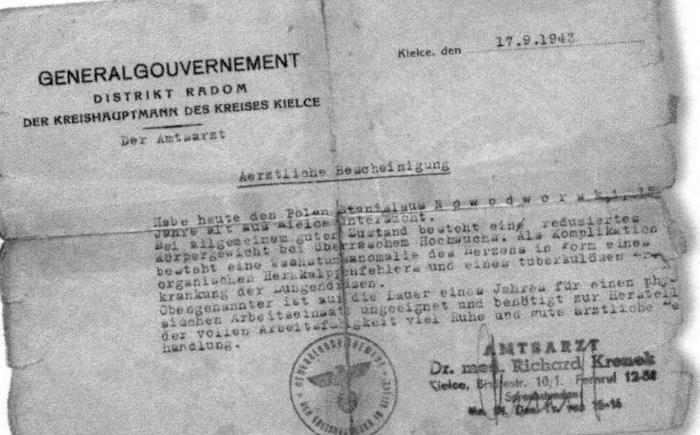

GENERALGOUVERNEMENT
DISTRIKT RADOM
DER KREISHAUPTMANN DES KREISES KIELCE

Der Amtsarzt

Kielce, den 17.9.1943

Aerztliche Bescheinigung

Habe heute den Polen Stanislaus N o w o d w o r s k i , 15 Jahre alt aus Kielce untersucht.
Bei allgemeinem guten Zustand besteht eine reduziertes Körpergewicht bei überraschem Hochwuchs. Als Komplikation besteht eine Wachstumsanomalie des Herzens in Form eines organischen Herzklappenfehlers und eines tuberkulösen Erkrankung der Lungendrüsen.
Obengenannter ist auf die Dauer eines Jahres für einen physischen Arbeitseinsatz ungeeignet und benötigt zur Herstellung der vollen Arbeitsfähigkeit viel Ruhe und gute ärztliche Behandlung.

AMTSARZT
Dr. med. Richard Krenek
Kielce, Bracistr. 10/1. Fernruf 12-56

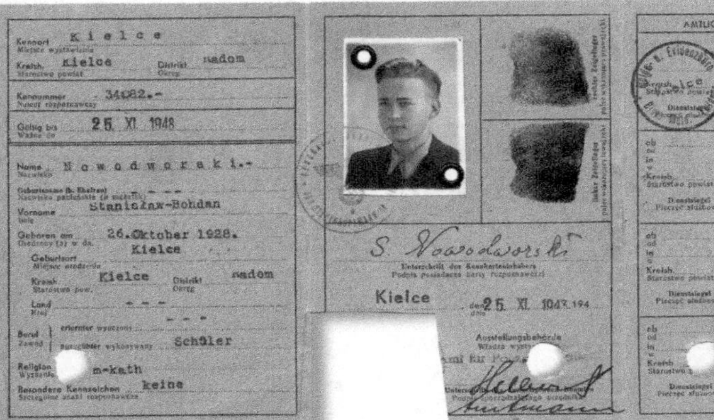

Kennort / Miejsce wystawienia: K i e l c e
Kreish. / Starostwo powiat: Kielce Distrikt / Okręg: Radom
Kennummer / Numer rozpoznawczy: 34082.-
Gültig bis / Ważne do: 25. XI. 1948

Name / Nazwisko: N o w o d w o r s k i.-
Geburtsname (b. Ehefrau) / Nazwisko panieńskie (u mężatki): - - -
Vorname / Imię: Stanisław-Bohdan
Geboren am / Urodzony (a) w dn.: 26.Oktober 1928.
Geburtsort / Miejsce urodzenia: Kielce
Kreish. / Starostwo pow.: Kielce Distrikt / Okręg: Radom
Land / Kraj: - - -
Beruf / Zawód: erlernter / wyuczony: - - - ausgeübter / wykonywany: Schüler
Religion / Wyznanie: röm-kath
Besondere Kennzeichen / Szczególne znaki rozpoznawcze: keine

S. Nowodworski
Unterschrift des Kennkarteninhabers / Podpis posiadacza karty rozpoznawczej

Kielce den 25. XI. 1943
Ausstellungsbehörde / Władza wystawiająca

AMTLICHE VERMERKE UWAGI URZĘDOWE

Der Kennkarteninhaber wohnt / Posiadacz karty rozpoznawczej mieszka
Kreish. Kielce Strasse / ulica Brzeźna 15
Dienstsiegel / Pieczęć służbowa
Unterschrift der Meldebehörde / Podpis urzędu meldunkowego

ab / od
in / w
Kreish. / Starostwo powiat
Strasse / ulica
Dienstsiegel / Pieczęć służbowa
Unterschrift der Meldebehörde / Podpis urzędu meldunkowego

STADT KIELCE
2 ZŁOTY 2

The Anchor – the symbol of hope – was also the emblem of the Polish Home Army. It is made up of letters P and W, the first letters of the Polish words meaning 'Poland fights on'.

An Anchor painted on the base of the Polish Airmen Memorial in Warsaw. Soon after this photograph was taken Germans destroyed this memorial.

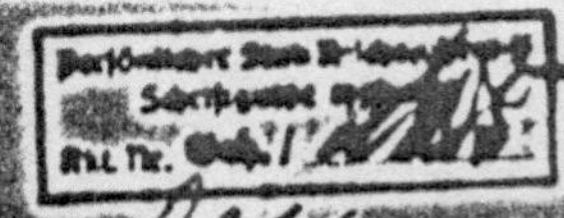

Aktennotiz für SS-Obergruppenführer W o l f f

Ich bitte, mit General Z e i t z l e r über die schlechte Stimmung in den höheren Offizierskreisen und das sichtbare Auftreten der Parolen der ausländischen Sender zu sprechen und ihm nahezulegen, hier unbedingt einmal für die Statuierung eines Exempels zu sorgen. Es muß einmal auch ein höherer Offizier, der sich in dieser Richtung schuldig gemacht hat, vor das Kriegsgericht gestellt und zum Tode verurteilt werden, um damit das vergiftende Abhören ausländischer Sender für längere Zeit wieder zu unterbinden.

H. Himmler

Feld-Kommandostelle
10.Dezember 1942 R./V.

175/140

SAP 161-6-12/375

Himmler's message to *SS-Obergruppenführer* Wolff: Please speak to General Zeitzler [Chief of Army General Staff] about the bad morale among higher officers who openly repeat formulations heard in enemy radio broadcasts, and advise him about the necessity of making an example of somebody. He must put one of these officers … before a Court Martial which will pronounce a death sentence. This will put a stop for a long time to the listening to the poisonous foreign broadcasts.

Chapter Six

Polish Operation 'N' – Humble Beginnings

Before the war, Poland, like Britain, did not have a Ministry of Propaganda. The decision to form one was taken one week before the German invasion. There was not enough time to implement this decision beyond appointing the minister and his deputy. Just like the Foreign Office, the Polish Ministry of Foreign Affairs was interested in external propaganda, and, like the SIS, the Polish Intelligence Service (generally known as the 'Second Bureau' – obvious French influence – abbreviated in Polish in everyday speech, to *Dwójka* – 'the Deuce') had its own ideas about anti-Nazi black propaganda. They differed, nevertheless, from the SIS on the questions of timing and of the media to be used. The SIS was convinced that the right kind of propaganda would not only shorten the approaching war but might even, if started early enough, lead to the elimination of the Nazi regime and prevent the war altogether. They intended to use only leaflets.[1] Poles, on the other hand, being afraid of an overwhelming German retaliation, did not envisage any peacetime leaflet campaigns. They wanted to use only radio. They were thinking of a chain of black mobile short-wave transmitters that would meander along the Polish–German frontier, making it difficult to prove that they were broadcasting from Polish territory. Again, war came too soon for this plan to be put into operation.

According to German sources, during the September 1939 campaign, three kinds of Polish leaflets were dropped on the advancing *Wehrmacht*.[2] Polish military historians do not confirm this, and there are no records of such leaflet sorties by the Polish Air Force. One of these three leaflets looks like a black one.[3] It is addressed to *Deutsche Soldaten* ('German Soldiers') and is signed *Deutsche in Polen* ('Germans in Poland'). It asks a series of questions, such as: 'Do you know that French, English and Polish aircraft are bombing your towns? That France has occupied the Saar? That the English have landed in Danzig? That all your successes in the field are only the result of a ruse by the Polish General Staff – that the farther you advance, the more disastrous will be your defeat?' All this was so blatantly untrue that it could only expose the authors to ridicule. One cannot help thinking that perhaps this was exactly the intention and that the leaflet was a German 'double black'. The other two leaflets must have been the result of private initiative and could have been dropped from private aircraft. The subsequent history of Polish resistance abounds in examples of private enterprise.

A few hours before Warsaw surrendered on 27 September 1939, the Polish resistance movement was officially born. In accordance with instructions received from the commander of the Polish armed forces, then interned in Roumania, foundations were laid for the creation of the largest underground army in occupied Europe. Originally it was called *Sšužba Zwycięstwu Polski* ('Service for Poland's Victory') but soon it was renamed *Związek Walki Zbrojnej* (ZWZ – 'Armed Combat Association') and eventually, in 1942, it became known as *Armia Krajowa* (*AK*, the Home Army). Germans thought that the military defeat would humble the Poles and break their spirit. They were wrong. Even before the last shots were fired, underground organisations were springing up spontaneously all over the country – hundreds of them – but only *ZWZ-AK* was under direct orders of the head of the Polish armed forces and of the Government-in-Exile, located first in Paris and later in London. Gradually it absorbed most of the smaller, local organisations. Only the communists and the implacably anti-communist nationalist organisations would not recognise *AK*'s authority.

The very first black operations were carried out by the commander of the *ZWZ* Warsaw District.[4] During the First World War he served in the Austrian army and remembered the devastating effect of the British propaganda. He decided to emulate Lord Northcliffe. He did not even seek the approval of the *Komenda Gšówna* (*KG* – 'Central Command'). Since his only reprographic machine was a mimeograph, the output was not very impressive. It consisted of leaflets and of a satirical magazine. The main theme of both were the differences between the opulent lifestyles of the members of the *NSDAP* (*Nationalsozialistische Deutsche Arbeiter Partei* – the Nazi Party), *SS* and *Gestapo* on one hand, and of the hard-pressed front-line soldiers on the other. He hoped to drive a wedge between these two groups. The distribution of the printed matter targeted houses and flats occupied by Germans, German offices and restaurants.

Warsaw was not the only place where black propaganda operations were initiated spontaneously. In Cieszyn (Silesia) mimeographed subversive leaflets started to appear in January 1940.[5] In the district of Poznań (western Poland) German soldiers and civilians began receiving subversive leaflets as early as December 1939. One of these leaflets called upon the soldiers to organise soldiers' councils. Germans in Nowy Targ could read the monthly *Der Freie Deutsche* ('The Free German'), which was also distributed by post to Germans in the Kraków area.[6] In Kraków itself, where the principal German authorities of the *Generalgouvernement* (that part of German-occupied Poland that was not incorporated into the *Reich*, abbreviated to *GG*) had their seat, two periodicals were being printed: *Germania* and *GG Nachrichten*. There were many more examples.

The *ZWZ* Central Command observed these activities and especially the operation in Warsaw, with great interest. The commander, General Rowecki (cover name 'Grot'), appreciated the importance of good black propaganda (in 1932 he wrote and published *Propaganda as a Combat Medium*). He realised that what was being done at the time in Warsaw and in the other places was unsatisfactory. Those responsible were not sufficiently conversant with the German language, culture, history, psychology and current conditions in the Services and in Germany itself to be able to produce convincing black material. What was more, after all the victories of 1939–40 the German soldier was full of enthusiasm for his country's leadership, and in terms of living conditions he was not doing badly. Seeds of discontent were falling on barren ground.

In November 1918, 'Grot', as a young officer with only a handful of men under his command, disarmed a German infantry company. The German soldiers were demoralised, and just wanted to go home. Now, 'Grot' and his staff were convinced that history would repeat itself, that a skilful propaganda campaign would destroy the *Wehrmacht* fighting spirit. Sound familiar? They expected that the ordinary soldiers would not come to the assistance of the security forces and of the administration, which would be the primary targets to be attacked by *AK* coming into the open.

'Grot' decided to set up a new, ultra-secret, professional propaganda organisation, whose output would contain no traces betraying its Polish origin. He called it *Akcja* 'N' – Operation 'N', N being the first letter of *Niemcy*, the Polish word for Germany. N as a symbol of the unknown made it even more apposite. Security was to be exceptionally strict, and the operation would be as self-contained as possible. No other branch of the Resistance was to be aware of its existence. The 'need-to-know' principle was to apply even to the top people in Central Command and in the parallel civilian underground organisation. This had the result that when Operation 'N' was in full swing, the *AK* intelligence service was reporting excitedly the emergence of several German resistance organisations. These reports were often accompanied by actual 'N' leaflets and other prints, obtained from German sources. Those in the know were delighted. Resistance organisations and intelligence services in other countries were also taken in and their mistaken views persisted, often for a considerable time. In 1961, at the International Congress on the History of European Resistance Movements in Milan, many 'N' publications were displayed as a genuine product of German resistance groups. Similarly, an 'N' poster signed apparently by the *SS* General Koppe – informing Germans living in the *GG* that because of the approaching Soviet Army they must get ready to be evacuated – was for years treated by the Hoover Institute (Stanford University) as a genuine German document.[7] As late as 1979, in a book published in eastern Germany, two periodicals produced by 'N', *Der Hammer* and *Der Frontkämpfer*, were listed as joint products of German and Polish communists.[8]

The products of 'N' did not have a monopoly to create confusion. Many of the concoctions created by British black operations were, for a considerable time, and some probably still are, accepted as genuine.[9]

The strict security surrounding 'N' did not prevent some penetration by *Gestapo* agents, but the *Gestapo* files available now indicate that the penetrations were only peripheral and did not cause any major disasters. In the case of fortuitous arrests, the 'cut-outs' and alarm systems worked well.

In February 1941 'Grot' reported to London that he had set up within the *BIP* (*Biuro Informacji i Propagandy* – Information and Propaganda Bureau) a new cell called *Akcja* 'N':

> The work of 'N' is calculated for long-term effects … its output will be attributable to German clandestine opposition groups. This should enhance its effectiveness and should be seen also as a proof of the strength of these groups … its publications can represent any political persuasion: social-democratic, communist, national-socialist, monarchist or separatist (e.g. Austrian nationalist). … The repressive measures against religion will be highlighted. … There will be also subversive prints, masquerading as official publications . . . Germans will be encouraged to spy upon each other, and to denounce each other.[10]

To head the new organisation, 'Grot' appointed Tadeusz Żenczykowski (cover names 'Kowalik', 'Kania', 'Zawadzki'), who was an excellent organiser and had the knack of selecting the right people to work for him. He did not have Sefton Delmer's amazing insight into the German psyche – nobody else on the Allied side had – but he was experienced in propaganda. He understood that an effective propagandist should pretend to belong to the enemy's camp, that he should persuade his addressees that they were suffering wartime tribulations because of the errors and the incompetence of their government,[11] that the German soldier would reject enticements and promises offered by enemy propaganda but if he was addressed 'in the name of Germany', it would not make him feel a traitor if he complied with whatever was suggested. He had to be convinced that the opinions presented to him were those of his fellow countrymen. Loyal and patriotic soldiers will, in the company of their comrades, whinge about anything – meagre rations, stupid leadership, infrequency of furloughs, absence of female company, general mismanagement – but should they discover that these sentiments are fomented or encouraged by the enemy propaganda, they would immediately close ranks and give that propaganda short shrift. So 'N' had to operate under the labels of all sorts of fictitious German resistance organisations, both civilian and military. None of the leaflets or other prints were to be anonymous. The same names would be used repeatedly, creating the impression that the given organisation was not ephemeral and was growing in strength. Nothing was to give an indication of their Polish origin. Over eighty such fictitious organisations were created.

The object of the propaganda addressed to the members of the German administration of Polish territories would be to disrupt and to sabotage the efficient working of the German war machine and to slow down the economic exploitation of the country. Fake orders, instructions, circulars, appeals and invitations to meetings would create chaos and misunderstandings. The administration and the party organisation would be ridiculed and their authority undermined. Some of the operations would not be black. German officials would be warned that all instances of persecution of Poles were being recorded and that their punishment would be merciless and unavoidable.

The original brief given to the new black organisation was to attack the *NSDAP*, *Gestapo* and all security and police formations – the *SS*, *SD* and *Schupo*, etc. – but gradually the *NSDAP* became the principal, if not the sole target.[12] Civilian, non-party Germans and the *Wehrmacht* as a whole were to be left alone, but individuals or groups identified as dangerous to Polish interests were considered legitimate targets. Originally it was intended not to send black propaganda materials to those groups that were being attacked, but eventually some materials were addressed to members of the *NSDAP*, in the hope of causing a split in the Party.

The new organisation was not to give any indication of a connection with the rather ineffective operation conducted until then in Warsaw. To achieve this, it was decided to shut down the latter immediately and have a break of at least six months before starting anew. It was hoped that this lacuna would prevent the German authorities from connecting the two operations. It would also give the new organisation time to create a framework for its activities. Further, it was felt that the run of German successes could not last for ever, that eventually they must suffer setbacks that would give the black propaganda a better chance of being effective.[13]

The new organisation was to have four divisions: Operational Infrastructure, Research, Editorial and Special Operations.

Operational Infrastructure was to organise and maintain a network for gathering information relevant to 'N', and a distribution network. This meant setting up courier routes reaching to Norway, France, Italy, Yugoslavia and as far due east as conditions would permit. Later a separate Distribution division was created which became responsible for the distribution inside the *GG*. Couriers (also called 'inspectors') had to be provided with appropriate documents, so that they could travel all over Europe. This meant organising a facility to forge a multitude of the ever-changing essential personal documents. Couriers needed not only official IDs, passports, passes and various permits, but also documents issued in connection with their ostensible travels by government organisations or by German companies, such as movement orders, introductions, recommendations and purchase orders. To produce them various forms were needed, company letterheads, seals, stamps, examples of signatures. They were either stolen from German offices or were forged. Only one class of couriers did not need any special documents: train guards and engine drivers. German railways employed many Poles, also on long-distance trains. The destinations of the parcels they carried were mainly in Germany but they were also making deliveries to contact addresses in France, Italy and the Balkans.

The task of the Research division was to study National Socialism as a political and social phenomenon, to seek out its structural contradictions and ideological difficulties, to become familiar with its specific jargon, methods of reasoning and the characteristics of its leading personalities – their foibles, peccadilloes and especially their more serious transgressions. It was to gather information on German history and geography, on the development of the language and its dialects, on the background of current events, on the situation of various social groups – anything that could be useful in the creation of fictitious opposition circles of all political shades, and in producing subversive propaganda on their behalf.[14] It was imperative to know the exact current psychological state of the Germans generally and the state of the morale of the troops in particular. An excellent source of this information was the correspondence between the soldiers at the Russian

Front and their families and friends at home.[15] All these letters were passing through Poland, and Polish postal officials had access to them. Letters were opened, photographed and sent on to their destinations with very little delay. The information obtained from all available sources enabled the Research division to suggest to the editors suitable subjects as well as the idiom to be used. It was a laborious process, which only began to produce real results from the summer of 1942.

The editorial team was made up of experienced journalists, acquainted with German affairs. Nevertheless, they lacked detailed knowledge of these affairs. That knowledge would come later from the Research division, but they felt that they could not just sit idly waiting for that moment, they felt that they had to work out some guidelines themselves. After many hours of discussions they concluded that in spite of Hitler's military successes, there must exist in Germany a feeling of dissatisfaction, especially among the working class and among those whose family life was disrupted by the war, especially since an end of that war was not in sight; these feelings would be unavoidably reinforced by mounting casualties, by women being obliged to work in factories, by general shortages.[16] Furthermore, in the last free German election, nearly 15 million people did not vote for Hitler. Some of them were later locked up in concentration camps and others emigrated, but millions were still at liberty in Germany, hopefully still opposed to Hitler. True, they were frightened, their spirit of initiative paralysed, but surely, given the right impetus, active opposition would emerge. It was thought that Operation 'N' could create this impetus by producing a regular clandestine paper, representing the social-democratic ideology from the Weimar Republic period. This ideology would be acceptable not only to the socialists but also to the communists and to the liberal bourgeoisie.

Another line of attack was to be based on the conviction that there must exist a significant discord between the majority of German generals on one side and Hitler, *NSDAP*, *SS* and the *Gestapo* on the other. The predominantly aristocratic German generals were surely only pretending to support the upstart corporal. Further, there must exist among soldiers and non-Party *Wehrmacht* officers a feeling of dissatisfaction with the privileges enjoyed by the *Waffen-SS* and by the Party members in the *Wehrmacht*, who usually had safe administrative or staff jobs. Operation 'N' must encourage these feelings. It also had to create doubts as to Hitler's professed military genius.

At the beginning it was proposed to produce two monthlies: *Der Hammer*, representing the social-democratic ideology, for the German civilian population; and *Der Soldat*, which would pretend to be the organ of a clandestine military, anti-Hitler organisation – for soldiers and officers of the *Wehrmacht*. In time, the list of periodicals grew to exceed ten titles. Each one was given a distinct political profile in line with its supposed pedigree, and had to be able to address convincingly a given class of people. Their common task was to highlight, each one from its own point of view, current events that impinged upon the great majority of Germans, such as the incompetent rule of Hitler and his party, reverses on the front, casualties, sufferings of the front-line soldiers and of the families being bombed at home. All publications, even those endeavouring to maintain a serious image, also had their 'humour and satire' corners – sometimes bitter, often risqué, but always scathing.

There were also quite a few one-offs. A periodical, i.e. a publication appearing seemingly regularly, always in the same format, maintaining the same line and the numbering of its issues, encourages the readers to trust the strength of the organisation behind it. This is an important aspect of propaganda. But this format could not be used in every case, it could not serve to express every manifestation of opposition thinking. Some of these manifestations could emerge from small groups, not having at their disposal the means to publish regularly. This assumption of the multiplicity of opposition forms led 'N' to the printing of one-off leaflets and booklets.

The original proposal to print the two monthlies was accepted, but two problems remained to be resolved: should the articles be written in German from the outset, or should they be written in Polish, then translated into German; and should one print using gothic or Latin founts? The first reaction of the editors, who were all fluent in German, was that they should write in German, but on reflection they decided against it. The German they learned at school and at universities was *Hochdeutsch* (literally 'high German', also called *Bühnen Deutsch*, i.e. 'stage German'), used on a daily basis only by the upper and professional classes, the intellectual élite and on the stage. Average Germans would speak in local dialects, and soldiers had their own, rather profane jargon. The editors could not manage either. Fortunately, appropriately qualified translators were found: some were born and brought up in various parts of Germany and were professional translators, and one had served in the German army during the First World War.

It is surprising how close the two black operations – British and Polish – were in their approach to the job. They shared also some of the difficulties.

So far as the presentation was concerned, those in charge of 'N' thought that gothic founts would be more convincing but they were practically unobtainable in Poland. Then it was noted that German publications were increasingly using Latin script. So it was decided to use the latter. Unfortunately, as it turned out, the printers found some gothic founts and the first number of *Der Hammer* appeared partly in gothic, as did a leaflet signed by the *NSDAP Erneuerungsbewegung* (Party Renewal Movement). Unfortunately – because when copies were handed over to the *Gestapo* by loyal Germans, the less than perfect use of the gothic founts gave the first indication that Poles may be involved. A four-page analysis of the print, prepared by the *Gestapo* in Šódź, came to the following conclusions:

1. The author is to be found in German circles.
2. The originating print shop is in possession of Polish founts.
3. The printer is a professional.
4. The compositor is most likely a Pole.[17]

The game was also given away by a number of mistakes in typesetting, caused mainly by the compositors confusing capital letters G and E, R and N, B and V, E and G. In the gothic founts these letters do look alike, but a German compositor would never confuse them. In addition, the founts used to print the non-gothic part of *Der Hammer* were identified as of Polish origin, so it was deduced that the non-German compositor most probably was a Pole. On the other hand, the report added, judging by the contents and the construction of the text, the author must be an experienced German propagandist.

So the report was both bad news and good news, but since it came to light only after the war, the editors were not aware that it praised their work. Perhaps eventually they did notice the giveaway mistakes, but several more leaflets were printed in gothic.

With the help of the Research Division, the proficiency of the Editorial Department was improving all the time. Eventually the highest German security authorities had to take notice. On 9 November 1942 the chief of the *Gestapo*, Heinrich Müller, signed on behalf of Himmler a circular on the subject of subversive publications printed in German: 'During 1941 the subversive publications contained many linguistic errors. Now they are without exception written in good German, free of any mistakes. Their contents and presentation are perfect for achieving a subversive effect ... they come by post, mainly from Warsaw, addressed to individual Germans.'[18]

From February 1941, the *ZWZ-AK* commander was submitting to London detailed reports on the activities of 'N'. In a report dated 15 April 1942, he described the Special Operations division brief: 'To conduct moral subversion among Germans both in Poland and in the *Reich*, which is to go beyond the limits of printed propaganda. This means denouncing individual Germans to their authorities, spreading damaging rumours, creating mix-ups and misunderstandings adversely affecting their morale, undermining their confidence. In general the object is to create chaos and to encourage personal intrigues. The basis of all these operations is provided by our extensive card index of all Germans in Poland. It contains also details of many Germans in the *Reich*, of families of soldiers fighting on the Russian Front and of soldiers killed there.'[19]

This card index contained the details of about 30,000 Germans in *GG* alone, listing not just their names and addresses but also particulars of their families, employment, relations with other Germans and with Poles, their interests, misdemeanours and their animosities in private life and at work. Basic data for this index were obtained through Polish employees of Food Offices, where both *Reichsdeutsche* ('proper' Germans, mainly from the *Reich*) and *Volksdeutsche* (ethnic Germans, born outside the *Reich*) had to register to obtain their food ration books, graded according to their category: the most privileged were the *Reichsdeutsche* and then there were four descending categories of *Volksdeutsche*. A priceless source of information was a copy of the *NSDAP* 'Who's Who', obtained by an 'N' cell in Silesia. It listed all Party members, with their Party membership numbers, addresses, positions and brief CVs. Its possession was restricted to high Party officials and some government departments. The same cell also procured telephone directories from all over Germany. As a result, Operation 'N' was basing its activities on a solid database – just like *Gustav Siegfried Eins*.

The Distribution Division that covered the *GG* acted as a wholesaler: its couriers, mostly women and girls, delivered the leaflets and other prints to regional 'N' cells. There were about twenty of them, servicing fifteen regional cells.[20] Each made two or three deliveries per week. They travelled by rail, carrying as personal luggage parcels weighing usually 10, 15 or 20 kg.[21] Rail travel was dangerous but no other means of transport were readily available to Poles. Since nobody could possibly survive on the meagre official food rations, thousands and thousands of people were making a living and helping the town dwellers to survive by bringing provisions from villages to towns. This trade was, of course, forbidden and, if caught, a 'smuggler' could end up in a concentration camp; if he – or more frequently, she – was lucky, just the 'contraband' would be confiscated. Passengers and their luggage were often searched. 'N' prints were more dangerous to carry than illegal prints in Polish, since any German policeman could see immediately what they were. There were isolated cases when a policeman, having been ordered to look for butter and bacon, was simply not interested in any printed matter. Taking into account the number of trips the couriers made, surprisingly few were caught, and a system of 'cut-outs' prevented further arrests. The basis of this system was that the courier would collect the consignment from a person unknown to her, identified only by a password.

Special Operations and both Distribution functions had an important partner in the *Szare Szeregi* (clandestine Scouts), who ran their own distribution system.[22] This system was entirely separate from 'N'; except at the very top, there was no contact between them, they were not even aware of each other's existence.[23] The *Szare Szeregi* network covered also eastern Poland and reached as far west as Berlin. Part of the distribution in the GG was in their hands, as were a number of special operations, such as Street Propaganda and Operation Tse-Tse. The latter, a nuisance operation, targeted individual German families and made their lives miserable by threatening telephone calls, abusive letters, blocking keyholes, breaking windows, tarring front door-handles, summoning undertakers. Street propaganda meant chalking and painting of slogans and putting up of posters. One such operation turned into a duel with the German propaganda. From mid-August 1943, in all Polish towns, the word *Oktober* started to appear on the walls. Germans were receiving mysterious telephone calls, the caller just saying '*Oktober*' or sometimes adding: 'Just you wait.' The idea was to get the Germans to worry that something terrible would happen to them in October. It had associations with their October/November 1918 debacle. Their propaganda machine counter-attacked: instead of obliterating the inscriptions, they were expanded to read: *26 Oktober 1943* and on a line below – *4 Jahre* GG, meaning that on 26 October 1943, four years of GG would be celebrated. (GG was established on 26 October 1939.) The paint was hardly dry when the word *nur* ('only') started to appear in front of the figure 4. Game to *Szare Szeregi*, but the match went to the Germans: in October the terror, especially the number of public executions, reached a new high.

An easy but nevertheless a very satisfying modification was applied to the slogan *Deutschland siegt an allen Fronten!* ('Germany is victorious on all fronts!') by changing the letter 's' in *siegt* to the letter 'l'. The result meant: 'Germany is down on all fronts!' It was especially easily done if the slogan was written in the gothic script, in which letters 'l' and 's' are similar.

Although it has little to do with black propaganda, I must mention the most ubiquitous result of our street propaganda, the symbol of resistance – the Anchor. It was made up of the letters 'P' and 'W', standing for *Polska Walczy* ('Poland Fights On'). We chalked and painted our Anchor wherever we could. Every time I saw one it gave me a warm feeling. By the spring of 1944 Germans gave up trying to obliterate them. Our Anchor was victorious!

The regional 'N' cells were responsible for the distribution in their areas. There was one aspect of distribution where there was some overlap between Distribution and Operational Infrastructure divisions: supplying German soldiers, both in the *GG* and closer to the Russian Front. The simplest method was to plant the prints, normally singly but occasionally in small batches, in passenger and goods wagons of trains going East, as well as in military vehicles that were expected to be driven in the direction of the front. Ideal places were marshalling yards and military vehicle repair shops that employed Poles. Polish printers working in a print shop producing magazines for the *Wehrmacht* were inserting leaflets into copies of *Die Armee Zeitung, Die Panzerfaust* and *Der Stosstrupp* before they were despatched to front units. Poles working in the cloakrooms of German messes stuffed leaflets into greatcoat pockets and planted them in lavatories. In many streets there were containers for donated magazines for despatch to soldiers fighting in the East. 'N' donated thousands of magazines, with suitable enclosures. Other containers were for books for soldiers in hospitals. Books donated by 'N' had some pages replaced by *Der Soldat* or by leaflets.

German civilians were not neglected either: they could pick up copies of 'N' prints in the lavatories of their offices and in restaurants. They received them also by post or just found them in their letterboxes.

Operation 'N' rapidly became a sizeable organisation. 'Grot' reported to London on 16 July 1942 that the number of people working for 'N', excluding *Szare Szeregi*, was 948, of whom 48 ran the centre (the 5 divisions) and 410 were in the *GG* distribution network, dealing, on average, with 17,000 prints per month. The western area – Polish territories annexed to Germany and the *Reich* itself (called the *Altreich*) – were looked after by about 40 people, dealing with just under 4,000 print items per month, while the eastern area – Polish territories occupied by the Soviet Union in September 1939 –had about 50 people distributing about 1,400 prints per month. *Szare Szeregi* distributed over 4,000 prints per month.[24] By the end of 1943 these figures were considerably higher.

One rather important element of an operation based on the printed word was not an organic part of the 'N' organisation: the reprographic facility. In spite of the stress on the importance of being self-contained, it had to use print shops operated by *BIP* (*Biuro Informacji I Propagandy*), the Polish *AK* propaganda department of which 'N' was a secret part. *BIP* had eleven print shops (with cover names from W1 to W11) which, in 1943, were using an average of 2½ tons of paper

per month.* 'N' was using several of these shops, but in time W1 became their near-exclusive printer. They also continued to use W5, which produced plates, and one print shop that specialised in forgeries. The index of all clandestine print shops in Warsaw has 147 entries, and the underground press registers show about 1,200 titles, of which approximately 330 were printed, while the rest was produced by duplicating or as carbon copies.[25]

All resistance organisations were always on the lookout for printing presses. So were the Germans. In Sącz, a small town in southern Poland, they closed down a print shop. A list of the inventory was made and the usual lead seals were put on the doors. One evening a lorry arrived. The seals were broken, two handprinting presses were replaced by chaff-cutters, and the seals were successfully replaced.[26] The number of machines tallied with the inventory and there were no repercussions.

The regular *Meldung Wichtiger Staatspolizeilichen Ereignisse* ('Report on Important State Police Events'), issued in the autumn of 1943 lists, under the heading 'Leaflets of the Polish Resistance Movement', sixty-three leaflets and periodicals in Polish, and eighteen leaflets and periodicals in German.[27] It is interesting that on 10 April 1943 the Šódź *Gestapo* had already compiled a list of 119 'Subversive prints in German, presumably issued by the Polish Resistance'.[28]

A clandestine reprographic facility had very little in common with normal printing establishments. It was usu-

* One source, J. Ślaski, *Polska Walczaca*, p. 289, gives a figure about ten times higher, but this is difficult to accept. According to J. Rzepecki, *O wydawnictwach Akcji N*, p. 162, paper consumption peaked at 5t per month. Grot in his report to London of 1 March 1943 (Studium Polski Podziemnej, *AK w dokumentach*, Vol. 2, p. 439) states that in the preceding 11 months 28t were used.

ally a small room in a basement, a loft, a bombed-out house, a storeroom of a mechanical workshop or, less often, in a peasant's cottage. Bigger resistance organisations, with more ample resources, 'N' included, would build false walls in cellars, excavate bunkers under houses (in one instance several dozen cubic metres of soil were carried out for disposal in attaché cases), and make provisions for damping down noise and vibrations. Since power was strictly rationed, metered private supply could not be used, and surreptitious connections had to be made to the street cables. The constant coming and going of people, usually carrying parcels, had to be camouflaged by some sort of a commercial activity (it was called a 'mask'). All the print shops run by *BIP* had letterpress machines, but more than half of all the clandestine reprographic facilities could not boast anything better than a duplicator, mostly homemade at that. In 1944, *BIP* were very close to notching up an occupied Europe record: had it not been for the outbreak of the Warsaw Rising, they would have installed a rotary press! Purpose-built premises were ready, equipped with alarm systems and all mod cons, even with an escape tunnel for the printers, in case of a *Gestapo* raid. The press, purchased in Czechoslovakia, was brought to Kraków in *Wehrmacht* lorries and was waiting there for shipment to Warsaw.[29] According to some sources, it did manage to reach the city. Its main use was going to be after the liberation, should the retreating Germans destroy all the non-secret newspaper printing presses. There are no records to explain how this incredible operation was carried out. It would have been called W12.

In the case of 'N' publishing, it was not just the physical working environment that was different from normal publishing, but the production stages were too. The main cause of the difficulties was the distance separating authors and editors from the print shop. The former were in the town centre and the latter in the outskirts. The person in charge of W1 would collect the typed scripts from a contact in the city centre. If stopped and searched, a script in Polish would not usually constitute a hazard, unless the German policeman spoke Polish, but when it was in German it could be a disaster. On safe arrival at W1, the compositor would work very carefully, making sure there were no errors. Hand proofs were made and taken back to the town centre for proofreading by the editors. Collection date and time of the corrected proofs were agreed and in due course they were brought back to W1 so that printing could commence.

Another difficulty was due to the lack of appropriate German founts and type sizes. For instance, the only way to produce many large letter titles was with the help of plates. The same applied to illustrations and, in the case of the satirical periodical *Der Klabautermann*, which was in colour, for every drawing three zinc plates, mounted on wood blocks, were needed. They were produced by W5, which specialised in plate-making. The packages were quite bulky.

Obviously, illegal printing was a very high-risk occupation. What made it especially dangerous was the overlapping of people with several functions: a print shop would service various branches of an organisation or even other befriended organisations; it would be known to people who were involved in setting it up and in servicing its machine; these people, in turn, would have contacts with other branches of the organisation and with other organisations. If a person with multiple contacts was arrested and made to talk, the damage he or she could cause was incalculable. Printers had to expect attacks from many directions. They were armed but when the camouflaged entrances were discovered and the *Gestapo* did arrive, their chances of survival were nil.

By the spring of 1944 the total number of 'N' prints came to over a million. This does not sound impressive compared to the tens of millions of leaflets produced weekly by the Allies, but, considering the conditions in which 'N' worked, it was no mean achievement. Moreover, the effectiveness of distribution was different: whereas practically every 'N' leaflet hit its target, only a minute fraction of the leaflets dropped over Europe was read by those for whom they were intended.

The basic 'N' tactics tried to create the impression that both the civilian and the military German oppositions were widely spread and that they had many varied roots. It tried to create a picture of numerous, discrete groups. For this purpose the individual publications presented different points of view, both in respect of political programmes and in respect of tactics. They even indulged in polemics among themselves, for instance an allegedly social-democratic organ would come out decisively against the possibility of a military dictatorship, while the ostensibly military-national ones would maintain that only such dictatorship was capable of overthrowing Hitler and achieving an honourable peace. In the summer of 1943 *Der Soldat* suggested that Field Marshal von Mannstein should become a military dictator, while a leaflet allegedly signed by *Luftwaffe* officers called upon Göring to get rid of Hitler and assume power as the head of a military government; at the same time the social-democratic *Der Durchbruch* (successor of *Der Hammer*) was furiously attacking Göring.

As we know, 'N' was going to kick off with two regular publications: *Der Hammer* and *Der Soldat*. Of course, there was no certainty that they could be published regularly, so they were not numbered consecutively and readers could blame any breaks in the numbering on distribution difficulties. Barbarossa, the German attack on the Soviet Union on 22 June 1941, changed the priorities and two weeks later a leaflet for the German soldiers on the Russian Front went into distribution (3,000 copies). It was signed: *Soldatenverband 'Freiheit der Ostfront'* (Soldiers' Association 'Freedom of the Eastern Front'). It tried to dampen the euphoria of the initial successes in the field and it condemned the Nazi Party for having started another war that would result in many German casualties. There are no reports of German reactions to this leaflet, but one can imagine that in the enthusiasm of the rapid and seemingly unstoppable advance, the only reaction would be derisive rejection.

Chapter Seven

Operation 'N' – Rise and Fall

Another event that disrupted the original planned publishing schedule was the mysterious flight of Hess to Scotland on 10 May 1941. Unlike the British powers-that-be, but just like Delmer, 'N' thought that it would be a mistake to ignore such a propaganda opportunity.

'N' had been plotting all sorts of intrigues aimed at breaking up the unity of the Nazi Party and at encouraging infighting between its various factions, and Hess did cause considerable confusion within the Party: after all, he was Hitler's deputy. The latter's assertions that Hess lost his mind were not very convincing. 'N' decided to aggravate this confusion by creating a new pro-Hess faction called *NSDAP Erneuerungsbewegung* ('Party Renewal Movement'). The assumption would be that Hitler and his clique had perverted and betrayed the National Socialist ideals whose guardian was Hess; that Hess was against the war with the Soviet Union and that he was organising his own faction within the *NSDAP* just as Röhm did in 1934; that since Hitler had had Röhm murdered, he could do the same to Hess; that Hess found out that Himmler was after him and had to flee to save himself.

All this was quite feasible, and the 'N' editors decided that, with their help, Hess would now issue an appeal to Party members, dissuading them from attacking the Soviet Union, as the only outcome could be a defeat on a Napoleonic scale. He would call for the removal of Hitler as the only way to save the *Reich* and the Party from a shattering catastrophe, and he would enjoin all patriots and true believers in National Socialism to support the Renewal Movement.

The two-page leaflet was printed on these lines, ending *Heil Hess!* It was datelined 'Munich', the birthplace of the Nazi movement, and 4,000 copies went into distribution at the end of July 1941. The second 'Hess' leaflet, written in a similar vein, appeared on 28 August. In total six similar leaflets were printed over a period of eighteen months, all criticising Hitler and appealing to Party members to join the Renewal Movement. The last leaflet of the series, of January 1943, with Hess's photograph on the front page, gave in detail the programme of his party: the top priority is to get rid of Hitler and to conclude a peace treaty; only Hitler and his cronies will be held responsible for murders and persecutions, not the German nation; those responsible for murdering Jews will appear before a court made up of Germans and of representatives of other nations but not of Jews; Germany will keep part of Czechoslovakia and western Poland; the fate of Lorraine and Alsace will be decided by plebiscite; all European countries will join a common market.

Preparing these leaflets was not easy. Their author, Zygmunt Ziółek, remembers: 'These appeals signed by Hess had to be not only convincing from the point of view of their political contents, but they also had to be written in the habitual form and style of his speeches and appeals, which were very well known to the German public. They were all available in print and could be found on the bookshelves of most party members. The possibility of being unmasked as a "Polish Hess" had to be avoided at any price, since that would mean the end of our operation.'[1]

The monthly *Der Soldat* was addressed to soldiers. Its aim was to convey to them that within the *Wehrmacht* did exist and was functioning a powerful and patriotic organisation, whose object was to take the control of the armed forces away from the incompetent Party officials and to restore it to the professionals who knew how to lead the nation to victory. It was scathing about the behaviour of the security and administration officials in the occupied territories who were bringing dishonour to the good name and to the uniform of the German soldier. The first issue, bearing No. 7, was printed in July 1941. There were two articles: about Hess fleeing to Scotland, presented as his protest against a war on two fronts and about the idiocy of attacking the Soviet Union, in spite of Napoleon's experiences of 1812 and of the difficulties encountered in that area by the German army during the First World War. There were also some smaller pieces about the lifestyle of members of the *Gestapo*, *SS* and *NSDAP* and some jokes in the barrack-room style: some risqué but most outright pornographic. The editors spared no effort to create a unique style, different from all the other 'N' products. This principle was applied to all periodicals, so that their common provenance would not be noticeable, but the editors of *Der Soldat* were especially strict in this respect.

After some research the editors decided that the man best suited to lead their anti-Hitler conspiracy would be Field Marshal von Reichenau. He had been Hitler's man since 1933 and was a distinguished commander. On the Russian

Front he commanded the Army Group South. It was thought that 'unmasking' von Reichenau as the head of the conspiracy would shock both the Party and the *Wehrmacht*: if a man that close to the *Führer* turns against him, then things must be going really badly for Germany. The mistrust of the Party towards the army would deepen dramatically, with far-reaching consequences.

The Christmas 1941 issue of *Der Soldat* carried von Reichenau's photograph, and it was argued in an extensive article that he was the only man who could save Germany. It ended with the slogan: 'With Reichenau – for a different, better Germany!'

A fortnight later the *OKW* announced that Reichenau had had a heart attack and died on a train – Hitler's personal train. He had been returning to his post, after visiting the *Führer*. Another version reported that, having survived a plane crash, he had died of a stroke.

'N' could not believe their luck. Although there was no proof that Reichenau's demise was linked to the article, they received congratulations from General Sikorski in London and even from Churchill.[2]

'N' decided now to designate General Erich von Mannstein as the head of the opposition within the army. The organisation he was supposed to lead was named *Soldatenbund Hindenburg*. The revelations in *Der Soldat* followed a similar pattern as before, but they failed to harm von Mannstein or his career. Nevertheless, it continued on the same tack by presenting the deaths of *Luftwaffe* generals Udet (suicide, after a quarrel with Göring) and Jeschonnek (suicide), of Colonel Mölders (air accident) and the Minister of Armaments Todt (air accident), as executions of the leaders of the opposition.

The success of Operation Reichenau had an unexpected result. The British propaganda took up the theme on identical lines. 'N' was afraid that this would suggest to the Germans the existence of close links between the two operations, destroying the patriotic image and the credibility of the fake military conspiracy. *Der Soldat* was suspended. It was replaced in March 1942 by a similar monthly: *Der Frontkämpfer*. *Der Soldat* was resurrected in September 1942 and both continued to appear until January 1944. There was another reason for the suspension of *Der Soldat*: it was hoped that the German authorities would conclude that von Reichenau's death was a serious blow to his organisation, which needed time to regroup.

The innovation in *Der Frontkämpfer*, as compared to *Der Soldat*, was the inclusion of in-depth articles on the production of war material by both sides. The May 1942 issue discussed aircraft production from September 1939 to September 1942. The July issue was devoted to merchant vessel construction, and the issue that followed to tank production. They all showed that Germany had no chance of catching up with the production capacity of the Allies. Also, whereas *Der Soldat* addressed all soldiers, *Der Frontkämpfer* focused, in accordance with its title, on the soldiers on the front line. The plight of these soldiers was contrasted not only with the luxuries enjoyed by the *NSDAP*, the *Gestapo* and the *SS*, but also with the cushy comforts enjoyed by the shirkers sheltering in the rear echelons.

Der Frontkämpfer proposed a new candidate to head the alleged anti-Hitler *Wehrmacht* conspiracy: Field Marshal Fedor von Bock. The leader in the July 1942 issue bore the title 'Generals against Hitler' and carried von Bock's photograph. It discussed the differences between Hitler and his faithful on one side, and the front-line generals on the other. It took up this theme again in the October issue with an appeal headed 'Field Marshal, you can trust us' and signed 'The front-line fighters in the East'. It was precipitated by von Bock being deprived by Hitler – for the second time – of his command.

The January 1943 issue opened with an appeal of another resistance organisation created by 'N': *Soldatenbund Ost* ('Soldiers' Association East'). It disclosed the existence in the army of an old junta of generals, listing those who were against Hitler and those who were for him. Nevertheless, in spite of all these efforts to incriminate various generals as enemies of Hitler, none came to any harm.

The first issue (actually bearing No. 13) of the four-page *Der Hammer* was printed at the end of July 1941 with a print run of 4,000 copies. The front page carried a message that was repeated on the front pages of all subsequent numbers: 'You know very well who to thank for this war … the peace is up to you.' It contained three articles and several small items. The general tenor was: the situation is hopeless, defeat is unavoidable, the Party is corrupt, no effort is made to spare soldiers' blood, soldiers' families in Germany are being bombed by the British, German women have to work in factories, German propaganda cannot be trusted, the strength of Britain and of the USA continues to grow.

The ideas promoted by *Der Hammer* were feasible, its distribution – in the Polish areas annexed to the *Reich* (Upper Silesia, Poznań, Pomerania) and in the *Reich* itself – efficient, but somehow it did not strike the right chord with its readers. After many discussions the editors came to the conclusion that the reason was two-fold: the originator was too nebulous and the category of the addressees was not clearly defined.[3]

In the Hess affair there was a clear leader – Hess himself – and an obvious target – members of the Party, who were being told exactly what they should do: organise cells of the new party. *Der Soldat* professed to represent actual persons – Reichenau, Udet, Todt – and was appealing to the soldiers fighting on the Russian Front to overthrow Hitler, get rid of the Party crooks and create a better Germany. *Der Hammer* lacked these attributes. The organisation behind it was anonymous. It was addressing its message to the 'working classes', not a very precise concept. Its contents were too general and enigmatic to elicit a response. It did not make any suggestions as to who should actually overthrow Hitler or who should create a better Germany. Some members of 'N' thought that donning the mantle of the Communist Party might produce better results.

The arrest of the editor of *Der Hammer* in July 1942 precipitated the decision to close it. It was replaced by *Der Durchbruch*, also of a social-democratic orientation. Its main slogan was 'Peace in the West – Victory in the East'. Its first issue proclaimed: 'We will sort out things in our country ourselves. With our own German hands, without any help from the Anglo-Saxon criminals or from the soviet rabble.' Unfortunately, it still did not manage to touch the right chord and, after its distribution network in Upper Silesia and in Czechoslovakia was betrayed to the *Gestapo*, it was decided to discontinue its publication. No further attempts were made by 'N' to publish a social-political monthly for the Germans.

Right from the beginning, the 'N' editors wanted to print a fake issue of a German magazine. They could remember the First World War success of the fake *Frankfurter Zeitung*, which was smuggled into the Kaiser's Germany and distributed through normal channels. By February 1942 they had chosen their victim: the satirical illustrated magazine *Erika*. Its illustrations were just black and white and the format would not cause any problems either. The 'N' version was going to be a special issue, dated 1 April 1942. 'N' was fortunate in having an illustrator who had the knack of copying the style of any German illustrator or cartoonist. It was decided to satirise Hitler, the Party, the *Gestapo* and the *SS* in an absurd way, acceptable on April Fool's Day. Some copies were made available in Warsaw to newspaper kiosks that actually sold them quite openly. The main item informed readers that Hitler had given birth to a son and that the greeting *Heil Hitler!* was to be replaced by *Heil Hitler und Sohn!* There followed cartoons illustrating the serious situation both in the *Reich* and at the front, jokes and witty sayings. There was also 'The Prayer of the Third *Reich*':

> Dear God – make me blind
> So that I cannot find the truth.
> Dear God – make me deaf
> So that I shall believe all the lies.
> Dear God – make me dumb
> So that I shall not find myself in Dachau.
> Make me blind, deaf and dumb
> So that I shall fit in the Third *Reich*.

The fake *Erika* was a resounding success. It changed hands among soldiers and officers at fifty times the price of the genuine article.

Another successful forgery was that of the magazine *Bilder für die Truppe* ('Pictures for the Troops'), published by *OKW*. Two issues were produced in 1943, faithful imitations of the original, except for the subject of the illustrations: the cruelties of the war and the appalling conditions endured by front-line soldiers.

Erika's success encouraged the editors to start a satirical magazine. Their superiors gave their approval in May 1942. It was to be called *Der Klabautermann*. This was the name, in naval slang, of a shipboard spirit, a harbinger of misfortune. Its style, layout and general appearance were those of typical German satirical magazines. It had much in common with the leading satirical magazine *Simplicissimus*. On the cover of the first issue was a drawing of a German town being devastated by bombing, the burning houses stretching out long skeleton arms, while crosses, representing the graves of the fallen, cascade on Hitler's head. It was exactly in the manner of the leading German illustrator Matejka and bore his signature. There were political anecdotes and cartoons, jokes, funny and macabre stories and, of course, pornographic drawings and tales. So far as the latter were concerned, *Der Klabautermann* was even more inventive than *Der Soldat* or *Der Frontkämpfer*. The issues that followed continued this pattern. The last issue appeared in April 1944.

From August 1942, Germans living in the *GG* had 'their own' bi-weekly: *Die Ostwache*, supposedly published by the local German opposition. It was aimed at inciting the *Reichsdeutsche* against the *Volksdeutsche* and vice versa, disclosing corrupt practices, scandals and disputes between higher officials, and tried to discredit those functionaries who, from the Polish point of view, were the most harmful. It described the persecution of the Polish population and criticised the inadequate protection of German civilians in the case of a Polish rising, warning of the certainty of revenge, when the civilians would have to pay for the crimes committed by the *Gestapo* and high Party officials.

The Polish *Volksdeutsche* were presented with their own monthly, *Die Zukunft* ('The Future'), adorned with an ominous logo: a hangman's noose. Many of them could not really speak German, so the title was printed both in German and in Polish with the text in Polish. They were reminded repeatedly of their treachery, and threatened with revenge (Poles heartily despised the Polish *Volksdeutsche*, more than they hated the *Reichsdeutsche*). After the Stalingrad fiasco there was no hope for Germany or for them, said *Die Zukunft*, and it called upon them to attenuate their guilt by changing their attitude and by cooperating with the Underground.

In addition to the periodicals, 'N' printed numerous one-offs, from stickers and single-page leaflets to thirty-two-page booklets. Of the latter, three were especially in demand among German soldiers: *Der Rote Terror* ('The Red Terror') with Stalin on the front page, which contained descriptions of German crimes in Poland; *Der Grösste Lügner der Welt* ('The Biggest Liar in the World'); and *Der Windmacher* ('The Braggart'), which had Churchill on the cover but inside contained quotations from *Mein Kampf* and from Hitler's speeches, exposing his contradictions, lies, conceit, loss of contact with reality and his sheer stupidity. Copies of the last two were sent by courier to London and were presented to Churchill by General Sikorski. Copies were also posted to ten of the highest Nazi dignitaries, including Hitler, Goebbels and Göring.

There were leaflets signed by the South-German Freedom Association, Liberty and Peace, Soldiers' Association Hindenburg, Soldiers' Association Potsdam, Soldiers of the *Luftwaffe*, Polish and German Social Democrats and many, many fictional others. A leaflet signed by a 'Group of *NSDAP* women in Cologne' disclosed the immoral carryings-on of German women who were having affairs with foreign workers, and appealed to husbands, fiancés, fathers and brothers serving in the *Wehrmacht* to write to their women telling them to behave themselves. This delicate subject was mentioned again about a year later, in a leaflet under the title: 'Health advice of the *NSDAP* Medical Association'. Very gently the reader was told that the anger and 'zoological envy', seen with increasing frequency in soldiers' letters home, were totally out of place. They should think of the future of the nation. The *Führer* wants more children. Disagreement is tantamount to treason!

Another leaflet, also addressed to soldiers and supposedly signed by Goebbels, tried to justify the necessity of a strict censorship, but it painted also, as if inadvertently, a grim picture of the situation at home. A leaflet signed by the so-called Association of German Front Soldiers quoted casualty figures, actually obtained by *AK* intelligence: in February 1942 they averaged 10,970 per day. Let us put a stop to this madness, they appealed. No more gigantic plans to conquer the world. We have less and less of everything, except those killed in battle, invalids, widows and orphans. The pseudo-official leaflet 'Ten Commandments' obliged soldiers who belonged to the Party to spy upon their comrades and to report any manifestation of disloyalty to the regime.

During the winter of 1942, a leaflet was produced in which 'the well-known Berlin physician Dr Lippert' explained the nature of frostbite, how to recognise it and how to treat it. It was all good medical advice. He also referred casually to the terrible conditions suffered by soldiers on the front line, but he did it so vividly that it was tantamount to an incitement to desertion. Especially as his recommended ointments were not available in the *Wehrmacht*. This *Kälteschäden* ('frost damage') leaflet had the appearance of an official publication, and many soldiers kept it folded in their pay-books. At about that time *AK* intelligence discovered that soldiers who were badly wounded or seriously disfigured by frostbite were not being sent to hospitals in Germany, since doing so would have a deleterious effect on the morale of the population. Special hospitals and convalescent centres were prepared for them in occupied territories. One could well imagine that in extreme cases keeping them alive would not be a priority. So another leaflet purported to disclose secret instructions issued by the Party to medical officers, advising them the threshold condition due to wounds, sickness or frostbite beyond which the soldiers were not worth saving and should be put out of their misery by painless injections. This would also reduce the burden of cripples and invalids that would have to be carried by the postwar society. Other leaflets again gave advice on ways to simulate sickness and on how to evade Military Police checkpoints when deserting.

Three leaflets were concerned with religious questions. One, under the title *Gott mit uns! Staat ohne Gott!* ('God with us! State without God!') described the persecution of the churches in the Third *Reich*. The second protested against restrictions and closures being imposed on the church, and the incarceration of priests. The last one was a sermon, allegedly delivered by the Bishop of Münster, describing the persecution of the church by the authorities.

Leaflets in Italian for Italian soldiers in transit or waiting to be sent to the Russian Front were to encourage a friendly attitude to Poles, to discourage further participation in the war, to undermine their loyalty to Mussolini and the Fascist Party and to drive a wedge between them and the Germans. They were issued in the name of Italian anti-fascist organisations. For instance, at the end of 1942, a leaflet known as *L'Asse* ('Axis') or as *Il Padrone e il Servo* ('The Master and the Servant') came out on behalf of a leftist group, *Italia Liberata*. It presented Mussolini as Hitler's humble servant and at the same time as a murderer of hundreds of thousands of Italians who had perished fighting Hitler's war. A leaflet under the heading '*Soldati!*' and over the signature of an Italian opposition group, *Italia Reale* (supporting the monarchy), appeared in 1943 calling for the overthrow of Mussolini and for the conclusion of a separate peace. The unfortunate outcome of these leaflets was that many soldiers deserted, but for an Italian to hide in Poland was very difficult. Most were caught and executed.

There were similar leaflets for Hungarian, Bulgarian and French soldiers, as well as for *Wehrmacht* soldiers from Austria and Czechoslovakia.

Many stickers were produced. One simply said: *Nur für Deutsche* ('Only for Germans'). This was the inscription one could see on anything that was reserved for the exclusive use of the *Herrenvolk*: better restaurants, first-class railway compartments, front carriages of tramcars, even better benches in the parks. These stickers, however, were stuck to lampposts. Germans were at first nonplussed: 'this is stupid, they were saying, surely it is impossible to make the lampposts shine only for us'. Then the *Pfennig* dropped: the stickers were not reserving the lampposts for them as sources of light, but as gallows. Furious, they started scraping them off. Another sticker, with Hitler's picture and saying: 'So who is this?' was used to complement a German poster showing Churchill (with a thick cigar, of course) over the legend: 'Arsonist of the World'. Poles really enjoyed seeing a German poster of a huge ear with the warning: 'Beware! The enemy listens!' supplemented with a little rhyme:

And I shall whisper in your ear:
Germany's end is very near!

When German boasts of soon having in action a new, devastating weapon failed to materialise, 'N' posed the question:

> *O du dumme, braune Affe,*
> *Wo ist deine neue Waffe?!*

('O you stupid brown ape, so where is your new weapon?!'). It impressed both Poles and Germans.

General 'Bór'-Komorowski's report to London for the last quarter of 1942 must have been written with some satisfaction:

> Among the more important achievements was the setting up of 'N' cells in Gdańsk [Danzig], Gdynia and Szczecin [Stettin]. These cells plant our prints on board of naval and merchant vessels, both German and flying other flags (e.g. Swedish or Finnish). For instance, of late, leaflets were planted on board of the *Servegobol* due to sail to Sweden and of an ammunition ship sailing to Finland. … We highlight problems which worry both the front soldiers and the civilians at home. … During this period we produced 24 prints, including the following periodicals: three issues each of *Der Frontkämpfer*, *Der Sozialdemokrat*, *Der Durchbruch* and of the satirical *Der Klabautermann*; also six issues of *Die Ostwache*, for Germans in Poland. … We produced nine different leaflets, one of them for Italian soldiers. … Distribution is both by letter and by planting, the preferred targets of the latter being barracks, military hospitals, railway stations, trains, car parks, German restaurants and cinemas. Military rail transports are a favourite.[4]

Special Operations were calculated to create chaos, misunderstandings and despondency. On one occasion they even managed to start among the Germans a real panic (the 'Koppe' poster). Practically each operation was different, and surprised the German authorities. Hardly a week passed without forged communications of some sort being sent out.

One of the most effective operations was carried out in 1942. Factory managers in the Warsaw district received instructions that the Nazi Labour Day on 1 May was to be a holiday. The order came typed on the normal letterheaded paper of the Labour Bureau and was couched in impeccable Nazi style. There were no reasons to doubt its authenticity. It was sent out at the last moment, so that when the Labour Bureau discovered what was happening, it was too late to stop it. Most factories in and around Warsaw were closed for the day. The production losses were comparable to those produced by a minor RAF raid.[5]

On another occasion all German households in Warsaw received a communication on Party notepaper instructing each family to bring to the German *Bürgermeister*'s office a food parcel for wounded *Wehrmacht* soldiers. The contents were precisely specified. On the appointed day a huge crowd congregated around the Town Hall. Officials would not let them in, claiming no knowledge of such an order, the loyal citizens berating them for not knowing their own dispositions. *Gestapo* arrived and proceeded to interrogate everybody. This took the rest of the day. When the German housewives, who constituted the majority of the crowd, were eventually allowed home, they were loudly cursing the chaos and the incompetence of the authorities.

A similar operation targeted German farmers around Warsaw. A letter was sent to 264 of them, supposedly from District Governor Fischer, suggesting that to celebrate the approaching *Führer*'s birthday they should bring to the Party area office a present for him: two hens and twenty eggs. The day and time were specified precisely. The same for everybody. The traffic jam around the area office, caused by some 200 horse carts, was monumental. So were the arguments between the angry farmers and the helpless officials.

Chaos was also achieved by sending out 931 call-up papers to *Volks-deutsche* living in Warsaw, telling them to report, again on the same day and at the same time, to the governor's office. This scam was repeated later in Silesia but in a refined form. The recruits were asked to: report to the Town Hall that they were leaving their homes; obtain a release from their employer and train their replacements; obtain confirmation of their professional qualifications; surrender their food ration books, obtain travel food coupons for three days and surrender any other unused ration coupons. They were instructed to report to a school in a town about 100 miles away. This school did not exist.

When *AK* intelligence discovered that the stocks of gas masks were insufficient to equip all Germans in Poland, a 'confidential' letter was sent out to all of them, on the appropriate headed paper and over the signature of the Chief of the Security Police in Warsaw, warning them that Russians were expected to use poison gases very soon and consequently every German should procure a gas mask within two weeks.[6] There were no gas masks in the shops and German administrative offices were swamped with enquiries, both by telephone and in person, and with pleas for help. Normal work had to be suspended. In desperation, the police chief issued a special proclamation, admitting that the original communication had been forged by the Poles and assuring his fellow countrymen that there was no imminent danger of gas attacks. Their reaction was not what he had hoped for. 'They've only just discovered that there aren't enough gas masks to go round,' they were saying, 'so they are trying to back out and are blaming the Poles.'

The gas-mask theme was continued by 'N' some months later, again by letters addressed individually, apparently from the local chief of police.[7] He informed the addressees that because of the continued danger of enemy gas attacks it was decided to issue gas masks to all Germans. Unfortunately, there was no certainty that the existing stocks would suffice to supply everybody, so a system of priorities would have to apply. Masks would be supplied to the following groups in this order:

1. Members of the *NSDAP* and their families.
2. Government officials and their families.
3. Families of soldiers fighting on the front line.
4. Other Germans from the *Reich*.
5. *Volksdeutsche*.

Dates were given on which members of particular groups should report to the local police stations to be fitted out. Only the first group would have nothing to pay. Of course there were no gas masks to collect, so more chaos ensued, more angry scenes and more bad blood between the privileged and underprivileged groups.

A similar approach was used and a similar effect achieved in the case of a circular addressed to German firms and administration offices by a 'Dr Kundicke, Special Plenipotentiary for the Prevention of Typhoid Fever'. He painted in vivid colours the appalling effects of an epidemic, and regretted to advise that there was a shortage of vaccines, which had to be restricted to officials in the defence industry and in the political administration. Their families would be eligible only in exceptional circumstances. Orders for vaccines should be sent, concluded the letter, accompanied by certified lists of eligible persons to the Government Institute of Hygiene in Berlin and at the same time the amount due should be paid into a specified bank account.

The Social Security organisation was, like all institutions under German management, well known for its tenacity in collecting contributions. It would never admit to having committed an error and it always managed to exact its dues. When a householder engaged a domestic servant, he had to report this fact and he became responsible for the payment of the contributions. The appropriate forms were printed and, on behalf of several hundred Germans, 'N' reported to the Social Security that they had engaged servants – in many cases more than one. After a while payment demands started to arrive. The outraged recipients spent many hours writing letters and arguing with the officials and berating their inefficient organisation. Social Security reciprocated with flying control visits, which further enraged the victims. It was easier to pay up and many did, but this did not assuage their anger nor did it strengthen their faith in the system. In many towns German ARP wardens were summoned for briefings. Quite a few working days were wasted.

Highly exaggerated tax demands were despatched on forged Tax Office forms, usually asking also for income and other details for the previous two or three years.

Police and *Gestapo* dignitaries were advised on appropriate post office forms to present themselves in person to collect parcels addressed to them. The unsuccessful efforts to trace the 'missing' parcels caused many angry words to be exchanged.

The confusion created by all these fake orders and instructions caused Governor Fischer to send out a circular, warning

Germans against orders forged by Poles. It had the effect that 'N' had hoped for: from now on, whenever a German received an inconvenient instruction or order, he would simply disregard it, on the excuse that he had taken it for a Polish forgery. More confusion!

On four occasions – twice in Warsaw and twice in Kraków – 'N' managed to publish pseudo-copies of official Polish-language newspapers (Poles used to call them 'the viper press'). To ensure a brisk demand and at the same time to delay identification, they all carried sensational headlines on their front pages, which, like all the other headlines, were not anti-German. The texts were, however. On 21 March 1943, the 'N' version of a 'special issue' of the Warsaw *Nowy Kurier Warszawski* announced: 'Spain declares war! Spanish planes attack Gibraltar!', while the articles that followed disclosed the catastrophic situation of the Third *Reich*, described the true military and political situation in Europe and informed readers of the successes of the Polish forces in the West. It caused quite a sensation. Copies were changing hands at forty and more times the normal price. When the Germans realised what had happened, they started raiding all print shops equipped with rotary printing machines. In fact, the whole issue, 10,000 copies, was printed on a flat-bed letterpress. The attention to detail was so great that even the serrations, characteristic for the output of rotary machines, were reproduced with the help of a specially made knife.

A little over a year later another 'special issue' was produced, this time proclaiming: 'German forces enter Sweden!' The two fake issues of the Kraków *Goniec Krakowski* were both produced in 1943. In each instance, the distribution of 3,500 copies was carried out by 100 of the *Szare Szeregi* scouts, 10 to 15 minutes before the genuine edition was delivered to the kiosks.

The efficiency of many institutions and offices – both government and commercial – was severely impaired by denunciations, sometimes anonymous, more often seemingly signed by fellow Germans. To be taken seriously, denunciations had to contain some truth. The card index of Germans in *GG* included all sorts of useful information on conditions and relations in particular offices, on friendships and animosities, on quarrels between dignitaries and between lower grades, on frauds, thefts and bribe-taking. Every denunciation included one or two real facts, which could easily be checked, followed by false accusations. In every case at least three letters were sent: the first to the highest authority of the given institution in Berlin; a few days later to the highest level in the *GG*; and lastly to the immediate boss of the accused. This method ensured that several people in three different offices would be wasting their time dealing with the case. Three separate files would be set up, there would be correspondence between the three levels. Possibly a police authority would become involved, again on three levels. Then the accuser denies having written the letter, the accused protests his innocence and responds with counter-accusations. More files, more correspondence. Many friendships are broken and the office atmosphere is irrevocably poisoned. In most cases, all concerned end up feeling resentful towards everybody else. Those in authority, having burned their fingers, now tend to treat all denunciations with great suspicion, the genuine ones included. It was hoped that a similar effect would be created when denunciations of non-existent Poles were sent by the hundred to the *Gestapo*.

A novel approach was used in conjunction with the *Winter Hilfe* ('Winter Help' – a charity) operation. Several thousand letters, ostensibly from district governors, were sent to Germans all over the *GG*, inviting them to support this good cause. Attached to the letter was a questionnaire, the completion and return of which, said the letter, would help to make this action more efficient. The rather inquisitive questionnaire was designed to make it difficult to understand, to make the victim lose both his temper and his confidence in the authorities.

When a securities print works in Germany was destroyed in an air raid, some of its production was transferred to a print works in Kraków. One of the Polish employees, who was in the *AK*, reported that he could obtain small quantities of some of the prints, including special forms, with watermarks (no *AK* print shop had the facility to produce convincing watermarks) and embossing, which were used to summon VIPs to meetings and conferences. Just what 'N' needed! Using the *NSDAP* 'Who's Who', officials who held key positions in the war effort were selected. They were now sent invitations to important meetings in distant locations. A director of an armaments company, say, in Essen would be asked to attend a conference in Vienna, and one in Vienna to go to Hamburg. The invitations arrived always at the last moment, so that there was no time to conduct any clarifying correspondence on the subject. The VIPs' frustration when, after having spent long and tiring hours on a train, they were told that there was no conference, can only be imagined. In 1944, when the German railway system was severely disrupted by air raids, their travels could take several days.

A hard-hitting and certainly not a charitable operation targeting the families of soldiers fallen at the front was based on the 'In Memoriam' newspaper pages. There are no indications whether this operation was suggested by London or whether it was started independently, in parallel to what Delmer was doing. In most cases the 'In Memoriam' notices included the home addresses of the fallen. Letters were written, ostensibly by the mates of the dead, telling the bereaved families that the departed were not, in fact, killed in battle but, for instance, by the *SS*, for having refused to take part in mass murder of Russian women and children, or by the Military Police because they were too exhausted to walk while retreating, or through the ruthlessness of an officer who, as a punishment for having badly polished boots, forbade the soldier to take cover during artillery bombardment etc. Sometimes the writer would claim that the soldier concerned was not dead, but had defected to the partisans. This operation was carried out especially relentlessly and vigorously in Šódź.*

It is worth mentioning that the 'N' cell in Šódź was the most active of all 'N' cells in the *Reich*. Not only was it able to distribute any quantity of 'N' material sent from Warsaw, but also, having its own printing facility, could reprint. They could also boast of a unique achievement in organising an actual cell of a fictitious German anti-Nazi movement. 'Anatol', who was in charge of the Šódź 'N', kept the local *Wehrmacht* Motor Depot under observation until he identified a number of likely candidates to become members of the *NSDAP Erneuerungsbewegung* – the supposedly pro-Hess secret movement. He selected five of them and started sending them appropriate 'N' leaflets. When none of them was observed taking these leaflets to the *Gestapo*, each was sent a letter informing him that the movement had been watching him for some time and now would like to entrust him with a most important mission. Meeting times (naturally different ones) and places were given, as were recognition signs to be used. Only one did not turn up. Those who did were disap-

---

* Before the war the second largest Polish city, nicknamed 'Polish Manchester' because of its textile industry. It had a large German population and in 1939 it was incorporated into the *Reich*.

pointed – there was nobody for them to meet. A couple of days later they received letters apologising, with the explanation that it was a test of their good faith. Eventually, 'Anatol' brought about a meeting of two of the candidates and then of the whole group. He never met them face to face; contact was by post and dead-letter boxes. He was sending them supplies of leaflets for distribution and instructions on recruitment. The cell continued to grow. Soon he was asking for, and receiving, weapons and ammunition.

After six months the *Gestapo* pounced. It was understood at the time that two soldiers were executed, several imprisoned and more sent to the front. The cause of the disaster transpired only after the war, when *Gestapo* records became available: none of the original candidates went to the *Gestapo* but one had reported the approach to his commanding officer. The *Abwehr* and the *Gestapo* jointly took charge of the operation and ran him from the start as their agent.[8]

The Special Operations division of 'N' also had a section called the 'Moral Terror Committee'. It made itself visible to the Germans as 'The Special War Tribunal', so its operations were not actually black. Its aim was to frighten the occupier.

A typical operation would start with selecting from the card index a few hundred Germans who were nastier and more dangerous than the rest. They would receive official-looking notifications (letterheads with the Polish Eagle – but naturally without an address – and signed by someone such as Commissar Malinowski or Grabowski) informing them that, as a result of information received, their names were placed on a list of Germans suspected of acting in a way detrimental to the Polish people. A week or so later a second missive would arrive, informing them that an investigation of the allegations had begun. After a longer interval they would be told that the investigation was completed. Next would come the news that the Tribunal would consider the case on a certain date and finally: the verdict and the sentence. Invariably – guilty and death. The whole process would take several weeks. The impression had to be created that the matter was serious, and that it was a thorough investigation.

Of course there was no investigation, no court. In very many cases the accused would mend their ways; some even offered substantial cash donations to the *AK*. When it was thought that the change of the attitude of the accused was genuine he would be informed that the proceedings were being suspended, subject to his continued good behaviour. Otherwise he would receive a confirmation of the sentence and a further notice that it was not subject to a status of limitations; also, that in view of the continuing German atrocities, the Polish State had decided to adopt the German rule of *Sippenhaftung* ('collective family responsibility'), and consequently, should he try to avoid the carrying out of the sentence, his family would be executed instead.

It was, of course, another empty threat; the Polish Resistance had no plans to introduce collective responsibility. The object was to make the recipient realise that the German 'law', as applied to Poles, had no moral foundations. Operation 'N' had no power to pronounce sentences and no organisation to carry out death sentences. Polish Resistance did possess a judicial branch that could pronounce death sentences on deserving Germans, which were then carried out by the executive branch (*Kedyw*). The Moral Terror Committee added substance to their threats by claiming in the letters to their 'clients' the credit for carrying out these death sentences.

Not many Germans were able to stand up to these threats. Those who could not or would not mend their ways, usually asked to be transferred to another country. A request to be moved, supported by the letters they received, was always granted. It was noticed that the replacements, who always knew the reason for the change, invariably behaved much better.

There was also a 'Commissar for the Eradication of Germanhood in Poland'. His job was to act against Germans who had appropriated Polish government or private property. Using official-looking notepaper, he would inform the wrongdoer that the property in question would be taken from him and restored to its lawful owner, in accordance with the 'Polish Wartime Retaliatory Statute'. (There was no such statute.) Should the property be damaged, the current unlawful owner would be punished. The range of punishments included the death penalty. Such letters were sent sparingly and, as a rule, were taken very seriously by the recipients.

Probably the most spectacularly successful special operation was the already mentioned 'Koppe' poster.[9] Early in 1944 'N' came to the conclusion that the moment was near when a Soviet breakthrough would make it necessary for the Germans to evacuate the *GG*. A suitable poster was printed, in the usual Nazi style, and distributed to 'N' cells throughout the *GG*. The poster was addressing all Germans and it was signed by the 'Commander of the *SS* and of the Police in the *GG*', General Koppe. He was also the Secretary of State for security in the 'government' of Hans Frank.

At the time this poster appeared, all Germans were aware that the Russian Front was creaking, that *Gestapo* men and policemen were being daily gunned down in the streets of Polish towns, that military trains were being blown up and that Polish roads, especially those crossing forests, were just as dangerous for Germans as the front line. The German administration was not yet in total chaos, but gloom, despondency and fear were widely spread. When the poster was displayed in all major cities of the *GG* on 24 February 1944, it surprised some Germans, who 'did not realise that things were that bad', but it was taken very seriously. The leading sentence did not leave any room for doubts: 'Herewith, all German nationals are ordered to leave the *Generalgouvernement*.' Then the very involved legal basis of this order was given. The poster explained that the evacuation would be carried out in two phases. The first phase was to commence immediately, and applied to *Reichsdeutsche* families and to all those Germans whose presence in the *GG* was not indispensable to the war effort. The second phase, said the poster, would be announced by individual letters. It could commence without any warning and would probably be carried out in very difficult conditions.

Panic ensued. Within hours railway stations were besieged by German men and women with their children and hastily packed luggage. German offices were in total chaos. Telephone lines were jammed and nobody could get through to higher authorities. Officials were asking for – and were paid – salaries in advance. Soon most offices were deserted. A drastic decision was taken by the commander of the police in Wieliczka (a small town near Kraków), who ordered his men to drive west at top speed. A few days later they were found somewhere in Austria. They were never seen again.

Only in the late afternoon did the authorities manage to contain the panic. It was not just a good practical joke. The German administration was paralysed for most of the day and individual Germans who succumbed to the panic suffered a considerable psychological shock and later some not inconsiderable unpleasantness from higher authorities.

Having fallen victim to several forged 'official' instructions, the average German would begin to view with suspicion anything emanating from his authorities and would become less eager to follow their orders. When reprimanded, he would claim that they looked to him like another 'Polish scam'. He would regard the authorities as incompetent and would blame them for allowing the situation to get out of hand.

The distribution of 'N' materials outside the *GG*, already mentioned, does merit a more detailed description. One of the main considerations when planning the distribution was to create the impression that all these materials originated in the *Reich* and were imported into the *GG*. This was to suggest to the readers that German resistance groups were strong, competent, well organised and had a long reach. It was also in the interest of 'N' that German security should concentrate their enquiries for as long as possible away from the *GG*. To maintain the credibility of the *Reich* provenance it was imperative that no material should be made available to German 'clients' in the *GG* before it appeared in the *Reich*. To reinforce the impression that the flow of the materials was from Germany proper to the East, couriers were bringing from Warsaw to the *Reich* prints in bulk, which were then planted singly in passenger and goods trains and in troop trains going to the Russian Front. Some of them would be found by security, some would be handed in by loyal finders, confirming the impression that the flow was West to East. There were reports of German railwaymen being arrested.

But this deception could not last for ever. According to a report by the Šódź *Gestapo* of June 1942: 'The leaflets are presumably produced in the *Generalgouvernement*, since single leaflets keep surfacing there a few days earlier than here.'[10] A later *Gestapo* report of 1 October 1943 (*Meldungen wichtiger staatspolitischer Ereignisse*) describes mass arrests in Biašystok, which enabled them 'to gain a good picture of the N-organisation, which is run centrally from Warsaw and, in addition to obtaining military and industrial information, has the task to subvert the German nation and the *Wehrmacht* through the production and dissemination of printed matter. This printed matter, which is produced in Warsaw, is delivered by couriers to destinations in the *Reich*. There it is despatched by post to persons especially selected as suitable targets. It was found also that this N-organisation recruited *Reichsdeutsche* as couriers to central Germany.'[11] This report is mistaken only in one respect: its author assumed that Operation 'N' was similar to the German 'N', which stood for *Nachrichten* ('intelligence'). But Operation 'N' never took part in any intelligence-gathering, except for its own use.

When fully developed, the 'N' network in the *Reich* had about thirty cells, from Hamburg to Munich, from Cologne to Leipzig. It had six centres (Berlin, Hannover, Brunswick, Bremen, Hamburg and Kassel) where the couriers were delivering their consignments. The consignments consisted of prints in bulk, which would be partly used by the centres and partly forwarded to the individual cells, and of prints in pre-addressed envelopes, for posting from different places. The addressees would be both in the *Reich* and in the *GG*. The couriers were mainly Poles from Silesia working as engine drivers or guards, but there were also other Poles, speaking perfect German, who were provided with uniforms of high-ranking railway officials and appropriate documents. The centres and cells were run mainly by Poles from Silesia, also working for the German railways or related enterprises, or by Poles whose parents emigrated from Poland to Germany.

A lot of thought was given as how best to use the precious prints that were to be delivered by post to individually selected persons, in the course of geographically defined campaigns. It was decided to concentrate on towns of between 20,000 and 100,000 inhabitants. Larger towns were excluded because it was realised that in smaller localities news spreads fast, whereas in larger ones it gets diluted and may just evaporate. A target of 1 per cent of inhabitants was thought sufficient.[12] The envelopes would be of all sorts of shapes and sizes, addressed in many different handwritings and posted from different towns in Germany. The results of the last German elections in 1932 and 1933 were studied and a voting map of Germany was produced, showing, district by district, the political preferences of the electorate. It was assumed that even after ten years the basic political prefer-ences of the electorate would be still the same. Materials displaying a social democratic colouring would be despatched to areas where the social democrats did well before 1933, and the 'Hess' leaflets would be sent where the *NSDAP* had a majority. Obviously, it was absolutely necessary to know the results of at least the first campaign. The II Bureau was requested to suggest a locality where they had an observer who would be able to submit a report. They suggested several names, from which München-Gladbach was selected.[13]

The II Bureau report did arrive eventually. It was quite encouraging. For several days the received prints were the main topic of conversations. People were speculating who were the real instigators and why their town was chosen. Some dutifully surrendered the prints to the police. The *Gestapo*, the *SD* and the *Abwehr* were alerted. They were all worried about the leaflets that were not surrendered. People were stopped and searched in the streets, and houses were turned over. A dozen people were arrested but eventually they were all released without being charged. The post office was ordered to open all letters. They were too late. By then all the leaflets had reached their destinations.

For the first six months of 1943, Operation 'N' was in top form. And then things began to go wrong. General 'Bór's' report to London for the period 1 July to 30 September 1943 makes sad reading:

> This period has been especially difficult. The growing intensity of the German terror rips open gaps among our most active people. This is especially noticeable in the East, where the Soviet and Ukrainian partisan attacks coupled with German 'pacifications' caused such losses that e.g. in the Biašystok and Grodno areas there are no people left to carry on with 'N'. … Operation 'N' has been seriously scaled down in the 'annexed' territories.* The main reason are hugely increased difficulties with border crossing. One of our best couriers was arrested and we have difficulties with the procurement of suitable personal documents. … There are also bottlenecks in our print shops. No periodicals could be printed in July and August.[14]

A series of more serious disasters started in December of that year with the *Gestapo* raid on print shop W8. Four months later came the turn of W7 and then, in quick succession, all the other print shops were liquidated with the exception of the smallest one, W3. It could not be spared for 'N' work. Special operations that did not depend on printing continued until the Warsaw Rising on 1 August 1944. Some Operation 'N' activities continued in the provinces until the end of 1944.

The only attempt at black broadcasting took place during the Warsaw Rising. On 7 August 1944, a captured German medium-wave station was restored to operational status and, after some tests, was made available to the Operation 'N' team, who had been trained for such an eventuality. It worked on

---

* Polish territories incorporated into the *Reich* in 1939.

224 metres, the wavelength of the German *Weichselsender* station, located in Kraków.[15] Its target audience were German soldiers fighting in Warsaw. Germans reciprocated by impersonating *Bšyskawica* ('Lightning'), the Polish-language transmitter of the Warsaw *AK*.

It is interesting to note that the transmissions of the genuine *Bšyskawica* were jammed not by the Germans, but by a TASS (the official Soviet Press Agency) transmitter operating in the UK. It did not try to interfere with transmissions of the German *Bšyskawica*.[16]

'N' operations were also conducted from Switzerland. When Germany attacked France, the Polish army there was about 70,000 strong, but only one division, the 2 Foot Rifles under General Prugar-Ketling, was combat-ready. It fought well, holding its positions near Pontelier until its ammunition and food ran out. No re-supply from the French was possible and it withdrew in full battle order, with bayonets fixed, across the frontier into Switzerland. The conditions of the internment there were not excessively onerous. A number of young men were given the opportunity to start or to resume their university studies, a secret officer corps training unit was set up and there were even staff officer courses. Soon radio contact was established with London and a very successful intelligence operation began, sending to London information gleaned from their own sources in Germany.

In November 1942, the Polish General Staff in London instructed Prugar-Ketling to start his own Operation 'N'. In the best 'N' tradition it was to be quite separate from the intelligence operation. It was to concentrate on sending subversive leaflets by post to addresses in Germany, purporting to come from revolutionary German student circles, and on spreading rumours, which would be supplied weekly by London.

The intention was to incorporate it into the plan 'Martini' (see Chapter 8).

In January 1944, Prugar-Ketling reported that, during December 1942 and January 1943, he had been selecting and training staff and had purchased a German typewriter and a duplicator.[17] A supply of German stamps, envelopes and paper was obtained. He recruited two Polish civilians to look after the duplicating. Lists were compiled of German intellectuals and working-class people to be targeted. Letters began to be despatched in February 1943, averaging 500 per month. Rumour subjects, received in coded signals from London, were augmented by listening to the RU stations. Some rumours were fed to the Swiss press, including leading papers such as *Neue Zürcher Zeitung* and *Basler Nachrichten*; others were used in leaflets despatched to Germany. In autumn 1943 the operation had to be discontinued: the Swiss moved around the interned personnel and the 'N' team was broken up. Financially, the operation closed with a healthy balance. Of the approximately £2,000 received from London, less than a tenth was spent.

Sometimes the question is asked whether *AK* tried to identify 'good Germans' for the purpose of recruiting them. No such attempts were made, although there were instances of Germans offering their services. There was no shortage of Polish volunteers. German recruits would be regarded as a security risk and, above all, the hatred of all Germans was so deep that the rank and file would not take easily to German comrades-in-arms. There were some exceptions, but very few.

A case of an unintended Operation 'N' beneficiary came to light recently. Antoni W., who had spent over four years in Germany as a forced labourer, returned after the war

100 per cent disabled. Unfortunately he did not have any documents to support his claim for compensation. His plight was brought to the notice of a person who had access to some ancient 'official' German forms and office stamps made by Operation 'N'. Appropriate documents were produced and the German authorities immediately granted full compensation. *Se non è vero è ben trovato.*

CHAPTER Eight

British–Polish Black Cooperation

It appears that Poland was in 1939 Britain's first partner in planning a black propaganda campaign against Germany. Perhaps there were similar approaches made to other countries, but no documents confirming this could be found. On 19 July 1939, an SIS emissary arrived in Warsaw on a top-secret mission.[1] Even the British embassy was not informed of his arrival. He went directly to the head of the II Bureau (the Polish Intelligence Service) and explained how important – in the British view – propaganda would be in any future war with Germany. He did not come to discuss the nature of that propaganda, only to obtain II Bureau's agreement in principle to assist in conveying such propaganda to Germany from their side of Europe; should this be acceptable, then the first task would be to arrange permanent and secret communications between London and Warsaw.

Polish reaction was favourable, although the II Bureau reserved the right to examine and to reject each propaganda campaign proposal. They were afraid of an avalanche of counter-propaganda from Germany, which possessed superior technical means. Nevertheless, they offered to help in penetrating various parts of Germany that had significant

Polish minorities and where Polish intelligence networks were already in place. They were also prepared to print black German propaganda, as requested by Britain, in time of war, but in peacetime they would expect to be supplied with genuine German paper and founts, which they did not possess. They were very impressed by the technical plans of a hot-air balloon, brought by the emissary, which could carry leaflets when the wind blew in the direction of designated regions. They asked for several such balloons, as soon as possible, so that their meteorologists could test them. They also explained their plans to set up mobile short-wave black transmitters and asked whether Britain could supply such transmitters, since they did not have the facilities to manufacture them. The request was noted. Finally it was agreed that a special Polish liaison officer would be sent to London as soon as possible; he would be at SIS's disposal and would communicate directly with the II Bureau in Warsaw, without the Polish embassy in London being informed of the nature of his activities. The requested German paper and founts were ready by 23 August 1939 but the war prevented their despatch.[2]

It is not certain when the British and Polish wartime black propaganda organisations established contact, but it is thought that it was probably some time in the summer of 1941. Liaison and co-ordination between the *AK* and the Polish General Staff in London was in the hands of the VI Bureau. It also looked after all communications between *AK* and the British side, usually with the help of SOE. This channel worked very well, and it seems that, more often than not, PWE, when wishing to communicate with 'N', made use of it, rather than going directly to the VI Bureau. Unlike all other European resistance organisations, including those in France, *AK* was not run, nor even directed, by SOE. The latter's function was purely supportive. It provided technical aid, training, finance and matériel, but no personnel.

This arrangement spared the Poles such tragic and avoidable disasters as were heaped upon the Dutch, the Belgians and the French.* VI Bureau was run by pre-war members of the II Bureau, old hands at the intelligence and clandestine operations game. A typical SOE operative was intelligent, imaginative, enterprising and very brave, but the need to operate unobtrusively, to observe meticulously the rules and never to sacrifice security for the sake of achieving rapid and spectacular results, was not in his blood. It would seem that in this respect the SOE women, being less inclined to go for buccaneering exploits, were more professional. SOE security in the field was frequently deplorable, and unprofessional interconnections between circuits were only too common. SIS's dislike of SOE's character and methods sprang from the unfortunately justified fear that they would result in disaster.

SOE did its best to represent Polish interests, often quite vigorously, vis-à-vis the Foreign Office and other government departments and bodies. Its head, Brigadier Gubbins, who was known in Whitehall as 'Gubbinski', expected his officers working with European resistance movements to identify with the people they were helping. Most members of SOE and of PWE – even Delmer, who was rather left wing – were

---

* Between March 1942 and May 1943, 46 SOE agents and 544 containers of stores despatched to Holland fell directly into the hands of waiting Germans. SOE ignored the coded warnings sent from Holland as well as other aspects of the received signals that should have rung the alarm bells. Seventeen agents dropped by the French Section fell into the arms of the waiting *Gestapo*. Germans were running eight resistance circuits in Belgium. (M.R.D. Foot, 'What Use was SOE?', *RUSI Journal* (February 2003)

aware of the Soviet threat, and understood why Poles were afraid of the Soviet Union, but they could not go against official British policy.

On 29 July 1943, one of the members of VI Bureau reported that, during a meeting with the 'head of the British anti-German black propaganda department' (this must have been Delmer), the latter said: 'Soon we shall have a new struggle on our hands and both of us will be again on the same side. I don't believe in the Soviet democracy. It is really a dictatorship, just like Hitler's. But now it is too early to talk about these matters, we still have just one job to do …'

A unique privilege enjoyed by VI Bureau (and by all other Polish governmental bodies in London) was that their communications remained independent of SOE – until April 1944. From then on they had to provide English-language copies of all signals despatched. Ostensibly this was the result of the tightening of security as D-Day approached. Nevertheless, one cannot help feeling that the true reason was to make it more difficult for the unruly Poles to conduct any anti-Soviet activities. Subsequent events fully justified the Polish mistrust of Moscow.

In 1941 'N' wanted to carry out an operation that would boost Polish morale by showing that British aircraft could reach central Poland. At the same time, SOE, for reasons of its own, wanted the Germans to think that British bombers had a longer range than they had in reality. So a scheme was hatched. On a certain night, the RAF would bomb targets in the Poznań area (western Poland), which was then the absolute limit of the range of its bombers. Some leaflets would be also dropped. On the same night identical leaflets would appear over Warsaw and in several localities close by, suggesting that this was the true range of the British bombers. The problem was how to make it appear that these leaflets were dropped from the air. After some tests it was found that clusters of toy balloons with simple release mechanisms would do the job. The operation, triggered by a coded BBC signal telling 'N' that the RAF would visit the Poznań area that night, was carried out in early November 1941. It is not quite clear whether 'N' printed copies of a British-supplied original, or whether the leaflets came from Britain. Perhaps a mixture of both. The operation itself was considered a success. Nevertheless, according to a *Gestapo* report, based on the information received from a V-man (a *Gestapo* agent), 'the purpose of the operation was to create the impression that English* planes were over Warsaw'.[3] So the laboriously constructed deception did not work.

A few weeks later the RAF again dropped leaflets over Poland, this time without involving the Polish side. This sortie had unexpected repercussions. The Polish government lodged a vigorous protest with the Foreign Office on two counts: leaflet raids over Poland should not be carried out without its agreement; and the contents of the leaflets should have had its approval. The Foreign Office apologised promptly.[4]

It is not known whether the first-ever British leaflet sorties over western Poland on 15–16 and 16–17 March 1940 evoked a similar reaction or whether they were agreed with the Polish government, then still in France. The BBC reported these flights as 'reconnaissance', and the local *Abwehr* office reported to Berlin that leaflets were dropped in considerable quantities, containing a message from the British airmen to the Polish public: 'You are not alone in this war… we know how you suffer, but be strong … the day of liberation will come!'[5] They

* On the Continent, even now, 'English' is used often when 'British' is meant. During the war 'the English' frequently embraced all English-speaking allies, including the Americans.

were presumably produced by the Air Ministry's Propaganda Section. The Foreign Office recorded another date: 'Our aircraft succeeded on the night of the 7–8 March in reaching Poland with a special leaflet in Polish.'[6] Another memo, dated 16 March 1940, states that two aircraft flew over Warsaw, and that leaflet raids over Czechoslovakia and Poland were successful and much appreciated by the inhabitants.[7]

In 1940 there was no agreement on the subject of Polish leaflets, not even within the Polish government: Sikorski was keen on having them dropped, while Foreign Minister Kot was against it, although he would not object to leaflets in German, destined for the occupying forces.[8] Later in the war, *AK* advised London that dropping leaflets addressed to Poles would be counterproductive, the expected reaction being, 'Our morale does not need building up, we need weapons, not leaflets!' The subject of dropping leaflets over Poland remained a controversial one throughout the war. For instance, the British side thought that leaflets were a good cover for parachuting personnel and supplies, whereas Poles were convinced that they would only attract attention to such drops and could provoke German reprisals.[9] Details of leaflet drops, and of the numbers dropped, found in various sources, are also contradictory.

SOE and PWE received the first full report on Operation 'N' in early July 1942. It was based on the report from the commander of the *AK*, General 'Grot'-Rowecki, for the period from its inception until 15 March 1942.[10] It was acknowledged by Major Perkins, the head of SOE's Polish Section, who thought it of great interest. He passed it to the SOE German Section, who 'considered it most valuable and would like to cooperate closely'. With his reply to 'N', Perkins enclosed three samples of SOE black products, offering to supply them in any quantity, should 'N' consider them suitable.

There must have been other, undocumented contacts, initially perhaps not very smooth, since Colonel Wilkinson, SOE Regional Controller in charge of the liaison with Poles, referred to 'N' in an internal memo as 'infernally independent'.[11] Nevertheless, before long, the head of VI Bureau, Colonel Protasewicz (cover name 'Rawa'), was thanking Perkins for the materials and was asking for more. He suggested also that some materials could be broadcast for 'N' by the BBC.[12]

On 5 August 1942, a Major Thurston wrote to Delmer about 'N': 'The organisation is definitely doing something, and part of what they claim to be doing clearly fits with your scheme of things. It might be possible … to establish a satisfactory connection between GS1 and the black propaganda of the "N" Action.'[13]

At about this time 'Rawa' wanted to offer to distribute British propaganda materials in Germany via 'N'. He signalled 'Grot': 'Is there a possibility to carry out a propaganda campaign among Germans by posting private letters from diverse localities in Germany and in the occupied territories … you would receive the necessary materials from here …'[14]

'Grot's' response was not very enthusiastic: 'The format and the weight of some of [your] prints make them unsuitable for our distribution system which is based on paper of a lighter weight. What is more, the contents of some would not be appropriate for our target groups and areas.' Nevertheless, 'Grot' requested three copies of every British black print, to be used as templates. There was also an urgent need for *SS* founts (the letters were in the shape of acute-angled zigzags) of all sizes, since they could not be procured in Poland, and without them it would be difficult to pretend that the 'N' prints were originating in Germany. As far as printed leaflets were concerned, he requested a delivery every six or eight weeks of 10,000 to 12,000 leaflets, printed on thin paper, aimed at both the *Wehrmacht* and the German civilians. The subjects were to be general rather than particular, should remain topical for some time, and conform to the style and spirit of 'N'. The printing should be of high quality. Their purpose would be to throw the *Gestapo* off the scent: the high print quality would hopefully be regarded as an indication that the leaflets had not originated in a primitive underground print shop in Poland, but in a well-equipped print works in Germany. 'Grot' also asked for photographs of bombed German towns, destroyed tanks and aircraft, and any German personal documents and forms.

At SOE's request, on 1 November 1942, an 'N' Section was set up within VI Bureau, to facilitate communications. It was headed by Major Dziewanowski. This is how he described his brief: 'The task of Section "N" is to cooperate with PWE, where black propaganda is concerned. Its function in connection with PWE is to provide advice and liaison facilities. The head of Section "N" meets weekly a PWE representative to discuss propaganda items that are to be disseminated by "N" in Poland and by the "N" organisation in Switzerland.... These items are approved before transmission by the head of VI Bureau. ... Section "N" receives from Poland requests for information and materials which are then dispatched via VI Bureau ... '[15]

By the end of 1942, approximately 70,000 black leaflets and stickers were despatched to Poland, usually as padding in parachute weapon containers.[16] This quantity is insignificant compared to the number of white leaflets dropped over

Germany, but while most of the latter fell on fields and forests, none of the former were wasted, being delivered to individuals or planted in German public places.

Not all items requested by 'Grot' were supplied, however, and a similar list was received from Warsaw again on 27 February 1943.[17] It contained an additional request: that the BBC should quote from 'N' periodicals, referring to them as genuine products of German opposition, as this would enhance their credibility among German readers. Copies of this signal were forwarded to Sefton Delmer and to the head of the Polish Minorities Section,* Major Hazell. On 2 March 1943, 'Rawa' signalled 'Grot': 'Our friends appreciate greatly your Operation "N" and request that you increase its intensity.' A few days later Delmer promised to deliver the *SS* founts within a week, as well as most of the outstanding items.

According to a VI Bureau unsigned note, referring to a conversation with Hazell on 19 March 1943, 'the *SS* founts were received' but it does not say by whom.[18] Hazell is reported also as having stated that the British side would prefer to conduct the propaganda in Poland according to its own methods and using its own materials, which it considered to be of superior quality. This is the reason – continued the note – why requests for materials, including printing paper, submitted by 'N', were being satisfied reluctantly or even not at all. Nevertheless, before the end of the month, 'Rawa' was reporting to 'Grot' that he was despatching sample German forms and leaflets, and that he was promised the *SS* founts within a week, as well as photographs of German POWs, the results of RAF air raids and destroyed German military equipment; he would

* PWE section dealing with the resistance movement among Poles in France, cover name EU/P.

also have ready for despatch forged *Generalgouvernement* stamps with Hitler's face replaced by that of Frank's.* Their purpose was to suggest that, just as Frank (supposedly) replaced Hitler's image with his own, he would replace him as the new *Führer*.

These stamps arrived in Warsaw, probably before the end of March 1943. About 1,500 were delivered, although Wiesenthal wrote of 250 sheets of 20 stamps each. They were used between 11 and 19 June 1943 to mail from five different places to addresses mainly in the *Reich*. They were not used, as mentioned by some sources, to mail death sentences to deserving Germans. Most were intercepted but some got through. They caused enough of a stir to be discussed at one of Frank's regular conferences. According to the entry in Frank's diary for 17 June 1943: 'Director Lauxman reports that about 1,100 of these stamps were intercepted. All possible steps are being taken to prevent them from reaching the Reich. The resistance is using them to mail letters according to a definite plan. The denomination was cleverly chosen; in the past it had been used only occasionally and postal officials assumed now that it represented a new series… most probably they were printed by the London firm of Morrison†… Director Ohlenbusch‡ states that the letters are written in a most subtle way and contain many expressions used by the Governor General.'[19]

This event also merited a mention in the top-secret *Meldung wichtiger staatspolizeilicher Ereignisse*: 'From a number of towns of the *GG* were despatched recently leaflets in German, under the heading "*Reichsdeutsche!*" and signed "on behalf of the

* Hans Frank, Governor-General of occupied Poland which he was treating like his fiefdom. He was hanged in Nuremberg in 1946. The stamps were intended to have an analogous effect to those with Himmler.

† In fact they were printed by Waterlow & Sons Ltd.

‡ Frank's chief of propaganda.

Volksdeutsche in the *GG*". The envelopes were franked with two genuine 2-*Grosh** stamps bearing the face of the *Führer* and one counterfeit 20-*Grosh* stamp with the face of Dr Frank. Although stamps with the likeness of Dr Frank do not exist, the Post Office cancelled these stamps in the normal way and dispatched the letters to their destinations. The Post Offices in the *Reich* have been warned.'[20] As with the Himmler stamps, these Frank stamps are now very rare and have been fetching good prices since the war. The only known postwar additional supply reached the market in 1958, when an anonymous seller offered several sheets of twenty stamps to a stamp shop off the Strand in London. They were released to the market very gradually, mainly in Germany.[21]

It seems that, after the initial friction, SOE's attitude to 'N' mellowed rapidly. On 5 April 1943, Wilkinson wrote to Dziewanowski: 'Thank you very much for the two reports, which I have read with great interest. Your friends appear to be doing most valuable work and I hope that they will be able to make use of some of the ideas which we are sending them …'[22]

A month later, Delmer to Dziewanowski: 'Both Major Thurston and I have now read the reports on "N" which you have sent us and we should both much appreciate it if, when you next signal your contacts, you should tell them how pleased we are with the progress they report. If it were possible to obtain some samples of the counterfeit German documents which "N" Action has been producing, we should both of us very much like to see them … the work they are doing is more than appreciated here and the operations as reported certainly seem to be going along the right lines.'[23]

* 1 *Grosh* = 1/100 of 1 Zšoty (Polish currency unit). Before the war L1 = Zš20; in 1944 = Zš500.

'Rawa' reported to 'Grot': 'Our friends think highly of your achievements and request samples of your fake official German prints'; and on another occasion: 'We received from our friends their current propaganda instructions. They conform exactly to what you are doing.'

The term 'friends', when used by the British, meant 'Poles', and vice versa. Now 'Grot' was receiving every week a list of rumours to be disseminated through all 'N' cells. It was explained that some of these rumours might not make much sense but that they were being launched in conjunction and in support of wider propaganda campaigns. For example:

- Nazi Party authorities ordered the cancellation of all furloughs of Service personnel to heavily bombed areas of Germany in order to prevent a deterioration of their morale by the sight of the ruins, of the civilian casualties and of widespread pillaging.
- Evacuees from bombed areas are permitted to consider the accommodation they are allotted to be their property. When the rightful owner takes them to court to secure repossession, the case is thrown out.
- One of the reasons the German general anti-aircraft defences are so inadequate is because they are massed around Berlin.
- Soldiers' wives have to work in factories in terrible conditions. Their children, from the age of twelve, are forced to work either in factories or on land. Children are separated from their mothers.

A letter from Delmer to Dziewanowski, dated 14 May 1943, deals with the despatch to Poland of British propaganda themes: 'I have arranged that we shall transmit at dictation speed one or perhaps two leaflets for "N" Action on May 27th, 28th and 29th … If this method proves satisfactory, I think that we might repeat it on other occasions.'[24] No confirmation of reception is available but the transmission was confirmed in an unsigned 'most secret' memorandum of 1 July 1943: 'Wireless dictation of leaflet material and directives. The contents of two leaflets have been dictated for reception by N-Action contacts in Eastern Europe, who receive weekly directives by wireless and are reported to have a number of presses printing leaflets for dissemination among the German occupying forces.'[25]

Supplying samples of prints either way was not easy. 'N' prints had to be microfilmed and brought to London by courier. This was dangerous and could take anything up to two months. Most of the materials so sent would be out of date on arrival. Despatching materials to Poland was simpler by using parachute drops, but this method could be equally slow, since flights with supplies for the *AK* were infrequent. (Air Chief Marshal 'Bomber' Harris was still not keen to divert his aircraft from bombing, and the Foreign Office was afraid of upsetting the Soviet Union, which was most suspicious of the *AK*, with its allegiance to the Polish government in London.) Flights were not possible in summer due to short nights, and bad weather could prevent them at any time of the year.

Nevertheless, Sefton Delmer had nothing but praise for the co-operation he received from the Polish side. He wrote:

> The Poles, in my experience, were the cleverest operators of all. From their bases in Poland they travelled over the whole territory of the *Reich*. And it was to the Poles that SOE

> entrusted, on our behalf, the tricky job of posting letters inside Germany itself.* It was the Poles who posted for us to German provincial newspapers the papier mâché matrices with which we counterfeited the feature service of one of Goebbels's agencies. … It celebrated the fiftieth birthday of Admiral Dönitz. The article … was completely orthodox except for one sentence: 'As a consequence of the loss of an average of thirty U-boats a month over the last half year' – it said – 'the Admiral has recently lost some of his pristine youthful freshness'.[26]

At least one newspaper, the *Danziger Vorposten*, printed this article.

On 22 June 1943, Thurston wrote to Dziewanowski: 'We are particularly anxious to get as wide a distribution as possible of the malingering instructions … anything "N" Action can do to spread these instructions among German military and naval personnel, especially among those training for U-boat warfare, will be very much appreciated.'[27] This message must have been forwarded successfully to Warsaw, since some time later – the document is undated – 'Rawa' signalled Warsaw: 'Friends confirm considerable success of the malingering instructions. They express their gratitude and request continuation of the operation.'[28]

Thurston wrote also to Delmer: 'It is certainly encouraging to find that they can work on this sort of scale but at the same time I should feel we had made an enormous step forward if we could get them to think in terms of really operational black stuff.' Delmer replied:

---

* Actually, Poles did not have here a monopoly, SOE had other channels as well.

> I think it is absolutely amazing that a production as finished as the *Klabautermann* should be produced under the noses of the *Gestapo*, and it undoubtedly has a certain subversive value, especially the two inside pages … clearly for high-brows there is value in the application of the *Simplicissimus** technique against the Germans … Until you read the actual text, the *Klabautermann* looks like a German funny paper of about 1940, which, to my mind, is valuable for those who are of a reflective turn … while the style of the other stuff is crude and many grammatical errors are made,† there are some good subversive things and it is certainly impressive to see the facilities that must be at their disposal.

On 30 June 1943, General 'Grot' was arrested, denounced by a traitor, and was immediately flown to Berlin, where his chances of being freed by the *AK* by force were nil. He was succeeded as the commander of *AK* by General Komorowski (cover names 'Bór' and 'Lawina').

In July 1943, Dziewanowski described the tasks of his Section 'N' in greater detail:

> Co-operation with the Political Warfare Executive in the area of the black propaganda, i.e. propaganda that purports to flow from subversive elements in the enemy camp. Vis-à-vis the PWE, Section 'N' has a liaison and consultative function.
>
> On a weekly basis the Head of Section 'N' discusses with a PWE representative the propaganda themes to be

---

* German satirical weekly.

† It seems that Delmer was more demanding than the Germans themselves: an *RSHA* circular dated 9 November 1942 stated that the Polish subversive prints were written in good German.

> disseminated by 'N' in Poland and also by the 'N' organisation in Switzerland. There was a plan to set up an 'N' cell in France, but it was abandoned. The weekly propaganda themes, before being signalled to Poland and to Switzerland, must be approved by the Head of the Polish VI Bureau.
>
> Section 'N' also forwards to Poland British propaganda materials.
>
> Section 'N' receives from Poland requests for propaganda materials and equipment, does its best to obtain them and forwards the materials to Poland. In this case it deals with both black and white requirements.
>
> Plans for the future concern mainly an intensification of the propaganda activities. Their realisation will depend on the expansion of the co-operation on the British side.[29]

According to Ellic Howe, *Winterhilfebriefmarken* – bogus charity postage stamps produced by his organisation – 'were used for internal mail in Poland where Polish postal workers no doubt franked them with malicious pleasure'.[30] He probably means that part of Poland which was annexed to the *Reich*, since in the *Generalgouvernement* after the first month or two of the occupation, no Reichsmark-denominated stamps could be used.

On 6 July 1942, 'Rawa' advised Warsaw: 'Our friends suggest the following operation, aimed at curbing the German terror in Poland: report to us immediately any killings of Germans, including their names and functions. Our Polish and German programmes will then announce that those individuals were condemned to death for crimes committed. A few days later it will be announced that the sentences were carried out.' There is no record of 'Bór's' reaction to this proposal.

At about the same time, 'Rawa' urged 'Bór': 'Use widely the sticker *VOLKSSCHÄDLINGE*.* Grey lettering. The letters *SS* in black, in the shape of the *SS* emblem. The purpose is to create discord between the Army and the *SS*.'[31]

On 6 August 1943, 'N' received an unexpected accolade when 'Rawa' signalled 'Bór': 'Our friends propose to copy your periodicals for distribution in western Europe. Do you agree?' There is no record of the response, which must have been yes, or if this proposal was actually realised.

On 26 August, 'Rawa' signalled Warsaw: 'Field Marshal von Mannstein will be the German Badoglio.'† It was at about this time that *Der Soldat* had suggested von Mannstein should take over in Germany. It is not clear whether 'N' followed London's suggestion or the other way round, or perhaps both London and Warsaw came up with the same idea simultaneously.

Also that August, 'Rawa' again signalled 'Bór': 'Friends are requesting the widest possible distribution and display of the following appeal to Germans, to be signed by Frank.' The appeal was addressed to 'German fellow-countrymen and members of the *Wehrmacht*' and had an ominous title: '*Führer* is in danger!' Frank was warning that 'reactionaries' wanted to remove Hitler and to establish a military dictatorship, which would, contrary to the will of the people, enter immediately into peace negotiations. They were spreading false rumours that, because of his failing health, the *Führer* was no longer fit to carry out his duties. 'The German nation does not want peace, the German nation wants Victory!' It concluded: 'Report immediately any suspicious rumour, any suspicious

---

* National pest.

† Badoglio contributed to the fall of Mussolini and became the head of the new Italian government.

occurrence to the party, the police or the *SS*. Long live the *Führer*!' About 3,000 posters with this appeal were printed on bright red paper, just like all the official German announcements, and were distributed to 'N' cells in bigger Polish towns. The same was done in several occupied countries, the whole operation being orchestrated by SOE. Naturally, in every country, the posters bore the signature of an appropriate German official. There were also minor modifications of the text, to take account of local conditions. On 15 September 1943, these posters appeared simultaneously all over occupied Europe. In the German quarter of Warsaw alone, 159 were put up. This perfectly synchronised operation must have been quite a shock to the *RSHA*.

Truszkowski wrote to VI Bureau: 'Major Thurston has just seen a sample of the poster that "N" Action produced in Poland on the lines of our poster "*Der Führer ist in Gefahr*". … You did a very nice job of it and he wishes me to tell you that this project has now been carried out successfully in at least 5 different countries.'

This was the crowning glory of the cooperation between SOE and Operation 'N'. Soon after, 'N' suffered its series of disasters in Warsaw when Germans discovered nearly all the print shops, and its activity practically ceased. It did continue in the provinces, but only on a local scale.

In February 1944, the head of the Security Police in *GG*, Colonel Bierkamp, received a letter from the *RSHA* under the heading 'Subversive Transmitter *Świt*', advising him that 'the above transmitter is located in England and is presumably operated by Polish emigrants. Its tendency is undoubtedly pro-Polish and anti-Comintern. Its transmissions are received here.'[32] It is surprising that the German radio location service took so long to localise *Świt* (meaning 'the Dawn' in Polish, British cover name P1): it started transmitting in the autumn of 1942, pretending to be a mobile transmitter, operating from various locations in Poland. It is equally surprising that PWE's first Polish RU was not activated until the war had being going on for over three years. According to *AK* sources, German attempts to localise it started immediately when it was heard, but were probably frustrated for a long time by the conviction that it was transmitting from somewhere inside the *GG*.

This is how *Świt* was described in a top-secret memorandum from the head of the PWE Polish Section, Moray McLaren, to Sir Ivone Kirkpatrick, Controller of the BBC's European Service:

> P1 is the official station of the Polish underground movement and is located somewhere near Warsaw, though it is mobile in character. It started in October 1942 as a station intended to represent the views of General Sikorski personally, and purported to be run by his supporters in Poland. … The material was to be written by the staff under the direction of General Sikorski, with ourselves in the role of both censors and guiders. … After General Sikorski's death the station assumed a less personal character and became more official, i.e. it openly expresses itself as under the direction of the underground movement. … It can in the fullest sense be described as a cooperational RU. … The policy … allows it to answer attacks from the Union of Polish Patriots* but *Świt* is not allowed to attack the Soviet policy.[33]

A Draft Policy Directive, in the same National Archives file, lists the aims of *Świt*: 'to encourage and direct organised resistance against the German occupation; to discourage spasmodic and

---

* A communist organisation set up in the Soviet Union on Stalin's orders, which evolved eventually into a puppet government.

unorganised revolt such as would weaken the forces of organised resistance by inviting heavy reprisals; to sustain the morale of the Polish population; to attack the morale of the Germans in Poland.' For the latter purpose PWE 'supplied material for nerve warfare on German occupying troops'.[34] The directive also states, under the heading 'Policy and Method', that 'P1 will … emphasise strongly the desire of the Polish people for close friendly relations with Russia, now and in the future', and also that it 'will attack the activities of the Polish communists in Poland', without explaining how to reconcile these two patently irreconcilable tasks. The result was that, during the summer of 1944, *Świt* had frequently to go off the air, when the situation in Poland was too obscure or too delicate for the Polish staff to broadcast.[35] So far as the attacking of the morale of the Germans in Poland was concerned, for instance, according to the 'Report on Activities' for the month of May 1944, out of a total of 899 minutes of broadcasting time, 123 minutes were given to 'German Internal Problems and Attacks on their Morale'.[36]

Świt could not avoid crossing swords with a Polish-language RU broadcasting from Moscow, called Kościuszko. Ironically, Kościuszko was a Polish national hero who fought against Russia in the eighteenth century. Now his name was being used to represent Soviet interests and *Świt* was being accused of being 'a station of Hitler'.[37] After a while, people at PWE realised that even if *Świt* had never taken an anti-Soviet line, it would have been regarded with hostility by the Soviet Union.

The resistance in Poland ran on two parallel tracks: military and civilian. The military side, the *AK*, was under the command and control of its *Komenda Gšówna* (Central Command), which was responsible to the General Staff in London and ultimately to the Polish CiC, also in London. The civilian side came under the 'Government Delegate' who was just that: a representative of the government in London but with some executive powers. He was responsible for organising the country's administration, which would come into the open on liberation. He was also responsible for an organisation bearing the slightly oxymoronic name of Directorate of Non-Military Combat. Whereas Operation 'N' was entirely under military control (although the Delegate's own Propaganda Department did try – unsuccessfully – to take it over), Sikorski placed *Świt* under the control of the Ministry of the Interior in London (Polish Home Office). In Poland the head of the Directorate of Non-Military Combat, Korboński, who was also in charge of the civilian communication network maintaining contact with London, was made responsible for supplying *Świt* with information that would enable it to create the impression that it was located in Poland. To communicate with London, Korboński was using a private cipher, known in London only to one person and in Poland only to himself and to his wife, who was his cipher clerk. In Poland, apart from them, only the Delegate knew the secret of *Świt*'s true location. Later, for operational reasons, the head of the *AK* Propaganda Department was also let into the secret.

Świt transmitted on 31 metres twice a day: at 0800hr and 1910hr. Its editors liked to enter into polemics with a German-controlled Polish-language evening paper that appeared in Warsaw at 1600hr. Nobody, whether Polish or German, could possibly imagine that a response within 4 hours (taking into account the time difference) was possible, except from Warsaw itself or from a very close location. How was it done? Korboński had two of his men working for that paper and they were supplying copies of first proofs some hours before the paper would appear. Salient points were rapidly enciphered and radioed to London. A secure telephone line linked the Polish communications facility there to *Świt*, where there would be enough time for the duty editor to write his response and the censor, Major Brysson (who was also generally in charge), to approve it.

The same procedure was used to supply to *Świt* the latest news from Warsaw, for example new posters with lists of executed hostages, announcements of new regulations, sabotage and other operations carried out by *AK*. Sometimes the appearance of German radio-location teams in the vicinity of the transmitter forced the breaking of the contact with London. To cover the lack of current news, the next *Świt* transmission would be suddenly terminated with an apology and explanation that a German patrol was uncomfortably close.

Świt also supported the operations of the Moral Terror Committee by disclosing the names of the perpetrators of atrocities and by warning them that they would not escape punishment.

The Polish team numbered five or six writers/presenters. They had to follow the general PWE directives but were never ordered to write about specific subjects. One topic was taboo: criticism of the Soviet Union. They could respond to attacks by the Moscow 'Patriots', but those who stood behind the 'Patriots' enjoyed total immunity. No transmission ever went out live: everything was recorded. This procedure was apparently introduced after the Free French started to depart from the censored and approved texts in live broadcasts.[38] The technical side was entirely in British hands.

The raw materials for the broadcasts were supplied in profusion. As many as 200 pages of monitoring extracts of all world stations arrived every day, with discrepancies and contradictions in German broadcasts clearly marked. Recordings of the transmissions of the Moscow 'Patriots' were also made available daily, as were reviews of the world press. The Foreign Office supplied, reconstructed, Goebbels's weekly propaganda directives, as well as copies of general instructions issued to the British press. *Świt* also received reports prepared by British censors, based on intercepted letters from abroad, as well as reports from the 'Patriotic School'.* The Polish Ministry of the Interior supplied copies of the Polish clandestine press and information on the conditions in Poland. An important input was provided by couriers and other persons arriving from Poland who could describe from personal experience the prevailing conditions, atmosphere and mood, and who could give the team invaluable help in keeping up with the changes in the spoken everyday language.

PWE had a high opinion of the station, as can be seen from McLaren's report of 15 May 1944: '*Świt* is doing a good job of work in keeping the Polish government in touch in a propaganda way with the Polish underground movement, and it is a useful card to hold up our sleeves. I make the strongest possible case for its retention and would regard its closing down at the present stage as lamentable.'

The secret of *Świt*'s location was unavoidably discovered by the German and Soviet radio-location services, and rumours concerning its true location started eventually to circulate among the London Poles, but those involved did not reveal its secret until after the war. *Świt* was closed down in November 1944.

Sometimes it was said that *Świt* was Churchill's gift to Sikorski, but, after studying the surviving documentation, one cannot help having the feeling that it was in fact an instrument

* British interrogation centre for all arrivals from occupied Europe.

created by the British side to weaken the Polish resolve not to give in to Soviet demands, whether territorial or political.

On 19 September 1943, 'Rawa' signalled 'Bór': 'Last year our friends activated in England a Polish radio station, ostensibly broadcasting from Poland. From the Polish side the Ministry of the Interior has been involved in the production of the programmes. Now our friends approached the Polish CiC with a suggestion that we should collaborate with this station as well. The CiC agreed to a trial period … and we are sending our people there. We would like *Świt* to broadcast programmes useful to you, so please send daily, if possible, two to three subjects to be mentioned, with suggestions how they should be presented.'[39] 'Bór's' reaction is not known.

Another Polish-language RU, *The Voice of Polish Women* (cover name P2), arrived on the air towards the end of 1943 and continued until 30 May 1944. McLaren in his memorandum of 15 May 1944 described it thus: 'It is staffed by women and is intended to give voice to the active struggle taken by the women of Poland. It should be stressed that it is non-official in character … and it is a purely PWE activity with the exception that the Polish Prime Minister knows about it, and we have agreed that we should have his personal approval of any woman who joins the staff. … It confines itself mainly to propaganda material rather than news, its location is not defined but is generally supposed to be further west than P1, somewhere in the Poznań area.'

According to its original brief, one of its objects was 'to attack the morale of all Germans in Poland', and the target audience was the clandestine press's listening posts.[40] It was to be 'non-political'. Presumably the author of the brief meant 'non-party-political'. A Foreign Office internal memorandum stated also that 'it will represent resistance to Germany as a religious crusade'.[41] The exceedingly sensitive author of one of the comments to this memorandum, expressed an anxiety that such a 'Christian' appeal might be regarded in Moscow 'as anti-Soviet, as much as anti-German' and much care must be taken to represent it as the latter. It is not surprising that, with such a nebulous brief, *The Voice of Polish Women* failed to impress its audience and it was taken off the air after a total of 115 broadcasts.

The interdepartmental strife was endemic in London, not only within the British governmental organisations but also within most of the Governments-in-Exile, including the Polish government. It was one of the reasons why a very ambitious Anglo-Polish black propaganda project had to be abandoned. It was the 'Plan Martini'. The idea came from General Sikorski, who, in the autumn of 1942, proposed an intensive infiltration of black leaflets into Germany, using Polish channels.[42] The area to the east from the Berlin–Prague line would be serviced from Poland by 'N', and the area to the west, by Polish centres in Switzerland and in France. An Anglo-Polish meeting on 6 October 1942 accepted this proposal but decided that PWE would be responsible for the production of the propaganda material, with the Polish members of the team having only an advisory function. This was unacceptable to Sikorski.[43]

The British reaction to this objection was accommodating, but other difficulties appeared. On the Polish side the operation was to be controlled by the Ministry of Foreign Affairs and not by VI Bureau. The Polish General Staff did not like this, and neither did the Ministry of National Defence. The Ministry of Foreign Affairs started immediately planning an increase in Martini's scope by including Italy. They wanted also to set up a cell in Portugal, but it turned out that they did not have a proper organisation even in France. PWE and SOE objected to increasing the size of the operation, since this would make it easier for the Germans to detect it.

The 'N' cell in Switzerland was operative at that time, but it is doubtful whether it could have increased its throughput dramatically. The initial enthusiasm of the British side slowly evaporated and, before long, Plan Martini was abandoned.

There were very few problems when *AK* and 'N' were cooperating with the Polish General Staff and VI Bureau, and, through the latter, with SOE and PWE. It may be democratic and laudable for the military to be controlled by civilian authorities, but one cannot help thinking that the Martini debacle would have been avoided had the whole show been run by professionals.

Chapter Nine

Why Did We Achieve So Little?

In modern warfare, with its exponentially growing complexity, it is impossible to quantify the contribution to victory, or to defeat, made by its particular elements, and especially by the non-material elements. The 'what if …?' approach can never provide an unequivocal answer, irrespective of whether the 'if' relates to the non-occurrence of an actual event or to the occurrence of a hypothetical event. In some disciplines, or in some situations, the calculation of probabilities can be based on exact science but in warfare the multiplicity of variables makes it a hit or, more frequently, a miss affair. Some events do come to mind, whose results are generally accepted as incontrovertible, for example the Hiroshima and Nagasaki bombs saved at least 200,000 Allied casualties, or the handing over to Britain by Polish cryptologists of the Enigma secrets they had solved, which saved the Bletchley Park code-breakers about two years' work, making it possible to win – just in time – the battle of the Atlantic.

As far as the effectiveness of black propaganda is concerned, it can be clearly seen only in a few instances of mainly operational black. For instance, the counterfeit *Skorpion* was 100 per cent successful in subverting the original, which was well received by German soldiers, causing its discontinuation; Aspidistra's intrusion operations did create a measure of the intended chaos; the Koppe poster produced by Operation 'N' did cause a panic among the civilian Germans in occupied Poland; 'N' succeeded in establishing among German soldiers in Šódź a real branch of a fictitious anti-Nazi organisation.

These were not spectacular achievements in the overall context of the war. But the black operations were not designed to be spectacular. They were designed to corrode and erode the enemy's morale, his will to continue the fight – not to annihilate him in one fell swoop.

According to the American social scientist, Lerner, no serious study of the effectiveness of psychological warfare operations could be made after the war, since there did not exist a 'conceptual frame of reference, which could have provided a unifying context for the diverse operations it conducted ... no adequate theory of opinion existed upon which a scientific programme could be built'.[1] This could not be done retrospectively since not enough relevant data were recorded. Lerner adds with regret: 'In view of the kinds of data required and the importance of the time factor in data about effectiveness, it is unlikely that any such overall study of Psychological Warfare can ever be made.' German authors shared (I think) this view: 'Propaganda went to war with the disadvantage of not being in possession of an effects model that could serve as a benchmark.'[2] Expressed in terms used in statistics, no chi-squared tests were possible, since there were no data empirically observed nor theoretically derived available.

During the later stages of the war the Allied propaganda warriors based the assessment of their endeavours, to a great extent, on the results of interrogations of POWs. It can be argued that even had the Allied interrogation officers been allowed to question the POWs directly about the effectiveness of covert operations – which they were not, lest they expose these operations as sponsored by the Allies – then the great majority of attempts to evaluate in this way the effects of black propaganda would have been pointless anyway. They would be pointless because, ideally, these effects should be subliminal, that is to say the targets should not be aware that they were subjected to black operations, that certain ideas were planted in their minds. Even should they come to realise eventually that their minds had been surreptitiously invaded, they probably would not want to admit it, maintaining that they had formulated these ideas themselves, which, of course, they could have done. Thus the interrogator would be no wiser. Even when the interviewee does his best to cooperate, if he was subjected to both violent and non-violent forms of attack, he cannot possibly be unequivocal about which was responsible for his actions or, if both were to blame, in what proportions. Further, his replies and opinions cannot but be subjective, so it is difficult to imagine how a report based on them could possibly be objective.

Because of its very nature, a successful black operation should leave no trace for the interrogator to evaluate. We seem to have reached here a *reductio ad absurdum*: if the effect of an event is capable of being evaluated, then, *ipso facto*, the intended event – a successful black operation – did not take place and so must be classified as a failure. Of course, if the observed behaviour of groups of targets corresponds to the intentions of the black operation to which they were subjected, one could assume that the operation was a success. But again, this would apply only to operational propaganda, when a specific and rapid effect was intended, and only in those rare instances where no other influences were involved (other propaganda, the tactical situation, cohesion within the group, type of leadership, availability of supplies, physical condition, etc.), as, for instance, in the case of counterfeit instructions to enemy soldiers or civilians purporting to come from enemy military or civilian authorities. In other words, one must avoid the pitfall of assuming that any act that corresponds to a psychological warfare stimulus is its result, simply because it followed the stimulus (*post hoc propter hoc*).[3] There is no doubt, that during the last months of the war, the interaction of sophisticated propaganda and of military setbacks and disasters did affect the morale of the German troops, but it is impossible to assess the relative importance of the two elements, and especially of the black component of propaganda.

In the case of non-operational, strategic, long-term black propaganda aimed primarily at modifying attitudes, the inevitable interaction of other factors makes most attempts to assess its effectiveness rather unrealistic. But then, there is for instance no doubt that, because of the effects of the long-term black and grey, German officers taken prisoner were more forthcoming: 'You seem to know everything about us anyway, so there is no use hiding anything', they were telling their interrogators.

A further difficulty arises from the fact that the purpose of a significant proportion of British black propaganda was to make its targets refrain from undertaking certain actions rather than make them do something. The great variety of detailed objectives of black propaganda and the diversity of means employed make a clearly correlated classification of causes and effects quite impossible.

As far as the controversy about the respective effectiveness of white and black propaganda is concerned, there is one aspect that reduces the chances of it being resolved, to nil: the lists of objectives and the themes used to support them were practically identical in both operations. They differed only in the treatment of the themes and the contexts in which they were presented.[4] So how can one decide how to apportion the credit for the success of a particular operation? This situation may be regarded as slightly paradoxical: two operations are conducted with an impenetrable wall separating them, but their effects are so intertwined that it is impossible to classify them according to their origin. Nevertheless, some British and also some German[5] historians are convinced that the Allied white propaganda, and especially the BBC, was more effective than black or grey.

Having said that, the logical thing to do would be to give up writing this book or, at least, to pen 'The End' right here. But I shall persevere. The available evidence is only circumstantial, but evidence nevertheless. No better evidence – for or against – is available.

Those in Britain who thought that white propaganda was more effective than black, assessed it from their own, British, point of view. They knew little about the German national character and nothing about the German social and individual psychology. They assumed, incorrectly, that German reactions, when exposed to the same stimuli, would be identical to the British reactions. But a typical German would not be fired up by concepts of 'freedom' or 'democracy',[6] especially that the claims of the 'Grand Alliance' that it was fighting for democracy were not very convincing: after all, one of the 'Big Three' was a totalitarian dictatorship, not better than Nazi Germany, and the remainder, the 'Lesser Allies', had no real say, even in matters that vitally concerned them. The average German could see nothing wrong with being a member of a disciplined society. Remembering the exaggerations of the First World War British atrocity propaganda, this time he would take similar or even worse accusations with a pinch of salt. He was immune to the great majority of political and moral arguments. He could not understand how anybody could denigrate Hitler, the man who had restored the national pride, who brought Germany stability, full employment, satisfactory living standards, good roads, glory on the fields of battle, who created – in the eyes of the majority – an effective shield against communism. He did not know or did not want to know the dark side. Of course, the economic and industrial base for all these achievements had been there already, but Hitler managed to unify the nation and to persuade the citizens that sacrifices (viz. the 'Guns v. Butter' slogan) were necessary for the common good.

There seems to exist here a certain similarity with the average German's attitude to Bismarck's reputation, especially after his death. Bismarck never attempted to hide his hate of parliamentary government, of democratic ideals, of socialism, of liberalism. In politics he was dictatorial, arrogant and more than forceful. Nevertheless, he was revered as the father of the German Empire, even by many liberals. After his death, German hankering after an equally great and strong leader did not stop until 1933.

The average German did not know or did not want to know the dark side of the way his country was run. In the conversations I had, during the last months of the war, with ordinary, decent Rheinland villagers either of my age or considerably older – those in between were either in the forces or were dead – the 'difficult' subjects were never mentioned, not even indirectly. They never brought them up and I had the feeling that they would not want me to do so. I felt at ease telling them, for instance, about partisan ambushes in Poland, when *Wehrmacht* soldiers taken prisoner would be released (minus their weapons and uniforms), while members of the *SS*, *SD* etc. would be summarily executed, but I could not bring myself to talk of *Gestapo* interrogation methods, of public executions by hanging or shooting, of conditions in concentration and extermination camps. It was not so much because of a fear of finding myself in a concentration camp for 'spreading malicious gossip', but rather because of my fear of being met with disbelief and denial. On the other hand, I was never asked to explain why the Polish partisans treated ordinary German soldiers and the members of security forces differently. Perhaps, after all, my interlocutors did know or could divine the reasons, but preferred to ignore them or, at least, to leave them unsaid.

Even during the last months of the war, over 50 per cent of surrendering German soldiers were declaring their faith in the *Führer*. A similar proportion believed that war-winning miracle weapons were just round the corner. Allied interrogation officers described this attitude as a 'manifestation of irrational wishful thinking'.[7] But perhaps that wishful thinking was not always irrational. For instance, had the fighter-bomber version of the first-in-the-world operational jet fighter Me 262 been delivered to the *Luftwaffe* in sufficient numbers before D-Day, the invasion might have been repulsed.[8] When Göring revoked his 1940 ban on all development work on new, truly revolutionary, aircraft types it was too late. Without this ban the outcome of the war in the air could have been different.[9] Nevertheless, whatever successes the *Luftwaffe* could achieve, Germany could not prolong the war beyond August 1945, when it would have become the atom bomb's first target.

Both in Britain and in Germany propaganda was sometimes called 'the fourth arm'. This was an exaggeration, taking into account the contributions to the war effort made, for instance, by intelligence and deception, contributions that probably exceeded that of propaganda.

Not everybody who was involved during the Second World War with black propaganda, became convinced of its merits. For instance, Richard Crossman, who joined the Ministry of Economic Warfare in 1940, and later became the assistant chief of the Psychological Warfare Department at SHAEF, expressed in his August 1952 RUSI lecture 'grave doubts whether black propaganda had an effect in any way commensurate with that of ordinary propaganda from the enemy to the enemy', the reason being that 'psychological warfare means imposing one's will on the enemy. If you want to impose the British will, or the Anglo-American will, or the Allied will on the enemy, then it has to be *your* will that you are imposing – and black propaganda, of course, is carefully not yours.' Crossman said also that since black propaganda had to be entertaining, it probably, in fact, improved enemy morale. Later he became less critical of the operation for which he had been responsible.

It is surprising that an experienced propagandist like Crossman was talking about overtly 'imposing one's will on the enemy'. This would not be effective propaganda. Effective propaganda is about causing your target to act according to your will, but without him being aware of it. Being imposed upon always evokes a negative reaction.

The superb performance of the German propaganda machine in France in 1939–40 was described in Chapter Two. The preparatory softening up of the enemy, the cooperation of white and black and of all propaganda media, the dynamic handling of the operation, deserved full marks. The *sine qua non* of a really successful propaganda campaign – victories in the field – was also there. The mutually reinforcing, positive feedback of the two campaigns produced remarkable results.

Nevertheless, not everybody in Germany shared this opinion. According to a confidential internal *Auswärtiges Amt* memorandum of 2 February 1943, entitled *Wer wird siegen?* (Who will win?): 'German propaganda maintains that the fact that the German soldier could trample over a nation whose will to resist was broken, was due to its erosive influence during the winter of 1939/40. The collapse of France was in fact unavoidable on other grounds ... just like the collapse of Rome ... due to the democratic rot and Jewish corruption ... the process of decay which brought France down had nothing to do with our propaganda ... it commenced long before.'[10]

The anonymous author is scathingly critical of German propaganda: 'It has never understood how to strike the right chord to ensure the necessary resonance in another nation. It could never win us new friends, it could never overcome any hostile influences.' Perhaps the author should not blame so much the German propaganda techniques as National Socialism itself. There was nothing behind its slogans of 'New Order' and 'United Europe': no enticing vision of a New Europe, no plan how to achieve a fusion of the different cultures. True, after Stalingrad, an effort was made to unite the European nations under an anti-bolshevik banner, but it was too late and the memories of the previous four years could not be eradicated. To be fair, it should be noted that the Allied governments never presented their image of the postwar Europe either; they never disclosed their plans for Germany after they got rid of Hitler. The memorandum is a strange document altogether: German misfortunes are blamed mainly on Freemasons. It is pretty safe to assume that a copy was not made available to Goebbels.

Every propagandist is eager to know what is the impression – if any – he is making on the target audience. The reports received in Berlin on the effects of the German black stations broadcasting to Britain were few and far between. Nevertheless, a *Büro Concordia* internal memo of 17 October 1941 was remarkably optimistic:

> Recently we received a further report on the successes of the *Concordia* broadcasts from one of our collaborators, who set himself the task of popularising them. It covers the first three months of the New British Broadcasting Station's broadcasts ... It can be seen from the numerous convictions of our collaborators, as reported in the British press, that even to-day, we can count on a significant number of supporters. Currently four more Englishmen are in court charged with advertising NBBS's broadcasts and with disseminating by means of leaflets the news contained in these broadcasts. It is worth noting that all accused are convinced that this station is located in England ... That the English government is seriously worried about the effects of the *Concordia* stations is clear from its continuous and desperate efforts to represent them as tools of Goebbels.[11]

On 8 July 1942 the Foreign Office in Berlin received a similar report on the New British Broadcasting Station and the Workers' Challenge. It said:

The success of these two stations can be confirmed as follows: the English press reported in May 1940 that several persons were convicted for distributing leaflets advertising these stations. It was reported the previous autumn that thousands of such leaflets were distributed all over the South of England. ... In October 1941 a secret, widely spread political organisation was uncovered. It was called 'The Union of the Free' and it disseminated leaflets with details of the broadcasts of the German *Geheim Sender* ... The BBC has been forced to counter-attack. In daily broadcasts it points out that these stations put out Nazi propaganda. ... The popularity of these transmissions is due to the fact that their predictions always come true ... It was found that so far the identification of a station as a German transmitter does not affect its popularity. Even an extended propaganda campaign does not undermine the conviction that these stations are located in Britain.

There may have been more reports from Britain, but one can safely assume that they would have been in the same vein: of not much practical use to the psychological warriors and not a source of real satisfaction to Goebbels. The *Promi* chief was deeply frustrated with the ineffectuality of his propaganda directed at the British people. He did not expect much from leaflets ('The written word is not as magnetic as the spoken word'), but he was convinced that his radio propaganda, especially in the summer of 1940, would achieve spectacular results. He just could not understand why there were no such results and commissioned several psychological studies to explain the surprising resilience of the British.

According to the study on 'The Inner Strength of the British Empire' presented to Goebbels in April 1941,[12] the following characteristics provided the basis of the British morale, especially in critical moments: Dogged Resolution, Muddling Through, Making the Best of a Bad Thing (calculated optimism, regarding Dunkirk and the bombing of English cities as a blessing in disguise), Sense of Humour, Being a Nation of Grumblers (thickens the skin), This Sacred Isle (national pride), the English Privilege (sense of mission, God-willed destiny as Crusaders, ideology of freedom).

These characteristics created a number of 'spiritual bastions', concluded the author. His advice was to destroy these bastions, employing all available military and propaganda means. Whatever the extent to which this advice was heeded, the results hoped for by Goebbels were not achieved.

Sir Reginald Leeper, in a paper of 18 July 1942[13] on the subject of black propaganda posed the question: Is it really effective? He gave the following answer: 'There is only one sound standard for judgement, viz. is there a carefully thought out plan for the work, are the various aspects of the work properly co-ordinated, is the execution deftly handled with an adequate background of information and understanding?' Surely, the reply to this question will only characterise the efficiency of the operation but not the effectiveness of the results.

In the absence of any objective and proven methods of measuring the effectiveness of Allied propaganda and especially of its black variety, the best one can do is to examine the intensity of the reactions, not only of the German propaganda but also of the German authorities, who should have had an idea of how dangerous that propaganda was to them. In any event it was never a total loss: whatever its effects on the target audience, it forced the enemy authorities to research those effects, compile reports, discuss possible countermeasures, implement those countermeasures and punish transgressors, etc. To do all this, resources had to be diverted from other areas, and in war resources are never over-abundant. Even if the message reached only a very few of the target audience, it would become known to all those involved with countermeasures, to policemen chasing and eventually bringing the transgressors to court, to various levels of the State authorities as the reports percolated higher and higher.

As soon as the Nazi Party came to power in 1933, it started working out ways of 'protecting' the population from foreign influences.[14] It was a reaction to the British 1918 propaganda campaign. Civil air-defence guidelines published in 1937, recalling the 1918 experiences, gave this warning: 'When Germany is attacked, our towns will be subjected again to a shower of similar rubbish. Steps must be taken now to make every German immune to this poison.' Immediately on the outbreak of the war, all foreign correspondence became subject to censorship. Individuals could no longer import foreign newspapers or foreign books on political subjects. A special law on 'Receiving of Wireless Transmissions' was promulgated on 1 September 1939. It imposed a total ban on listening to any station not under German control, including Italian stations. It applied to all parts of the broadcasts, including entertainment and even music. The standard penalty for listening was a term in a strict regime prison (prison for capital offenders). If there were mitigating circumstances, normal prison might be substituted. The wireless set was always confiscated. If the listener passed the information he had heard to third parties, he could be prosecuted under the law applicable to attempts to undermine the war effort, where the death penalty was the norm. He could be also charged with giving succour to the enemy or even with high treason. Rumours were spread that the authorities had equipment that could identify any station to which any set was tuned, and could locate the latter. Still, the number of people arrested for listening to foreign stations* was quite significant: 1,100 during the last four months of 1939, of whom 600 were convicted, and 2,197 during the first six months of 1940. In 1940 1,500 were sent to concentration camps and 20 were executed.[15] Confiscation of all sets

---

* In Germany this was called 'black listening'.

capable of receiving foreign stations was considered but was not implemented.

The listening ban applied also to the Services. Jamming of foreign stations was started and use was made of transmitters in occupied countries, but it could not be done on an effective scale without seriously impeding the reception of broadcasts of one's own radio network.[16] The position with regard to reading leaflets was, in theory, easier than the case of illegal listening: whereas listening itself became a criminal offence on 1 September 1939, the possession of leaflets did not become a crime until the spring of 1944, although the passing on of their contents was a capital offence, just like passing on of foreign radio information. In practice, since the eradication of leaflet-reading was in the hands of the *Gestapo*, anybody in possession of a leaflet could be accused of intending to pass on its contents and could find himself in a concentration camp, without the bother of a court appearance. A *Gestapo* circular of 4 February 1944, containing the new regulations, was ten pages long.[17]

The law of 1 September 1939 did not meet with universal approval. For instance the Minister of Justice Franz Gürtner* wrote to Goebbels, pointing out that 'this law will be regarded by the nation and by the world as an indication of a lack of trust between the government and the people, and of absence of confidence in one's own good cause'.[18] He criticised the harshness of the regulations and expressed a total opposition to the death penalty. There were similar representations from other highly placed personages, but the *Promi* minister held his ground.

* One of the early members of *NSDAP*; specialised in creating legal justification for Hitler's edicts.

In January 1942, regulations based on the law of 1 September 1939 were made more stringent. According to a circular issued by the Minister of State and Chief of the Chancery, Lammers,[19] Hitler decided to limit those permitted to listen to foreign stations, to the following: Göring, the Foreign Secretary, the Chief of Staff of the *OKW*, the most senior commanders of the *Wehrmacht*, the Home Secretary, Goebbels, the Minister of Post and Lammers. They could, in exceptional circumstances, extend this privilege to people working for them. The description of the application procedure was nearly a page long. Other ministers could be granted exemptions, again only in exceptional circumstances, on application to Hitler.

At the very beginning of the war, Goebbels wanted the German press to reproduce selected British leaflets, with a commentary showing them up as ridiculously inane. But he could not escape the classic dilemma of the propagandist: to copy, so as to make counter-attacking easier, or not to copy, to prevent an even wider dissemination of enemy propaganda. For instance, in September 1940 he instructed the press 'to polemise with the leaflet *Wer spricht die Wahrheit* [Who speaks the truth] but since it is presented in a very clever way, it should not be quoted literally'. Soon quoting was stopped altogether and an indirect method of counter-attack was adopted in the form of 'counter-whispers' which did not allude directly to the leaflets or to other sources of rumours; they were spread by Goebbels's 'word-of-mouth propaganda' home network. Some of these counter-rumours were just as fatuous as some of the British sibs: according to one of them, the baby of a couple who listened regularly to foreign stations was born with black ears. Later, during the last year of the war, this network was expanded in conjunction with the propaganda department of the *OKW*. It was also given another function: in competition with a network already run by the *Sicherheitsdienst*, it was to report on the feelings and thoughts of inhabitants of large cities.[20]

By 1944, *Promi*'s instructions to the media and to the Party activists were quite clear: 'In the press and in radio, the English arguments are to be demolished without any reference being made to the actual sources. On the other hand, at Party meetings and at public meetings, direct reference to the enemy leaflets may be made.' In time, Goebbels realised that no logical arguments could be found to counter the leaflets successfully. The press were forbidden to enter into any polemics. Keeping quiet came to be regarded as the best weapon.

The tactic of countering Allied propaganda without actually mentioning its source was noticed by PWE. Leeper wrote in a paper on 'Evidence of RU Reception' dated 1 January 1943: 'A study of the European press and broadcasting has frequently shown that answers have been given, without mentioning the source, to damaging rumours put out by our RUs. As those who study the press in PWE are not acquainted with the RU scripts, and as it would require a separate staff to read the press with this in view, evidence of this kind has not been fully sifted. In many ways these forced denials are the best proof of all, that the damaging rumour has had its effect.'[21]

During the first year or so of the war, British propagandists must have felt very frustrated, just like Goebbels did after June 1940. They were convinced that their appeals to the 'good Germans' to cause Hitler to give up his unreasonable war could not be more sincere, and persuasive, but the average German did not take these entreaties seriously, even considered them to be impertinent. They watched eagerly for indications of success in the reactions of German leaders but here they met only with ridicule. Nevertheless, Department EH took comfort in the fact that Hitler and Goebbels did not entirely ignore their efforts; it argued that this proved that Berlin was worried by British leaflets' possible effect.

The German white and black operations were more closely integrated than the corresponding British operations. Analogically, Goebbels in his reactions did not treat the two categories separately, which does not help to isolate and to identify the reactions to British black. Germans could see that the aims of British white and black were the same, so they saw no need to react to them differently. For instance we read in the *Radio Propaganda Situation Report* compiled by the Codes and Ciphers Department of the *OKW* about 'a new British black transmitter calling itself *The Radio of the European Revolution*' that 'ideologically moves along the same tracks as the general British broadcasts … also in its argumentation it follows them by and large, although in its formulations and style it does show a certain independence'.[22]

PWE would have been gratified to know that the subject of British propaganda had been cropping up during Goebbels's ministerial conferences[23] and in his diaries[24] more often than in his public statements. It was an irritating thorn in his flesh that he could not prevent the massive listening to foreign broadcasts, in particular British and Swiss, both at the front and at home, in spite of listeners being punished by penal servitude, concentration camp or occasionally even by death. Some upright Party members, who were tempted by the foreign stations, tried the excuse that they thought that the ban applied only to the 'weak and the malicious'.

At his ministerial conference on 11 January 1940, Goebbels condemned as too lenient the sentences for listening to and dissemination of foreign broadcasts, and demanded a few exemplary heavy sentences. He also banned the publication in the press of sentences of less than four years. A fortnight later he confirmed that the ban on listening applied to all *Wehrmacht* members: 'unless specifically directed by their appropriate superiors … to listen to such broadcasts in the line of duty … any German soldier exposing his soul and his spirit to such enemy propaganda is committing psychological self-mutilation'. On 19 April 1940 instructions were issued to the press to publish at regular intervals severe sentences on radio offenders. It was hoped that this would put a stop to a renewed growth of listening to foreign stations. At a conference six months later, Goebbels ordered that representations should be made to the Secretary of State Roland Freisler (later the infamous 'hanging judge' of the Peoples' Court in Berlin) about increasing the sentences on radio offenders: 'Listening to enemy broadcasts is an act of serious sabotage … it must be pointed out to the *Sicherheitsdienst* and to the police that enemy radio is again being listened to on an increasing scale'.

At another conference on 7 January 1941 the *Promi* minister stressed the great danger resulting from German troops listening to British stations: 'There are indications that British broadcasts … are now being listened to on an increasing scale by members of the *Wehrmacht* … there is a real danger of being contaminated by these enemy broadcasts. Major Martin was instructed to see to it that a categorical order is issued by the Chief of Staff of the *OKW*, on behalf of the *Führer*, prohibiting once again, on pain of heavy penalties, the listening to enemy stations.' Within two months all military wireless sets were adorned with bright yellow stickers carrying this message: 'Listening to foreign transmitters is a crime against the security of our nation. By order of the *Führer* it carries the punishment of long terms of penal servitude. Remember this, soldiers!' The stickers were reported as not being very effective.

At that time Sefton Delmer must have become a real nuisance, since on 7 April 1941 the Minister ordered that his name should not be mentioned ever again, either in the press or on the foreign radio service, the reason being: 'With his accurate knowledge of German conditions, Delmer tries to invest his very rude insults with an air of great verisimilitude and endeavours to inflate beyond all measure such disagreements as he may have accidentally got wind of, and then to play off one leading German figure against another.'

On 13 May 1941 Goebbels observed that 'the British stations are being listened to on a growing scale in the *Wehrmacht*, above all in the *Luftwaffe*, not for the sake of their spoken programmes but because of their jazz music: during the day the men usually tune in to *Radio Calais* which puts out that kind of music.' (So Sefton Delmer was right about the attractions of appropriate music!) 'Arrangements should be made for one or two transmitters to be provided for the broadcasting of light jazz dance music after 8.15 p.m. … listening to foreign transmitters must be ruthlessly stopped, even in the *Wehrmacht*.'

On 29 May 1941 Goebbels was back on the subject of the growing popularity of foreign stations: 'According to *Sicherheitsdienst* reports, foreign radio stations are again being listened to on a major scale. For that reason a few deterrent court sentences must be announced immediately.' An undated draft memo prepared by the *RSHA* revealed: 'Among the enemy stations preferred by listeners, the London transmitter must be named first; then comes Moscow and the recently activated *Gustav Siegfried I*.'[25] 'Black listening' continued to increase. According to Herzstein: 'By 1942 illegal reception of enemy broadcasts had reached in many regions crisis proportions.'[26]

Goebbels was not the only advocate of draconian penalties for 'black listening'. On 10 December 1942 Himmler sent the following memo to *SS* general Wolff: 'I would ask you to speak to general Zeitzler* about the unhealthy mood in the circles of higher officers and the noticeable cropping up in their conversations of the formulations used by foreign radio stations. An example must be set. A high-ranking officer who is guilty of this behaviour must be court-marshalled and sentenced to death. This should put a stop for a considerable time to the listening to poisonous foreign stations.'[27]

Goebbels described the current events in his diary more frankly than in his official statements. During 1943 Allied propaganda led to a certain anxiety and even to unrest among the German civilian population,[28] and Goebbels noted on 22 May: 'I have new reports on the mood prevailing in the country. There is nothing in them to be pleased about. … They all agree that the mood in Germany is suffering a temporary decline. … Because of the general internal tension, people are taking notice of the life style of the so called 'prominents'. Unfortunately some of the latter don't seem to care; their life style cannot be regarded as being in harmony with the current state of affairs.' So Delmer's angle of attack was again correct. Goebbels had been apprehensive for some time that enemy propaganda might succeed in driving a wedge between the Nazi leadership and the people. Widespread military reverses did not help.

Goebbels's worries about the civilian morale were echoed in a report issued on 18 June 1943 by the *OKH*. It noted that many front-line soldiers were returning from home leave

---

* Chief of the General Staff of the army.

deeply depressed by the defeatist mood of the civilians. The main cause of this mood was 'the constant listening to enemy stations by a regretfully large part of the population, and subsequent spreading of the information so obtained'.[29]

Nevertheless, the downturn of the mood did not lead to a collapse of morale. A defiant reaction to the Anglo-American bomber offensive and, above all, the counterproductive announcement by the Allies of the 'unconditional surrender' principle, created the foundations on which the German morale and the will to resist were rebuilt, just as the British morale and will to resist were reinforced in 1940.

Goebbels continued to confide his worries in the diary. On 25 May 1943 he wrote: 'There are reports … that many people are again listening to foreign stations. The reason for this, of course, is our completely obscure news policy which no longer gives people any insight into the war situation. Our reticence regarding Stalingrad directs listeners to bolshevik radio stations.' An entry on 16 August 1943 deals, for a change, with leaflets: 'In Berlin extremely ingenious leaflets are being distributed by an underground communist organisation. Psychologically, they are constructed in a very clever way and so are a bit of a problem. Thank God there are not a lot of them.' It is highly unlikely that these were communist leaflets. Most probably they were produced either by Delmer or by Operation 'N' and distributed in Berlin by Operation 'N'.

In November Goebbels had a new concern: 'This evening the so-called *Soldatensender Calais*, which evidently transmits from England … gave us something to worry about. The station does a very clever job of propaganda and from what is put on the air one can gather that the English know exactly what they have destroyed in Berlin and what they have not.' On 20 November he noted: 'Temporarily, the mood at the Front is worse than at home.'

On 27 September 1943, the Düsseldorf *Gestapo* wrote to its branches:

> For some time the spreading of rumours has been on the increase, no matter how silly they are. In many cases enemy broadcasts are the source. It is imperative to pursue the listeners more energetically and make an example of them. The number of arrests for 'black listening' during the first six months of 1943 has risen considerably in comparison to 1942, but still it must be assumed that not all transgressors were caught. Stiff sentences must be secured, to act as a deterrent. … Courts must be advised to deal with these cases expeditiously and without leniency. It is also important that they receive wide publicity in the press. … It is equally important that illegal listeners are found among the so-called educated classes, whose subversive intellectualism and cowardly weakness contribute to the spreading of rumours.[30]

Goebbels took the reports about the widespread violation of the 1 September 1939 ordinance as a personal insult.[31] He denigrated his fellow countrymen for being so common as to listen to Churchill's speeches, rather than accept an account of these speeches given by Fritzsche or himself. He condemned 'black listening' as contemptible, low and a display of ingratitude, showing a lack of confidence in the nation's leaders. He was equally upset by the high number of top Party and government officials who continued to try to obtain permissions to listen to foreign stations, but even more, when it transpired that radio monitors in his own ministry had been distributing their reports to unauthorised persons.

No wonder Goebbels expressed concerns about the ever-growing popularity of foreign stations: a 1941 *Gestapo* report obtained by the BBC put the number of its German listeners at 1 million; by autumn 1944 it was estimated at between 10 and 15 million.

By Goebbels's own admission, for his propaganda to be successful, it had to be supported by the *Wehrmacht*'s victories in the field. Without them, he could no longer maintain his reputation as a brilliant propagandist. When on the defensive, his counter-propaganda was not very effective. He became increasingly frustrated and angry with his fellow countrymen, because of their unresponsiveness to his efforts. He vented his anger by introducing harsher and harsher penalties.

Goebbels based his assessment of the effects of the hostile propaganda on reports submitted from various parts of the country by branch offices of his ministry, but his subordinates were usually interested more in protecting their own reputation than in presenting an objective assessment of public opinion. A district manager would be loath to admit that the morale in his district was not what it should be.[32]

Goebbels also received reports prepared by the Nazi Party network, which were not very professional and were again doctored at every level of the Party organisation. He relied as well, probably to a greater extent than he liked, on the *Meldungen aus dem Reich* (Reports from the *Reich*) prepared by his archrivals at the *RSHA*. This service was started when Hitler found out that on 1 September 1939 there were anti-war demonstrations in Vienna, which were not reported to him. He wanted to be informed truthfully about the mood in the country and these reports were, no doubt, more honest than other situation reports. Nevertheless, because of their very nature, they could not present the reality without bias. They were based on information garnered by V-men, *Gestapo*'s confidential agents, who would not necessarily enjoy the trust of the people whose confidences they wanted to draw out, who would not necessarily tell the whole truth and nothing but the truth. Further, as the information was percolating up the various levels of the organisation, it was being unavoidably edited, so that no shadows would be cast on the performance[33] of its members. The final editing was carried out by the head of *Amt III* of the *RSHA*, Otto Ohlendorf,* who did strive for honesty, without granting any favours, in line with Hitler's original instructions, but in Nazi Germany honesty did not pay. He made too many enemies, especially among the Gauleiters who did not like anybody else writing reports on what was happening in their fiefdoms, and after July 1944 *Meldungen* were discontinued. The weekly 'Home Intelligence' reports prepared by the British MoI had a similar basic purpose – to present the public opinion – but fortunately the ministry did not face similar obstacles in presenting the truth.

Meldungen reported in December 1943: 'All over the *Reich* people are frequently listening to the station Calais, in spite of strong interference. Its reports come up in many conversations and are widely commented. In many places persists an uncertainty whether this is an enemy, or a German station.' And a month later: 'What people have been saying during the last weeks about the military and political situation, was strongly tinged with pessimism … the voiced views on political and military events frequently tally with what the internal and external enemies are saying in broadcasts, in leaflets and in their whispered propaganda … their arguments find receptive

---

* Ohlendorf was better known as the commander of *Einsatzgruppen* in the Ukraine.

minds, since many people form of their own accord a dim picture of our present situation and of our future prospects.'

Goebbels's fears that enemy propaganda might succeed in setting the people against the Party were confirmed by *Meldungen*: 'Rumours are aloft that Ministers and District Leaders are moving out of towns to their country residences … while others drive every evening many kilometres to places unlikely to be bombed, and return in the morning.'[34] Similar 'most confidential' reports prepared by another department of the *RSHA, Amt IV* (*Gestapo*), informed that people were increasingly prepared to pay attention to enemy propaganda.[35] Another situation report prepared by the *SD* in June 1943 confirmed that people were picking up leaflets and were discussing their contents. In January 1945 it was reported to *Promi* that 'people's interest in leaflets is growing, especially in those containing statistics and maps … it was found on many occasions that these leaflets were being passed from hand to hand …' It should be noted that not one of these reports had ever stated that people's interest in leaflets and foreign broadcasts was waning.

The *OKW* did not want to be left behind the *SD* and also published several regular and one-off reports that dealt with enemy propaganda: in addition to the *Radio Propaganda Situation Report*, there were the *Nachrichten des OKW* (*OKW* News) and the *Wehrmacht Propaganda Lagebericht* (*Wehrmacht* Propaganda Situation Report) which wrote, for instance, on 6 March 1941:

> It must be said that the English subversive propaganda is based on exceptionally accurate intelligence information. Whatever is happening in Germany is being exploited in a crafty way, but since the authors do not understand the intellectual transformations that occur in Germany,

> their programmes, although technically quite outstanding, are incapable of making any impression on the masses. Nevertheless, these transmissions are capable of causing harm among certain intellectual circles as well as in the case of some primitively minded people, especially when they broach subjects that are, due to internal or external political considerations, too tricky to be handled by our counter-propaganda.

Quite a revealing report, especially the implication that 'English subversive propaganda' is being listened to by 'masses', and this as early as March 1941.

In addition to the confidential or secret reports with a very limited circulation, *OKW* published two periodicals: *Mitteilungen für die Truppe* (*MFDT* – Information for the Troops) and *Mitteilungen für das Offizierkorps* (*MFDO* – Information for the Officer Corps). While the former was available to any soldier and could be displayed on unit noticeboards, the latter was for officers' eyes only. Some of the contents could be used as material for company or platoon pep talks. Counteracting the enemy propaganda was the favourite subject of both publications. Between July 1943 and February 1945 it was given space in *MFDT* at least thirty-two times. During this period three issues were devoted entirely to counter-propaganda, one of them having twice the number of pages of normal issues. Judging by the continual exhortations of readers not to listen to enemy stations, read enemy leaflets and spread hostile rumours, these transgressions must have been quite common and their perpetrators did not take much notice of the appeals to desist, nor of the threats of severe punishment.

Issue No. 2 of the *MFDO* of February 1942 described quite accurately the British rumour operation (a PWE memorandum[36] quoted from it, describing it as a 'special secret document'):

1. The rumours are never accidental, but always spread according to a plan.
2. Moscow and London work together.
3. Rumour is an enemy weapon which is not used on its own. The enemy always couples it with the contents of his black broadcasts and leaflets. He is not stupid.
4. The rumours are psychologically very cleverly adapted to the weaknesses of the German people.
5. Guilelessness and the urge to show off are allies, upon which the enemy counts ... The enemy should not be given any chances, but he is given a chance every time this poison, carefully and craftily prepared by him, reaches and harms a circle of the German population.

In addition to the *OKW*, commanders of large units were also producing counter-propaganda bulletins and orders. For instance the Chief of Staff of the First Army issued in March 1944 a secret information bulletin for the use of unit commanders, under the title *Most Dangerous Enemy Propaganda – A Warning Against the So-called Soldatensender Calais*. This is the first paragraph of the three-page-long bulletin:

> Within our army command area is being heard – lately more and more strongly – a camouflaged enemy station which uses the cover name *Soldatensender Calais*. The manner in which this enemy propaganda operates must be described as highly dangerous, as it is not recognisable by primitive minds as enemy propaganda. The enemy station mixes genuine and invented news and at the beginning of its transmissions, usually presents the *OKW* communiqué, as

> well as the awards of Knight's Crosses. This way it achieves, in the case of simple listeners, a considerable credibility.

After giving more examples of *Calais*'s tricks, the bulletin offers advice on how to counter this propaganda.

On the Home Front, of the three channels used by the Allied propaganda, viz. radio, leaflets and rumours, the last one was probably the most expensive to fight. In the case of the first two, the police or the *Gestapo* acted on the reports received from their agents or on denunciations by malicious neighbours. Arrest, conviction, prison or concentration camp, occasionally an execution – that was all. The procedure in the case of rumours was more complicated: the chain along which they had travelled had to be established, the backgrounds, especially political backgrounds, of individual links had to be investigated, as well as any other relationships – professional, business, family, etc. The reports had to be submitted through official channels to the *RSHA* in Berlin, where they would be analysed and correlated. According to the instructions issued by the *RSHA* on 28 August 1941[37] these reports had to be prepared with an extraordinary attention to detail. A year later the *Gestapo* chief Müller had to issue a reminder: 'Recently there have been in circulation many rumours which were directed in an especially malicious way against the *Führer* and other leaders of the Party ... Other rumours aim to foment uncertainty and confusion in the *Reich* and in the occupied territories ... The originators and the disseminators of these rumours, who try in a malicious, spiteful and deliberately subversive way to undermine the resistance of the German nation, are to be apprehended and made available for further investigation.'[38]

There were many local initiatives to combat the pernicious rumours. District Party offices were issuing circulars and appeals, unit commanders kept reminding their soldiers of the poisonous effects of enemy propaganda. These efforts were mostly in vain, and occasionally they were even counterproductive. For instance, during the autumn of 1944 the Party authorities in Vienna decided to launch their own anti-rumour campaign. Suitable – they thought – articles were placed in the local press and were claimed to have the desired effect. *Promi*, on the other hand, was not at all pleased, since the articles actually spread the very rumours they were denouncing. Vienna was ordered to stop the campaign forthwith and to adopt the approved method of counteracting rumours with other rumours.[39]

To help fight the dangerously damaging rumours, at least three 'confidential' or 'secret' bulletins were produced. There was *The Propagandist* which drew attention to enemy leaflets and broadcasts that spread disturbing rumours, by publishing lists of popular rumours and concerns, with recommendations on how to counter them. The *Wehrmacht*, produced jointly with some State agencies the secret *Lügenabwehr* (Defence Against Lies), listing the false rumours making the rounds among the population, and providing suggestions on how to counter them.

The ever independently minded *Promi* published a similar bulletin, *Gerüchtespiegel* (Mirror of Rumours), which dealt 'only with rumours spread in German by enemy stations'. It gave the origin of every rumour, its full contents and detailed information on how to neutralise it. It was distributed to all special courts and to all units of the security services. I could locate only one issue, No. 4 of 1 July 1944, which lists eleven rumours of which one came from the *Atlantik* and the rest from Soviet stations.[40]

The profusion of the counter-propaganda reports may lead us to suspect that the editors' real purpose was to obtain a licence to listen to 'enemy propaganda'. In Berlin the social standing of possessors of these licences was enormous.

While the *Wehrmacht* fought on distant fronts, the counter-propaganda was conducted separately for the military and for the civilians at home. By the autumn of 1944 the front lines corresponded more or less to the German frontiers. The bulk of the forces were now on home ground. Soldiers were in direct contact with the population. Coordination of propaganda activities was not enough, they had to be unified. From October 1944 all anti-rumour campaigns were run jointly by *Promi*, *Wehrmacht Propaganda* and Party authorities.

In their efforts to gain some idea of the effects of their endeavours, PWE relied on 'Evidence of Reception' reports. These reports were based on the reactions of the German and neutral media, on information received from agents, both in Germany and in neutral countries, from the few people from occupied Europe who were managing to reach Britain, on captured documents and, especially, later in the war, on opinions elicited from POWs.

The evidence offered by these reports was mainly of the anecdotal type, for example 'The man in charge of the lighthouse in Cherbourg harbour reported that our *Nachrichten für die Truppe* were dropped over his place when the white flag already flew from the fortress … he was enthusiastic over them … ' (Evidence of Reception reports, July and August 1944),[41] or 'An officer on his rounds of inspection often found the men listening in groups on the service set to *Calais* … others listened regularly at places as widespread as Denmark, Bruges, Lublin and Bologna' (November and December 1944). Sometimes the presented evidence was inconclusive: 'An Allied Intelligence Officer visited a POW camp in October and found some 70 per cent of those he questioned to have been regular listeners of *Calais*' but according to another PWE report 'interrogations of a number of prisoners … showed that 50 per cent had listened to the *Calais* station'.[42] Sometimes it was contradictory: 'A traveller returned from Germany to Paris, reported that the flood of leaflets dropped by the RAF has had a great effect on the population' but 'According to a report from Bavaria the English aeroplane leaflet propaganda, so far from having done good, has done harm.'[43] The Evidence of Reception reports quoted many captured unit orders – from company to division – reminding the troops that reading of enemy leaflets and listening to enemy stations would result in severe punishment. They also noted with satisfaction that many POWs collected and kept various Allied leaflets and copies of the *Nachrichten für die Truppe*, and that *Calais* was listened to by U-boat crews at sea and in port; it had also a large audience among officers and men of the *Luftwaffe* and was even listened to in their messes.

Such facts, even when they could be verified, could not provide a basis for the quantification of the effects of Black propaganda. It is not clear whether this was realised by PWE, and consequently the interrogating officers were even instructed not to try to find out whether, and if so, to what extent, did the Allied propaganda influence the conduct of the German soldier who eventually did surrender. Or was PWE perhaps convinced that its products were so superbly and unavoidably effective that no further proof that they worked was needed, beyond the proof of reception?

There were two further factors that made the interrogation results even more inconclusive. Surrendering or deserting is a considerable psychological shock, which can change the soldier's priorities, his ways of thinking, and, in extreme cases, even his personality. The change is even more complex if external stimuli in the form of propaganda, whatever its colour, are involved. The cause and effect link may be, of course, reversed; surrender or desertion may be the consequence of a previous shock, physical or psychological. In either case, the man being interrogated is not the same man he was, when he was still fighting. His perception of the past events is not the same, as was his perception of these events as they were occurring. He will see his past behaviour in a different light and with the best will in the world he will probably be unable to describe his thoughts, reactions and decision-making processes exactly as they were then. Secondly, his answers may be distorted further by his conscious or unconscious desire to please his captors.

If you feel sorry for Delmer and Co. for not being able to form a clear picture of the results of their labours, please spare also a thought for the Operation 'N' people. They had no POWs to interrogate, no Evidence of Reception reports (whatever their worth) to guide them. On the other hand they had the satisfaction of seeing, often with their own eyes, the significant results of their special operations. Their 'Evidence of Reception' were reports compiled by the II Bureau, who were convinced that they were discovering proofs of the existence of German underground organisations, and also reports by their own people. They were primarily anecdotal, just like the PWE Evidence of Reception reports, and were forwarded in this form to London:

> In one of the factories in Šódź workers interrupted work and were reading in groups the *Volksgenossen!** leaflets. … It is reported from Toruń that soldiers are generally interested

* One of the pro-Hess leaflets produced by Operation 'N'.

> in the contents of our leaflets, they discuss them among themselves and in conversations with outsiders often use formulations lifted *verbatim* from them. … After leaflets were planted in military barracks it was noticed on several occasions, that soldiers kept coming back to the places where they had found them, obviously looking for more … 80 leaflets were planted on board of a navy training ship in Gdynia. When the commander ordered their surrender, only five were handed in. … In a town near Warsaw many soldiers have read the *Klabautermann*. They were denounced, and after an investigation, two were executed. … Drivers bringing damaged vehicles from the east to be repaired in the *GG* and taking back replacements, are looking for our leaflets. Often they are motivated by commercial rather than ideological reasons: in the Ukraine they barter them for food products which they then send home. We know one NCO who will take any number of leaflets to sell them over there for cash. He can get up to RM50 per print. … In the reading room of one of the officers' messes in Kraków a copy of the 'N'-produced *Erika* remained in the folder with the genuine *Erikas* for over a month', etc.[44]

The Hitler–Stalin pact was signed on 23 August 1939. Two sworn enemies became suddenly and, rather unexpectedly, bosom friends. Still, the *Gestapo* was not convinced that the Soviet manifestations of friendship were genuine. Its chief Müller warned in a circular of 22 December 1939 that the enemy subversive propaganda was being assisted by communists and marxists.[45] To old *Gestapo* hands this was something to be expected: during the previous years these two groups were the principal originators of illegal leaflets appearing in Germany. Not surprisingly, when the first 'N' prints made their debut, the security authorities assumed that they were the work mainly of communists or 'Moscow bolsheviks'.

The earliest available report of an 'N' print is a circular despatched on 18 July 1941 by the Radom *Sicherheitspolizei** to its sub-offices. It concerns a 'communist subversive print' under the title *Soldaten der Ostfront*. The circular gives a précis of its contents and concludes: 'It is interesting that the print does not hint at any sympathies towards the communist party or the bolshevik Russia. Presumably this was omitted to make wider circles susceptible to its message. There is no doubt that its authors should be looked for among communists.'[46] Another Radom circular, bearing a different signature, sent out barely a fortnight later, already positively identifies the originator:

> During the last fortnight the Polish resistance movement started again – as it did during the period November 1940 to January 1941 – to distribute subversive prints in German but in larger quantities and covering not only the *GG* but also the territories in the East. The distribution is by post, by the Field Post and by dropping into letter boxes of houses occupied by *Reichsdeutsche* ... The Polish resistance movement hopes to create among the *Reichsdeutsche* in *GG* the impression that both in the *Reich* and in the East a German opposition is alive and active. It hopes to shatter the German solidarity and to generate feelings of uncertainty, thereby supporting England's endeavours to weaken the German war effort. The English authorship of this propaganda can be taken as proven, since it has been ascertained that both the first wave of propaganda and the discovered plans of large-scale sabotage actions were instigated by England.

---

* Probably the most successful of all *Gestapo* District offices in their fight with the Underground.

The logic of the last statement seems a little suspect.

This attitude was typical of the great majority of Germans. They could not bring themselves to believe that Poles, whom they classified, at best, barely a rung above the *Untermenschen* ('subhumans'), were capable of planning and carrying out such operations. Even later, when the *Sicherheitsdienst* acquired some knowledge of 'N's' capabilities and presumably made this information available to other authorities, the *OKW* made no use of it and continued to the very end to maintain that all the leaflets and other prints were the products of 'Jewish–marxist–communist' propaganda. The likely reason is that in *OKW*'s probably correct judgement, enemy propaganda so labelled would be less effective than Polish or British propaganda.

And so we read in the *Nachrichten des OKW* (News from the *OKW*) No. 536: 'Until recently the Soviet-Russian propaganda used, in contrast to the British propaganda, roughly hewn tools so that the simplest mind could divine its intentions … now their subversive propaganda is much improved.'[47] Two examples of 'especially refined falsifications' are cited: *Urlauber Merkblatt* (Advice to those going on leave) and *Die zehn Gebote* (Ten Commandments for the National-Socialist Front Soldier). Both were in fact produced by 'N' and both were included in the list of *Leaflets of the Polish Resistance Movement* compiled by the *Sicherheitsdienst* towards the end of 1942.[48]

The following year the Propaganda Department of the *OKW* produced a 'Poison Folder' to 'assist unit commanders in their fight against the enemy propaganda'. German propaganda always tried to associate the phrase 'enemy propaganda' with the word 'poison' so that in people's minds the three words would become welded together. This folder contained among other items reproductions of eleven black prints, presented as of Soviet origin. In fact at least seven were 'Made in Warsaw' and one was Delmer's fake *Mitteilungen für die Truppe*. *OKW* continued on this path. *Mitteilungen für das Offizierkorps* of January 1944 credited 'bolshevik agents' with the printing of the 'N'-produced fake issues of *Bilder für die Truppe* and it referred to the *Merkblatt* (also 'N') which described the differences in food rations received by high Party officials and ordinary people, just as a 'leaflet disseminated in the occupied territories'.

The HQ of the *GG* Military District tried not to commit themselves: in their regular and detailed Situation Reports the all-embracing term 'enemy propaganda' is used. Titles of secured leaflets are listed but no opinion is ventured as to their provenance. Still, on one occasion the paragraph ends with a short note that 'a courier of the Polish resistance movement, who carried illegal prints, was detained'. Another report mentions:

> a strong increase in the activities of the enemy propaganda . . . many leaflets were thrown over the walls of military barracks … appeals were directed at the legionnaires [non-Germans] serving in the *Wehrmacht*, to desert and to join the bandit gangs* … incidents like the desertion on 19 September 1943 of thirty-one legionnaires with their weapons, and a similar desertion on 15 October of forty-two men who have taken with them 5 light machine guns, 11 automatic rifles, 41 rifles, 8 pistols and a considerable amount of ammunition, show clearly the dangers and the successes of the enemy propaganda.[49]

By the 1941 autumn, 'N' was causing concerns at the Šódź *Gestapo*. On 22 October its head cabled the head of the Poznañ

---

* The usual German term for partisans.

Gestapo: 'The distribution of leaflets in our District has recently increased enormously. Please press on with your investigations with the utmost vigour and identify as soon as possible the distributors of *Der Soldat*.' At about the same time his office produced a lengthy report on this subject: 'The Polish subversive propaganda in the German language has been intensified. ... Confidential sources of the *Sicherheitspolizei* have been tasked by their organisation to distribute larger quantities of the subversive leaflets by anonymous posting to Germans. The distribution covers the entire territory of the former Poland and so far has not been met with any counter-action worth mentioning. ... All the prints secured in this District originated in Warsaw, although this was masked by posting them in various localities.'

The report offers the fact, that the Polish underground press quoted from these leaflets, as proof of their Polish connection. It was a mistaken deduction, since the underground press was not aware of 'N's' existence and obtained the leaflets from their own German contacts. It continues: 'Especially noteworthy is the regular appearance of the newspaper *Der Hammer* in a socialist camouflage and of *Der Soldat*, whose latest secured issue displays communist tendencies. ... One must assume that these subversive publications are not without influence among both *Reichs-* and *Volksdeutsche* ... of the distributed prints only minute quantities are being surrendered to the authorities ... judging by what Austrians and Sudeten Germans are saying, this propaganda achieves concrete results among them and requires appropriate countermeasures.'[50]

From about this time – the end of 1941 – all 'N' prints were being correctly identified by *Gestapo* experts, but this was classified information which was never used by the German propaganda.

Concerns about the increased Polish underground propaganda activity were voiced at the *GG* 'government' sitting on 16 December 1941.[51] The head of the *Sicherheitspolizei*, Schöngarth, reported: 'This propaganda activity has grown to an extent unseen during the last two years … leaflets and periodicals in German were discovered in Kraków … they were disseminated mainly among soldiers … they were inciting soldiers to desert.'

A report prepared by the Radom *Gestapo* and distributed to all its branch offices in the spring of 1942 reflected a deep concern:[52] 'During recent weeks the distribution of subversive materials has reached unprecedented levels.' After listing six examples of such materials, the report continues:

> This well-planned subversive propaganda aims to create a feeling of an impending disaster not only among the German civilians but also within the *Wehrmacht*. Not without reason, it counts on the innocence of the normal *Reichsdeutsche* and on the not yet crystallised *weltanschauung* of the *Volksdeutsche*. All the *Sicherheitspolizei*'s attempts to counter this by suitably educating both, produced so far only insignificant results. … It is being confirmed again that the recipients of the subversive materials, even German civil servants, not only do not surrender them to the authorities, but even discuss them over drinks … it was found that the allegations of corruption were being accepted as true. Even if the conduct of the *Reichsdeutsche* provides currently the Poles with a motive to distribute such subversive materials, it has to be stressed, that according to the findings of our investigations, they contain extreme exaggerations … the effects of this subversive propaganda cannot fail to be noticed, both among the civilians and among members of the *Wehrmacht*. Numerous reports from V-persons confirm that an energetic counter-propaganda operation from our side is absolutely necessary.

Many other reports from different *Gestapo* branches expressed deep concerns with the low leaflet-surrender ratios (they had some idea of the distribution volumes from their agents) and with the uncritical acceptance of their contents by both *Reichs-* and *Volksdeutsche.* A report from the Radom *Gestapo* sounded quite desperate: 'If we do not achieve a 100 per cent surrender ratio, the Polish propaganda will win … the *Reichsdeutsche* take these materials – in the best case as 'curiosa' – back to the *Reich* and show them to friends. Subversive ideas are spread further. Soldiers bring them as 'souvenirs' and undermine the morale. I do not consider these dangers to be negligible.'[53]

Eventually *RSHA* in Berlin took notice and decided to take command of all anti-'N' operations. In November 1942 the *Gestapo* chief Müller issued a circular concerning 'subversive publications': 'In order to combat successfully this propaganda it will be now dealt with centrally, by the *Reichssicherheitshauptamt* Department IVD2. Consequently I would ask for all secured copies, together with envelopes, to be forwarded here, informing us at the same time whether the recipients have any ideas as to the identity of the senders.'

There followed a special instruction for police commanders in the *GG*: 'Since in all probability the subversive materials in German are printed in the *GG*, please conduct your enquiries with the utmost vigour. Exceptionally in this case, the possibility of losing V-persons should not be a consideration.'[54]

Five months later another *RSHA* circular ordered that: 'in future the subversive materials printed by the Polish resistance movement are not to be described as "published by communists"'.[55]

On 5 August 1943 the head of the Radom *Gestapo* issued the following order:[56] 'Any attempt to incite … is to be countered, if necessary, with the most brutal methods. In the case of moaners, defeatists and others who speak in a subversive way, with reference to the toppling of Mussolini, of the likelihood of similar events in Germany,* as well as in the case of the enemies of the State who engage in illegal written propaganda, it should be proposed to the *RSHA* to subject them to *Sonderhandlung*.† The executions will be announced by this office.'

It would seem that for some reason the head of the Radom *Gestapo* found it necessary to provide a pseudo-legal justification of these executions, which had been the norm, right from the beginning. Whereas people arrested for the possession of illegal Polish leaflets, for example, could sometimes get away with a concentration camp sentence, giving them a chance, albeit a slim one, of survival, those caught with 'N' materials were treated exactly like those caught in possession of firearms: the death penalty was automatic.

The examination so far of the extent of German countermeasures as an indication of the effectiveness of Allied propaganda assumed that the German perception of this effectiveness was correct. In fact this perception was not only dominated throughout the war by pre-conceived notions of an irresistible propaganda onslaught on 1918 lines, but was also shaped by field reports which, more often than not, were subjective and distorted. German reports to superior authorities, both civilian and military, served often as tools of empire building or to enhance the standing of the author. For instance, reports on actions against partisans in Poland usually exaggerated their losses, inflating both the numbers killed

---

* This was the theme of an 'N' leaflet.

† 'Special treatment' – euphemism for execution.

and the quantities of weapons captured. In a letter of 20 July 1944 the commander of 10 Army in Italy, General Vietinghoff, wrote to Himmler, reporting that as a result of a campaign by a *Kurt Eggers* propaganda unit under his command, the Polish 2nd Corps was ready to go over to the Germans.[57] And this just barely a month after Poles had taken the Monte Cassino monastery, suffering considerable losses. The purpose of many reports on Allied propaganda was to secure more assets to fight it.

During most of the war, first EH's and later PWE's rating of the Allied propaganda was the same as that by *Promi*: very high. The name itself of the PWE reports – Evidence of Reception – shows an exclusive interest in the propaganda reaching its targets, the implied assumption being that having done so it cannot fail to achieve the intended effect. Neither side entertained any doubts as to the efficacy of this propaganda, and both were convinced that exposure to it could not fail to produce results. British propaganda warriors would have been flattered, had they known how awe-inspiring their image was in Berlin. So what went wrong? Why did the hopes of one side and fears of the other not materialise?

Very few regular officers were involved in the British propaganda function, but still, in the best military tradition, it continued to fight – until Delmer's arrival – the previous war. But the political, social and psychological environment of 1939–40 was not the same as in 1918. Operation 'N' was different, so far as its special operations were conducted in response to developing situations and concurrent events, and produced ascertainable results. Nevertheless, these results, just like the few ascertainable results of British PSYOPS, were to the Germans, in the context of their total war effort, nothing more than a nuisance, insignificant pinpricks.

All historians cite the iron grip of the German security services as one of the main – if not the main – cause of the Allied propaganda's impotence. The *Gestapo*'s ruthlessness needs no proof, but what about the effectiveness of their methods? Defying increasingly sharp sentences and rising number of convictions, millions of 'black' listeners and readers of leaflets carried on undeterred. In May 1943 Goebbels came to the conclusion that it was his 'obscure news policy' that was driving the information-starved Germans to risk capital punishment, but he did nothing to remedy the situation. Perhaps the rest of the Nazi Establishment were incapable of visualising a different approach and the apparatus of enforcement and repression was simply unreformable. After Stalingrad, Goebbels's propaganda became even less factual, and irrational themes achieved prominence. The myths of Stalingrad, the 'Jewish-bolshevik world conspiracy' and 'Hitler's genius', became his leading motifs.[58]

A considerable proportion of Germans continued to expose themselves to enemy propaganda but, in spite of Goebbels's concerns, and whatever were their resulting doubts, which they may even have discussed with their friends, their thoughts and discussions were not translated into action. A convincing explanation would be that, except at the very end, those millions risking their necks were not really against Hitler and his party but only against the Nazi news policy. Listening to *Atlantik*'s news or reading it in the *Nachrichten*, they were satisfied with the 98 per cent or even just the 95 per cent that was true and correct. Perhaps, with practice, they learned to filter out the propaganda content. Most probably they felt also that being just passive recipients of news did not really make them criminals; on the other hand, active participation in any subversive or even just clandestine venture would, in their minds, constitute a transgression, unworthy of a disciplined citizen. All continued to be quiet on the German political Home Front.

During the second half of 1942, PWE thought that it could discern some signs of their efforts being successful. And then, in January 1943, came the 'Casablanca Declaration': Churchill and Roosevelt announced that to end the war, nothing short of an unconditional surrender by Germany would be acceptable. Both sides of the Alliance – East and West – had been quite neurotic about the possibility that the other side might conclude a separate peace with Hitler. The consequences of a separate peace with the Western Alliance would have been possibly more serious to the Soviet Union than the reverse would have been to the West. Still, the Foreign Office spared no efforts to prevent any possibility of upsetting Stalin, and pushing him back into Hitler's arms. Churchill had one aim only: to destroy Hitler. This single-mindedness did not blur his vision of other European issues – he was conscious of the threat from the East – but it prevented him from taking any serious and effective prophylactic measures against that threat. There was another, longer term, aspect of the conduct of war which highlighted the inadvisability of antagonising Stalin. The successful construction of the A-bomb was not yet a certainty and both Churchill and Roosevelt were hoping to persuade Stalin to make a contribution to the defeat of Japan.

The Soviet Union relied on agents and fellow travellers in high places in London and Washington to prevent any damage to its interests. Roosevelt was surrounded by them and with his health failing he could be easily influenced. And, no doubt, influenced he was. After the Casablanca Declaration Stalin could relax: the unconditional surrender principle was a guarantee that the West would now have to reject any German peace overtures. It was a death sentence for the millions of people who had to perish during the last years of the war: it was calculated, perhaps a little over-optimistically, that without the insistence on unconditional surrender, war could have ended two years sooner. We shall never know whether concluding peace with a Germany not totally defeated would have been better for the world.

The Casablanca Declaration was a disaster for PWE and a godsend for Goebbels. He could, without any fear of contradiction, tell both the civilian population and the troops that now all Germans were 'in the soup' together. He appeared to admit that some of his fellow countrymen did not like their rulers, but he assured them that, should the Allies win, their revenge would make the Treaty of Versailles seem Utopian.[59] Allied propaganda never contradicted the Nazi assertions that a dire fate awaited Germany if it was defeated. It could not do so without antagonising occupied Europe and the exiled governments in London. In 1918 the Allied propaganda blamed the German rulers, now it was saying that the people would bear the responsibility. Statements in Parliament warning the German nation that the longer it tolerated the Nazi reign, the greater would be its responsibility for the crimes committed in its name, did nothing to counter the fear, spread by Goebbels, of the consequences of a lost war.

British propaganda did not even mention Casablanca for nearly five months. It could never find an effective antidote. The anti-propaganda shield created gratuitously for Germany by the Declaration remained effective until the very last phase of the war.

The Casablanca Declaration made an equally deep impression on the *Wehrmacht* as on the civilian population. It strengthened further the military morale, which was already near shatterproof. The Allies did not seem to realise this until mid-1944. The SHAEF *Directive for PSYWAR* of June 1944 admitted defeat: 'It must be accepted that the German High Command has rendered the Army largely immune to the PSYWAR campaigns which proved effective in 1918, i.e. bolshevist propaganda, leading to soldiers' and workers' councils, and democratic propaganda leading to a revolt of the civilians under arms against the professional soldiers … no propaganda directed at the front line German soldier is likely to be effective unless it sounds and looks more positive and more authoritative than his own Army Order forbidding him to listen to it.'[60] So we have an admission that the SHAEF propaganda was of the 1918 vintage. The second part of the quoted passage is really a *non sequitur*: to be able to judge whether the Allied propaganda is more positive and more authoritative than his orders, the German soldier had first to disobey them and acquaint himself with that propaganda.

Less than a year after Casablanca, Allied propaganda had to deal with another difficulty. Eastern European countries began to worry that the West would abandon them to the Soviet Union, as it had abandoned Poland. According to a memorandum of 22 February 1944,[61] Hungary and Finland thought that whether they went on fighting or surrendered or even changed sides, their ultimate fate would be the same. They had no incentive to leave the Axis camp, just as Turkey had no incentive to join the Allies.

Throughout most of the war there persisted a strange concurrence of views of both sides on the efficacy of British propaganda. Both were convinced that it would produce outstanding results. But not for the same reasons.

The British thought that the average German could be made to act either by invoking high ideals or by appealing to his self-interest (Hitler's 'inner bastard'). German authorities were still mesmerised by the 1918 successes of British propaganda, and saw that from 1941 onwards it was copying and improving their own victorious methods of 1939–40. German security services, whose job it was to fight the enemy black, and whose own 'inner bastards' were probably overdeveloped, credited average Germans with similar characteristics, and expected them to act as desired by British propagandists. All three were mistaken.

It took a total and utter defeat in the field, and a breakdown of the military and civilian organisations to make the German morale plummet, but even then, on the Eastern Front, the fear of Russian vengeance spurred both officers and men to fight to the last cartridge. The basic strength of their morale was derived, in common with the general population, from the habit of discipline, especially strong among those who had been indoctrinated in the *Hitler Jugend*. Then there was the professional pride and the conviction of serving in the finest army in the world which, they believed, represented the embodiment of the highest physical and spiritual attainments of German culture. In the words of an old German song: '*Der Soldate, der Soldate/ist der schönste Mann/im ganzen Staate* … ' ('The soldier is the most handsome man in the entire land'). In most cases, however, the principal factor was the loyalty to the regiment and, even more, to the 'primary group', to one's mates – *Kameradschaft* – sentiments well understood and shared by the British soldier.

There was also another aspect, mentioned by Colonel Hans von Luck, commander of an armoured regiment: 'They [the soldiers of his regiment] were all keen to stay with the old gang, which for them meant protection and security.'[62] In February 1945, when his regiment was about to be moved from the Western to the Eastern Front, von Luck addressed his men: 'It will be our last battle. Forget all the slogans, about a "Thousand-Year *Reich*" and "Final Victory must be ours". From now on we are fighting solely for survival, for our homeland, our wives, mothers and children, whom we want to save from a fate none of us can imagine.' And fight they did. Magnificently. Both the old hands and the sixteen-year-old replacements.

By January 1945 German courts martial issued 25,539 death sentences for desertion, insubordination and subversive activity.[63] In addition, an unknown number of executions were ordered or carried out by drumhead trials, Military Police, *Sichercheitsdienst* and unit commanders. These figures seem high but as a percentage of the total of those serving, they are insignificant. Even the great majority of the pre-war communists could not resist the *Wehrmacht* ethos. They fought shoulder to shoulder with their old political foes and were equally unreceptive to Allied propaganda.

I am sorry Mr Delmer, but I must come to the conclusion that neither my own minuscule contribution to the Allied black operations, nor your gigantic one, did noticeably expedite the downfall of the Third *Reich*, although the cost of the collateral damage we managed to inflict – the time and efforts of the German security and propaganda authorities involved in counteractions – probably did exceed the cost of our black operations. Your operations were absolutely brilliant, but even you, with your exceptional feeling for and knowledge of German psychology of the interwar period, could not foresee the extraordinary resilience of German civilians and especially of soldiers. The Casablanca Declaration and the overwhelming fear of the deserved Russian retribution did not help. Allied psychological warfare did more than just fight the previous war, but the wartime psychology of the adversary was not understood sufficiently well to secure success. But even if the understanding were there, it does not follow that ways could have been found to shatter the German resilience.

Nevertheless, as a consolation, I must quote General Eisenhower, who wrote after the war: 'I am convinced that the expenditure of men and money in wielding the spoken and written word was an important contributing factor in undermining the enemy's will to resist and supporting the fighting morale of our potential Allies in the occupied countries.'

Nearly all PWE files were destroyed soon after the war ended. There is no record of any of the PWE top people, most of whom came from the City or from Fleet Street, making any effort to save them. Perhaps they even welcomed their records' destruction, because they wanted to obliterate any traces of their wartime activities and to restore in everybody's eyes their unblemished image of officers and gentlemen. Perhaps they also wanted to prevent others from finding out the details of their black techniques and operations which, no doubt, became well ingrained in their own memories. Well before the Victory Parade, to which Polish forces under British command were not invited, so as not to upset Stalin and his client government in Warsaw, they were successfully resuming their pre-war careers. One cannot but wonder to what extent the skills they honed during their years with PWE helped them to do well in peacetime.

British PSYOPS are now, officially, attributable. This means that the British government eschews black and grey propaganda. Nevertheless, it is to be hoped that in an emergency those responsible for the defence of the realm would not hesitate to employ any available means contributing to a successful outcome. To avoid being caught unprepared again, Britain should have in place skeletal PSYOPS structures for all types of operations, including the use of the Internet, which seems to be eminently suited to carry out grey and black operations. These structures should have both defensive and offensive Information Operations capabilities. We can but hope that they do exist.

Glossary

II Bureau	(Pol) The Second Bureau of the Polish General Staff, Intelligence
VI Bureau	(Pol) The Sixth Bureau of the Polish General Staff in London, responsible for resistance in Poland
AA	*see Auswärtiges Amt*
Abteilung	(Ger) department, section
Abwehr	German Military Intelligence Service
AD/Z	c/n SOE Director of Research
AK	*see Armia Krajowa*
Altreich	(Ger) Germany within its 1937 boundaries
Armia Krajowa	(Pol) the Home Army, the main Polish underground force, often called the 'Secret Army'
Auswärtiges Amt	German Foreign Office
BIP	(Pol) *Biuro Informacji i Propagandy* (Information and Propaganda Bureau), *ZWZ/AK*
'Bór'	(Pol) c/n, *see* Komorowski

Braddocks	c/n of incendiary devices, air-dropped for sabotage purposes
C c/n of head of MI6	
CD	c/n of Executive Director of SOE
CHQ	c/n of SO1 (Country HQ)
DE	c/n, also G2, of German language PWE RU, also called 'Neubeginn'
DNB	(Ger) *Deutsches Nachrichten Büro* (German News Agency)
Einsatzgruppen	(Ger) Murder squads which followed the front-line troops. First used in Poland in September 1939; later, in occupied Soviet territories, were killing mainly Jews
G2	c/n, also DE, of German language PWE RU, also called 'Neubeginn'
G3	c/n of Gustav Siegfried 1, German language PWE RU
Gauleiter	(Ger) District Nazi Party leader
Gesellschaft	(Ger) company (business)
Gestapo	*Geheime Staatspolizei* (Secret State Police), a department of RSHA
GG	(Ger) *Generalgouvernement* (Occupied Poland)
'Grot'	(Pol) c/n of Rowecki
GRU	Soviet Military Intelligence
GS	(Ger) *Geheim Sender* (secret transmitter)
GS1	*Gustav Siegfried 1*, German language PWE RU c/n G3
Heer	(Ger) army
Hellschreiber	(Ger) wireless teleprinter

Herrenvolk	(Ger) master race
Hitler Jugend	(Ger) Hitler Youth, organisation for boys
ISRB	Inter-Services Research Bureau (c/n for SOE)
ISSB	Inter-Service Security Board
ISSU	Inter-Services Signals Unit (c/n for SOE)
JIC	Joint Intelligence Committee
KG	(Pol) *see Komenda Gšówna*
Komenda Gšówna	(Pol) Central Command (of *AK*)
Komorowski Tadeusz	(Pol) general, c/ns 'Bór', 'Lawina', commander of *AK* 1943–4
Kriegsmarine	(Ger) navy
Kurt Eggers	(Ger) *Waffen-SS* propaganda unit
'Lawina'	(Pol) c/n, *see* Komorowski
LCS	London Controlling Section – deception coordination
Luftwaffe	German air force
MD	Mining and 'diversionary' equipment (drops to Poland)
MEW	British Ministry of Economic Warfare
MI5	British counter-intelligence
MI6	*see* SIS
MI(R)	Military Intelligence (Research)
MO1(SP)	Military Operations 1 (Special Projects) (c/n for SOE)
MoI	British Ministry of Information
NID	British Naval Intelligence Division
NKVD	(Sov) National Internal Affairs Committee, Soviet Intelligence and Security Service

NSDAP	(GER) *Nazionalsozialistische Deutsche Arbeiter Partei*, the Nazi Party
OKH	(Ger), *Oberkommando des Heeres* (High Command of the army)
OKW	(Ger) *Oberkommando der Wehrmacht* (High Command of the armed forces)
OW	c/n combat equipment (air drops to Poland)
P1	c/n, *see* Œwit
P2	c/n, *see* Voice of Polish Women
Periwig	c/n of a deception operation, intended to make the German security think that among foreign workers in Germany existed a powerful resistance organisation
PID	Politcal Intelligence Department of the FO
POW	Prisoner of War
Promi	(Ger) *Propagandaministerium* (Ministry of Propaganda)
Propagandatruppen	(Ger) army propaganda units
Protasewicz	(Pol) colonel, c/n 'Rawa', head of VI Bureau
PWE	Political Warfare Executive
'Rawa'	(Pol) c/n, *see* Protasewicz
Reich	German State
Reichsdeutsche	Germans born in the *Reich*
Reichsrundfunk	German State Broadcasting
Reichssender	German State Broadcasting Station

RKM	(Ger) *Reichskriegministerium*, pre-1938 War Office
Rowecki Stefan	(Pol) general, c/ns 'Grot', 'Grabica', commander of *ZWZ* and then of *AK*
RSHA	(Ger) *Reichssicherheitshauptamt* (Reich Central Security Office)
RU	Research Unit, c/n PWE black station
RUSI	Royal United Services Institute
SA	(Ger) *Sturmabteilung* (assault squad), 'Brownshirts', the strong arm of the Nazi Party
Schupo	(Ger) *Schutzpolizei* (protection police), urban constabulary
SD	(Ger) *Sicherheitsdienst* (security service), intelligence branch of the SS
Section D	Offshoot of SIS, precursor of SOE
Seelöwe	(Ger), 'Sea Lion', c/n for the German invasion of Britain
SHAEF	Supreme Headquarters Allied Expeditionary Force
Sikorski Wšadysšaw	(Pol) general, CiC of Polish forces in the West and Prime Minister of the Polish government in London. Died in a plane crash off Gibraltar on 4 July 1943
Sipo	(Ger) *Sicherheitspolizei* (security police), made up of the *Gestapo* and the Criminal Police

SIS	British Secret Intelligence Service, MI6
SO1	Propaganda branch of SOE
SO2	Subversion branch of SOE, made up of Section D and MI(R)
SO3	Short-lived planning branch of SOE
SOE	Special Operations Executive
SS	(Ger) *Schutzstaffel* (protection squad)
Standarte	(Ger) unit of the SA or SS, roughly equivalent to a regiment
Südstern	(Ger) 'Southern Star', c/n of a German propaganda operation aimed at subverting the Polish 2 Corps in Italy
Świt	(Pol) 'Dawn', c/n P1, Polish language PWE RU
Szare Szeregi	(Pol) 'Grey Ranks', wartime clandestine Scouts
TWZW	(Pol) Tajne Wojskowe Zakšady Wydawnicze (Clandestine Military Publishing)
UPC	Underground Propaganda Committee
V-man	(Ger) *Vertrauensmann*, (confidential agent) of the *SD* or Gestapo
Voice of Polish Women	c/n P2, Polish language PWE RU
Volksdeutsche	(Ger) ethnic Germans, born outside the *Reich*
Volkssturm	(Ger) German Home Guard
Waffen-SS	Militarised *SS*

Wehrmacht	German armed forces
Wiesenthal, Simon	the most persistent and the most successful postwar Nazi hunter
Zwiazek Walki Zbrojnej	(Pol) Armed Combat Association, predecessor of *AK*
ZWZ	(Pol) *see* Zwiazek Walki Zbrojnej

Notes

Archives & Libraries

AAA	**Auswärtiges Amt Archiv, Berlin**
AAN	Archiwum Akt Nowych, Warsaw
BA	Bundesarchiv, Berlin
BAMA	Bundesarchiv-Militärarchiv, Freiburg
BBC WAC	BBC Written Archives Centre, Caversham
BN	Biblioteka Narodowa, Warsaw
CAW	Centralne Archiwum Wojskowe, Warsaw
CBW	Centralna Biblioteka Wojskowa, Warsaw
IF	Institute Français, London
IFZ	Institut für Zeitgeschichte, München
IPMS	Polish Institute and Sikorski Museum, London
IPN	Instytut Pamieci Narodowej, Warsaw (Gestapo Archives)
IPN Ld	Instytut Pamieci Narodowej, Šódź (Gestapo Archives)
IWM	Imperial War Museum, London
LH	Liddell Hart Centre for Military Archives, London
TNA	The National Archives (Public Record Office), London
RUSI	Royal United Services Institute Library, London
SPP	Polish Underground Movement Study Trust, London
WBBH	Wojskowe Biuro Badań Historycznych, Warsaw

Chapter 1: Psychological Warfare

1. A. Huxley, *Brave New World* (London, Chatto & Windus, 1987),p. 11.
2. R. Bruce Lockhart, 'Political Warfare', *RUSI Journal* (May 1950).
3. R. Bruce Lockhart, *Comes the Reckoning* (New York, Putnam, 1947), p. 154.
4. L. Farago, *War of Wits* (London, Hutchinson, 1956).
5. M. Dewar, *The Art of Deception in Warfare* (Newton Abbot, David & Charles, 1989), p. 164.
6. Hans Fritsche, *Es sprach Hans Fritsche* (Stuttgart, Thiele, 1949), p. 193.
7. R. Evans. *The Coming of the Third Reich* (London, Penguin, 2004), p. 396.
8. Daugherty and Janowitz, *A Psychological Warfare Casebook* (Baltimore, John Hopkins University Press, 1958), p. 2.
9. T. Kochanowicz, *Na wojennej emigracji* (Warsaw, KIW, 1975), p. 79.
10. D. Lerner et al., *Propaganda in War and Crisis* (New York, GW Stewart, 1951), p. 429.
11. M. Lloyd, *The Art of Military Deception* (Barnsley, Leo Cooper, 1997), p. 147.
12. A. Hitler, *Mein Kampf* (London, Hurst & Blackett, 1938), Chapter VI.
13. S. Delmer, *Black Boomerang* (London, Secker & Warburg, 1962), p. 41.
14. Farago, *War of Wits*, p. 267.
15. LH, Dobrski 1/3.
16. J. Laffin, *Links of Leadership* (London, Harrap, 1966), p. 291.
17. V. Lenin, *Selected Works* (London, Lawrence & Wishart, 1921).
18. Farago, *War of Wits*, p. 268.
19. *Ibid.*, p. 273.
20. T. Pilcher, *War According to Clausewitz* (London, Cassell, 1918).
21. H. Wedel, *Die Propagandatruppen der Deutschen Wehrmacht* (Neckargemuend, Scharnhorst, 1962), p. 9.
22. K. Stolinski, *Counterfeiting of Currency by Frederic II* (London, privately published, 2001).
23. C. Berger, *Broadsides and Bayonets* (San Rafael, Presido, 1961).
24. K. Kirchner, *Bayern und der Frieden* (Erlanger, Verlag D + C, 1983), p. 17.
25. Farago, *War of Wits*, p. 260.

26. J. Keegan, *A History of Warfare* (London, Hutchinson, 1993), p. 347.
27. Laffin, *Links of Leadership*, p. 33.
28. J.-P. Gourevitch, *La Propagande dans tous ses états* (Paris, Flammarion, 1981), p. 7.
29. Wedel, *Die Propagandatruppen*, p. 12.
30. Letter to author from Service Historique de L'Armée de Terre.
31. T. Fontane, *Der Krieg gegen Frankreich 1870–71* (Berlin, 1875).
32. K. Kirchner, *Flugblätter, Psychologische Kriegsführung in 2 Weltkrieg* (Munich, Carl Hanser Verlag, 1974), p. 11.
33. B. Blau, *Propoganda als Waffe* (Berlin, Bernhard & Graefe, 1935), p. 40.
34. C. Roetter, *Psychological Warfare* (London, Batsford, 1974), p. 74.
35. Wedel, *Die Propagandatruppen*, p. 12.
36. TNA: PRO FO 898 52.
37. N. Davies, *Rising '44* (London, Macmillan, 2003), p. 460.
38. R.A. Haldane, *The Hidden War* (London, Robert Hale, 1978), p. 31.
39. J. Baker White, *The Big Lie* (London, Evans Bros, 1955), p. 108.
40. E. Howe, *The Black Game* (London, Michael Joseph, 1982), p. 25.
41. TNA: PRO CAB 65 1 215.
42. A. Brown, *Bodyguard of Lies* (London, WH Allen, 1976), p. 7.
43. Lecture at RUSI, 30 October 2001.

Chapter 2: German Black Propaganda

1. L. Paine, *German Military Intelligence in World War II* (London, Stein & Day, 1984), p. 12
2. Z. Zeman, *Nazi Propaganda* (London, OUP, 1964), p. 160.
3. *Ibid.*, p. 170.
4. J. Baird, *The Mythical World of Nazi War Propaganda, 1939–45* (Minnesota, University of Minnesota Press, 1974), p. 13.
5. E. Howe, *The Black Game* (London, Michael Joseph, 1982), p. 64.
6. O. Buchbender and R. Hauschild, *Geheimsender gegen Frankreich* (Hertford, Mittler, 1984), p. 26.
7. C. Roetter, *Psychological Warfare* (London, Batsford, 1974), p. 99.
8. M. Balfour, *Propaganda in War 1939–45* (London, Routledge & Kegan Paul, 1979), p. 428.
9. V.R. Berghahn, 'Wehrmachtpropaganda', *Revue d'histoire de la deuxième Guerre Mondiale*, No. 54 (1971).
10. Buchbender and Hauschild, *Geheimsender*, p. 34.

11. A. Boelcke, *Kriegspropaganda 1939–41* (Stuttgart, D.Verlagsanstalt, 1966), p. 166.
12. Buchbender and Hauschild, *Geheimsender*, p. 35.
13. Howe, *The Black Game*, p. 64.
14. Buchbender and Hauschild, *Geheimsender*, p. 53.
15. Howe, *The Black Game*, p. 62.
16. Balfour, *Propaganda in War*, p. 174.
17. www.radiofrance.fr/chaines/radio-france/musee.
18. Two-part programme broadcast on 8 and 9 January 1991.
19. Roetter, *Psychological Warfare*, p. 104.
20. D. Rossignol, *Histoire de la propagande en France 1940–1944* (Paris, Presses Universitaires de France, 1991), p. 50.
21. J. Baker White, *The Big Lie* (London, Evans Bros, 1955), p. 36.
22. Rossignol, *Histoire de la propagande en France*.
23. C. Coker, 'What Would Sun Tzu Say about the War on Terrorism?' *RUSI Journal* (January 2002), p. 19.
24. P. Linebarger, *Psychological Warfare* (Washington, Infantry Journal Press, 1948), p. 80.
25. J. Baird, *The Mythical World of Nazi War Propaganda, 1939–45* (Minnesota, University of Minnesota Press, 1974), p. 25.
26. K. Kirchner, *Krankheit rettet* (Erlangen, Verlag D + C, 1976), p. 89.
27. Buchbender and Hauschild, *Geheimsender*, p. 22.
28. Howe, *The Black Game*, p. 65.
29. Buchbender and Hauschild, *Geheimsender*, p. 58.
30. G. Krause, *Die Britische Auslandspropaganda* (Berlin, Stubenrauch, 1940), p. 70.
31. C. Levy, 'L'organisation de la propagande allemande en France', *Revue d'histoire de la deuxième Guerre Mondiale*, 9.
32. BAMA, RW4/249.
33. A. Boelcke, *The Secret Conferences of Dr Goebbels 1939–43* (London, Weidenfeld & Nicolson, 1967), p. 70.
34. R. Schnabel, *Misbrauchte Mikrophone* (Wien, Europa-Verlag, 1967), p. 93.
35. Howe, *The Black Game*, p. 66.
36. R.V. Jones, *Most Secret War* (London, Coronet, 1978), p. 114.
37. M. Dewar, *The Art of Deception in Warfare* (Newton Abbot, David & Charles, 1989), p. 168.
38. LH, Dobrski 14.
39. TNA: PRO INF 1/265 and 266.
40. Roetter, *Psychological Warfare*, p. 16.

41. J.A. Cole, *Lord Haw-Haw and W. Joyce* (London, Faber & Faber, 1964), p. 135.
42. Buchbender and Hauschild, *Geheimsender*, p. 37.
43. AA, 1782 E237639.
44. Schnabel, *Misbrauchte Mikrophone*, p. 133.
45. W. Kozaczuk, *Wojna w Eterze* (Warsaw, Radio I Telewzja, 1977), p. 97.
46. Kozaczuk, *Wojna*, p. 105.
47. Schnabel, *Misbrauchte Mikrophone*, p. 16.
48. C. Madajczyk, *Polityka III Rzeszy w Polsce* (Warsaw, PWN, 1970), p. 173.
49. J. Dobroszycki, *Reptile Journalism* (New Haven and London, Yale University Press, 1994), p. 144.
50. S. Lewandowska, *Polska konspiracyjna prasa* (Warsaw, Czytelnik, 1982), p. 379.
51. S. Piotrowski, *Dziennik H Franka* (Warsaw, Wydawnictwo Prawnicze, 1956), p. 235.
52. Madajczyk, *Polityka*, p. 168.
53. SPP, A.3.19.2/5.
54. TNA: PRO FO 898 61.
55. SPP, A.3.1.1.4 88.
56. Lewandowska, *Polska konspiracyjna*, p. 381.
57. BA, R55 20782.
58. Kirchner, *Krankheit Rettet*, p. 53.
59. S. Delmer, *Black Boomerang* (London, Secker & Warburg, 1962), p. 137.
60. J. Hosang, *Gezahnte Kriegspropaganda* (Sollingen, the author, 1954), p. 5.
61. TNA: PRO FO 898 101.
62. Linebarger, *Psychological Warfare*, p. 88.

Chapter 3: British Black Propaganda

1. P. Wright, *Spy Catcher* (New York, Viking Penguin, 1987), p. 327.
2. E. Howe, *The Black Game* (London, Michael Joseph, 1982), p. 2.
3. TNA: PRO CAB 16 127.
4. TNA: PRO CAB 23 99 325.
5. TNA: PRO CAB 23 96 375.
6. TNA: PRO CAB 23 99 325.
7. S. Rogerson, *Propaganda in the Next War* (London, Bless, 1938), p. 8.
8. TNA: PRO FO 898 426.

9. D. Garnett, *The Secret History of PWE* (London, St Ermin's, 2002), p. 17.
10. M. Balfour, *Propaganda in War 1939–45* (London, Routledge, Kegan, Paul, 1979), p. 90.
11. TNA: PRO CAB 66 2.
12. C. Cruickshank, *The Fourth Arm: Psychological Warfare 1934–45* (London, David-Poynter, 1974), p. 48.
13. TNA: PRO FO 898 6.
14. Garnett, *The Secret History*, p. 3.
15. Rogerson, *Propaganda*, pp. 58ff.
16. *Ibid.*, p. 129.
17. *Ibid.*, p. 80.
18. TNA: PRO FO 898 1.
19. TNA: PRO CAB 21 1071.
20. J. Beevor, *SOE: Recollections and Reflections* (London, Bodley Head, 1981), p. 15.
21. B. Wittek, *Der Britischer Aetherkrieg gegen das 3 Reich* (Münster, Fahle, 1962), p. 52.
22. Garnett, *The Secret History*, p. 10.
23. BA, R 58 268.
24. Garnett, *The Secret History*, p. 22.
25. B. Liddell Hart, *Defence of the West* (London, Cassell, 1950), p. 54.
26. TNA: PRO COS 40 390.
27. W. Mackenzie, *The Secret History of SOE* (London, St Ermin's, 2000), p. 60.
28. Garnett, *The Secret History*, p. 63.
29. *Ibid.*, p. xiii.
30. *Ibid.*, p. 79.
31. K. Philby, *My Silent War* (London, Harrap, 1963), p. 14.
32. M.R.D. Foot, 'What Use was SOE?', *RUSI Journal* (February, 2003).
33. Wittek, *Der Britischer Aetherkrieg*, p. 49.
34. TNA: PRO HS 4 170.
35. TNA: PRO CAB 21 1071.

Chapter 4: Sefton Delmer Creates a Radically New Concept

1. D. Garnett, *The Secret History of PWE* (London, St Ermin's, 2002),p. 18n.

2. S. Delmer, *Black Boomerang* (London, Secker & Warburg, 1962), p. 16.
3. W. Churchill, *The Second World War*, Vol. 3 (London, Cassell, 1948).
4. TNA: PRO FO 898 8.
5. BBC WAC, E2/344.
6. Delmer, *Black Boomerang*, p. 125.
7. Garnett, *The Secret History*, p. 41.
8. TNA: PRO FO 898 54.
9. J. Baker White, *The Big Lie* (London, Evans Bros, 1955), p. 62.
10. M. Balfour, *Propaganda in War 1939–45* (London, Routledge, Kegan, Paul, 1979), p. 465n.
11. Delmer, *Black Boomerang*, p. 37.
12. TNA: PRO INF 1 888.
13. E. Howe, *The Black Game* (London, Michael Joseph, 1982), p. 84.
14. Delmer, *Black Boomerang*, pp. 39ff.
15. Garnett, *The Secret History*, p. 43.
16. *Ibid.*, pp. 45ff.
17. Delmer, *Black Boomerang*, p. 69.
18. Balfour, *Propaganda in War*, p. 100.
19. Howe, *The Black Game*, p. 114.
20. Delmer, *Black Boomerang*, p. 46.
21. *Ibid.*, p. 62.
22. *Ibid.*, p. 64.
23. *Ibid.*, p. 66.
24. TNA: PRO FO 898 51, 220.
25. TNA: PRO FO 898 67.
26. TNA: PRO FO 898 178.
27. Garnett, *The Secret History*, p. 91.
28. *Ibid.*, p. 95.
29. Delmer, *Black Boomerang*, p. 80.
30. *Ibid.*, p. 85.
31. TNA: PRO FO 898 51.
32. Garnett, *The Secret History*, p. 208.
33. Delmer, *Black Boomerang*, p. 99.
34. *Ibid.*, p. 89.
35. *Ibid.*, p. 92.
36. Garnett, *The Secret History*, p. 379.
37. TNA: PRO FO 898 397.
38. Garnett, *The Secret History*, p. 440.
39. Delmer, *Black Boomerang*, p. 205.
40. TNA: PRO FO 898 67.

41. Howe, *The Black Game*, p. 140.
42. C. Cruickshank, *The Fourth Arm: Psychological Warfare 1934–45* (London, David-Poynter, 1974), p. 105.
43. SPP, A2.3.11.3. 26.
44. TNA: PRO FO 898 51.
45. Delmer, *Black Boomerang*, p. 123.
46. *Ibid.*, p. 187.

Chapter 5: Black Rumours and Black Leaflets

1. L. Farago, *War of Wits* (London, Hutchinson, 1956), p. 269.
2. LH, Dobrski, 14.
3. D. Garnett, *The Secret History of PWE* (London, St Ermin's, 2002), p. 214.
4. S. Delmer, *Black Boomerang* (London, Secker & Warburg, 1962), p. 94.
5. Garnett, *The Secret History*, p. 214.
6. TNA: PRO FO 898 70.
7. TNA: PRO DEFE 28 48.
8. Delmer, *Black Boomerang*, p. 128.
9. Garnett, *The Secret History*, p. 192.
10. LH, Dobrski 1/2.
11. TNA: PRO FO 898 67.
12. Delmer, *Black Boomerang*, p. 139.
13. M. Balfour, *Propaganda in War 1939–45* (London, Routledge, Kegan, Paul, 1979), p. 248.
14. O. Buchbender, *Die Vierte Waffe* (Lüneberg, Deutsche Studien, 1985), p. 148.
15. R.G. Auckland, *British Black Propaganda to Germany 1941–5* (Leeds, Psywar Society, 1989), p. 31.
16. TNA: PRO FO 898 183.
17. TNA: PRO HS 6 696.
18. Delmer, *Black Boomerang*, p. 130.
19. *Ibid.*, p. 143.
20. A. Ishoven, *Willy Messerschmitt* (Vienna, Paul Neff, 1975), p. 305.
21. TNA: PRO FO 898 397.
22. SPP, A2.3.11.3.
23. Garnett, *The Secret History*, p. 432.
24. TNA: PRO FO 898 501.
25. Delmer, *Black Boomerang*, p. 145.

26. O. Buchbender and R. Hauschild, *Geheimsender gegen Frankreich* (Hertford, Mittler, 1984), p. 111.
27. E. Howe, *The Black Game* (London, Michael Joseph, 1982), p. 242.
28. Lerner et al., *Propaganda in War and Crisis* (New York, GW Stewart, 1951), p. 264.

Chapter 6: Polish Operation 'N' – Humble Beginnings

1. TNA: PRO HS4 165.
2. K. Kirchner, *Flugblatt Propaganda im 2 Weltkrieg* (XV+ Vols, Erlangen, Verlag D + C, 1978), p. xiv.
3. K. Kirchner, *Flugblätter, psychologische Kriegsführung in 2 Weltkrieg* (Munich, Carl Hanser Verlag, 1974), p. 43
4. Z. Zióšek, *Dywersyjna propaganda antyhitlerowska* (WBBH III/50/27), p. 2.
5. H. Auderska and Z. Zióšek, *Akcja N* (Warsaw, Czytelnik, 1972), p. 11.
6. A. Filar, *Nasz czšowiek w Abwehrze* (Kraków, Zw. Lit. Pol., 2000), p. 61.
7. A. Kawczyński, *Unternehmen N* (Munich, Vierteljahrhefte für Zeitgeschichte, 1966), p. 68.
8. H. Gittig, *Illegale antifaschistische Tarnschriften 1933–1945* (Leipzig, VEB, 1972), p. 79.
9. W. Stevenson, *A Man Called Intrepid* (London, Sphere, 1981), p. xvi.
10. Studium Polski Podziemnej, *AK w dokumentach* (6 Vols, London, SPP, 1970–89), Vol. 6, p. 438.
11. G. Mazur, *Akcja dywersyjna N* (Wrocšaw, Ossolineum, 2000), p. 20.
12. J. Rzepecki, *O wydawnictwach Akcji N*, No. 2 (Warsaw, Wojskowy Przeglad Historyczyny, 1972), p. 233.
13. Rzepecki, *O wydawnictwach Akcji N*, p. 234.
14. Mazur, *Akcja dywersyjna N*, p. 7.
15. T. Bór-Komorowski, *The Secret Army* (London, Gollancz, 1950), p. 82.
16. Auderska and Zióšek, *Akcja N*, p. 38.
17. IPN LD 1/115 19.
18. IPN LD 1/110 8911 42.
19. Mazur, *Akcja dywersyjna N*, p. 56.

20. J. Rzepecki, *Organizacja i dzialanie BIP* (Wojskowy Przeglad Historyczyny, 1971), No. 4, p. 153.
21. Ziókek, *Dywersyjna propaganda*, p. 75.
22. G. Mazur, *BIP* (Warsaw, PAX, 1987), p. 115.
23. S. Broniewski, *Cakym Z.yclem* (Warsaw, PWN, 1983), p. 120.
24. Mazur, *BIP*, p. 61.
25. S. Lewandowska, *Polska konspiracyjna prasa* (Warsaw, Czytelnik, 1982), p. 260.
26. Auderska and Ziókek, *Akcja N*, p. 705.
27. BA R58 212.
28. IPN LD 1/110.
29. Ślaski, *Polska Walczaca* (Warsaw, PAX, 1985), p. 288.

Chapter 7: Operation 'N' – Rise and Fall

1. Z. Ziókek, *Dywersyjna propaganda antyhitlerowska* (WBBH III/50/27), p. 16.
2. *Ibid.*, p. 29.
3. *Ibid.*, p. 37.
4. SPP, 3.1.1.3. 3.
5. T. Bór-Komorowski, *The Secret Army* (London, Gollancz, 1950), p. 78.
6. *Ibid.*, p. 80.
7. J. Rzepecki, *O wydawnictwach Akcji N* (Warsaw, Wojskowy Przegląd Historyczyny, 1972), p. 264.
8. IPN LD, 1/118.
9. G. Mazur, *Akcja dywersyjna N* (Wrocšaw, Ossolineum, 2000), p. 26.
10. IPN LD, 1/115.
11. BA, R58 212.
12. SPP, 3.1.1.3.
13. J. Nowak, *Kurier z Warszawy* (London, Odnowa, 1978), p. 88.
14. Mazur, *Akcja dywersyjna N*, p. 137.
15. K. Malinowski, *Źošnierze Šączności walczącej Warszawy* (Warsaw, PAX, 1983), p. 198.
16. J. Zawodny, *Powstanie Warszawskie w walce i dyplomacji*, p. 40.
17. SPP, SK15/10.

Chapter 8: British–Polish Black Cooperation

1. TNA: PRO HS4 165.
2. TNA: PRO HS4 165.

3. IPN, 168/47.
4. SPP, A1.4.1.42.
5. BAMA, RW4/245.
6. TNA: PRO FO 898 6.
7. TNA: PRO FO 898 7 463.
8. TNA: PRO HS149 11/11/40.
9. TNA: PRO FO 898 454.
10. G. Mazur, *Akcja dywersyjna N* (Wrocšaw, Ossolineum, 2000),pp. 47ff.
11. TNA: PRO HS4 170.
12. SPP, 3.6.3.3/4.
13. TNA: PRO FO 898 224.
14. SPP, 2.3.11.1. 35.
15. Mazur, *Akcja dywersyjna N*, p. 131.
16. SPP, 2.3.11.3.
17. SPP, 3.6.3..2/26.
18. SPP, 2.3.11.3 65.
19. H. Frank, *Okupacja i ruch oporu w dzienniku Hansa Franka* (Warsaw, KIW, 1972), p. 162.
20. BA, R 58 211.
21. Information supplied by Mr Z. Bokiewicz, philately consultant.
22. SPP, 3.6.8.2.
23. TNA: PRO FO 898/224.
24. SPP, A2.3.11.3 75.
25. TNA: PRO 898 64 179.
26. S. Delmer, *Black Boomerang* (London, Secker & Warburg, 1962), pp. 132ff.
27. TNA: PRO FO 898/224.
28. TNA: PRO HS4 302.
29. Mazur, *Akcja dywersyjna N*, p. 131.
30. E. Howe, *The Black Game* (London, Michael Joseph, 1982), p. 217.
31. TNA: PRO HS 4 302.
32. BA, R 58 268.
33. TNA: PRO FO 898 51.
34. D. Garnett, *The Secret History of PWE* (London, St Ermin's, 2002), p. 183.
35. *Ibid.*, p. 184.
36. TNA: PRO FO 898 51.
37. Garnett, *The Secret History*, p. 207.
38. T. Kochanowicz, *Na wojennej emigracji* (Warsaw, KIW, 1975), p. 58.

39. Studium Polski Podziemnej, *AK w dokumentach* (6 Vols, London, SPP, 1970–89), Vol. 3, p. 135.
40. TNA: PRO FO 898 51.
41. TNA: PRO FO 371 34556.
42. TNA: PRO FO 898 224.
43. TNA: PRO FO 898 225.

Chapter 9: Why Did We Achieve So Little?

1. D. Lerner, *Psychological Warfare against Nazi Germany* (USA, MIT Press, 1971), p. 286.
2. O. Buchbender, *Die Vierte Waffe* (Lüneburg, Deutsche Studien, 1985), p. 124.
3. Lerner, *Psychological Warfare*, p. 289.
4. *Ibid.*, p. 266.
5. B. Wittek, *Der Britischer Aetherkrieg Gegen Das 3 Reich* (Münster, Fahle, 1962), p. 51.
6. TNA: PRO INF 1/888.
7. Buchbender, *Die Vierte Waffe*, p. 127.
8. A. Price, *The Last Years of the Luftwaffe* (London, Arms & Armour, 1993), p. 176.
9. D. Herwig and H. Rode, *Luftwaffe Secret Projects* (Hinckley, Midland Publishers, 2000), Introduction.
10. AAA, Inland IIg 1782–3.
11. R. Schnabel, *Misbrauchte Mikrophone* (Wien, Europa-Verlag, 1967), p. 100.
12. O. Buchbender and R. Hauschild, *Geheimsender gegen Frankreich* (Hertford, Mittler, 1984), p. 52.
13. TNA: PRO FO 898 63.
14. K. Kirchner, *Flugblatt Propaganda im 2 Weltkrieg* (XV+ vols, Erlangen, Verlag D + C, 1978), Vol. 6, pp. li ff, Vol. 5, pp. xxxiii ff.
15. TNA: PRO FO 898 101.
16. R. Herzstein, *The War that Hitler Won* (London, Hamish Hamilton, 1979), p. 405.
17. BA, R 58 268.
18. BA, R 43 II 639.
19. BA, R 58 268.
20. Buchbender, *Die Vierte Waffe*, p. 180.
21. E. Howe, *The Black Game* (London, Michael Joseph, 1982), p. 127.

22. BAMA, RW 4 2486.
23. A. Boelcke, *The Secret Conferences of Dr Goebbels 1939–43* (London, Weidenfeld & Nicolson, 1967).
24. Goebbels.
25. BA, R 58 953.
26. R. Herzstein, *The War that Hitler Won* (London, Hamish Hamilton, 1979), p. 404.
27. BA, NS19 1429.
28. Buchbender and Hauschild, *Geheimsender gegen Frankreich*, p. 52.
29. *Ibid.*, p. 53.
30. BA, R 58 268.
31. Herzstein, *The War that Hitler Won*, p. 405.
32. J. Baird, *The Mythical World of Nazi War Propaganda, 1939–45* (Minnesota, University of Minnesota Press, 1974), p. 38.
33. Kirchner, *Flugblatt Propaganda*, Vol. 6, p. lxxv.
34. Buchbender, *Die Vierte Waffe*, p. 164.
35. *Ibid.*, p. 184.
36. TNA: PRO FO 898 63.
37. BA, R 58 990 and IPN, 184/35.11.73.
38. BA, R 58 268.
39. Herzstein, *The War that Hitler Won*, p. 414.
40. BA, R 58 268.
41. TNA: PRO HS6 696.
42. TNA: PRO FO 898 64.
43. C. Cruickshank, *The Fourth Arm: Psychological Warfare 1934–45* (London, David-Poynter, 1977), p. 160.
44. SPP, 3.1.1.3 Meldunek Nr 178.
45. BA, R 58 268.
46. IPN, 168/47.
47. IFZ, ED 325/5.
48. BA, R58 209.
49. BAMA, RH 53–23/43.
50. IPN LD, 1/115.
51. H. Frank, *Okupacja i Ruch Oporu w dzienniku Hansa Franka* (Warsaw, KIW, 1972), p. 411.
52. IPN, 168/47.
53. IPN, 168/47.
54. IPN LD, 1/110.
55. *Ibid.*
56. IPN, 168/46.
57. BA, NS 19 2450.

58. Baird, *The Mythical World*, p. 40.
59. R. Bruce Lockhart, *Comes the Reckoning* (London, Putnam, 1947), p. 158.
60. TNA: PRO FO 898 178.
61. TNA: PRO HS 4 138.
62. H. von Luck, *Panzer Commander* (London, Cassell, 1989), p. 240.
63. WBBH VII/50/6.

Bibliography

Allard, P. *Der Krieg der Lüge*, Leipzig, List, 1941
Anders, W. *Bez ostatniego rozdziašu*, London, Gryf, 1959
Auckland, R.G. *British Black Propaganda to Germany 1941–45*, Leeds, Psywar Society, 1989
Auderska, H. and Ziółek, Z. *Akcja N*, Warsaw, Czytelnik, 1972
Baird, J. *The Mythical World of Nazi War Propaganda, 1939–45*, Minnesota, University of Minnesota, 1974
Baker White, J. *The Big Lie*, London, Evans Bros, 1955
Balfour, M. *Propaganda in War 1939–45*, London, Routledge & Kegan Paul, 1979
Barker, E. *British Policy in South-East Europe in the Second World War*, London, Macmillan, 1976
Beevor, J. *SOE: Recollections and Reflections*, London, Bodley Head, 1981
Berger, C. *Broadsides and Bayonets*, San Rafael, Presido, 1961
Berghahn, V.R. 'Wehrmachtpropaganda', *Revue d'histoire de la deuxième Guerre Mondiale*, No. 54 (1971)
Bergmann, K. *Achtung! Feind-Propaganda*, Erlangen, Verlag D + C, 1974
Bethel, N. *The War Hitler Won*, London, Allen Lane, 1972
Blau, A. *Propaganda als Waffe*, Berlin, Bernhard & Graefe, 1935
——. *Geistige Kriegführung*, Potsdam, Voggenreiter, 1937
Boberach, H. *Meldungen aus dem Reich*, Herrsching, Pawlak, 1984
Boelcke, A. *Kriegspropaganda 1939–41*, Stuttgart, Deutsche Verlagsanstalt, 1966
——. *The Secret Conferences of Dr Goebbels 1939–43*, London, Weidenfeld & Nicolson, 1967

——. *Wollt Ihr den Totalen Krieg?*, Stuttgart, Deutsche Verlagsanstalt, 1967

Bond, B. *Liddell Hart: A Study of His Military Thought*, London, Cassell, 1977

Bór-Komorowski, T. *The Secret Army*, London, Gollancz, 1950

Borodziej, W. *Terror i polityka*, Warsaw, PAX, 1985

Bramsted, E. *Goebbels and N.S. Propaganda*, London, Cresset, 1965

Briggs, A. *The War of Words*, London, OUP, 1970

Broniewski, S. *Cakym Z.yclem*, Warsaw, PWN, 1983

Broszat, M. *NS Polenpolitik 1939–45*, Stuttgart, Deutsche Verlagsanstalt, 1961

Brown, A. *Bodyguard of Lies*, London, WH Allen, 1976

Bruce Lockhart, R. *Memoirs of a British Agent*, London, Putnam, 1932

——. *Comes the Reckoning*, London, Putnam, 1947

——. 'Political Warfare', *RUSI Journal* (May 1950)

Buchbender, O. *Heil Beil!*, Stuttgart, Seewald, 1974

——. *Die Vierte Waffe*, Lüneburg, Deutsche Studien, 1985

Buchbender, O. and Hauschild, R. *Geheimsender gegen Frankreich*, Hertford, Mittler, 1984

Buchbender, O. and Schuh, H. *Die Waffe die auf die Seele zielt*, Stuttgart, Motorbuch Verlag, 1983

Buchheim, H. *SS und Polizei im NS-Staat*, Duisdorf, Studiengesellschaft Für Zeitproben, 1964

Butler, E. *Amateur Agent*, London, Harrap, 1963

Churchill, W. *The Second World War*, London, Cassell, 1964

Clausewitz C. *On War*, London, Penguin, 1968

Cloet, R. 'Les Directives de Goebbels', *Revue d'histoire de la deuxième Guerre Mondiale* (October 1966)

Coker, C. 'What Would Sun Tzu Say about the War on Terrorism?', *RUSI Journal* (January 2002)

Cole, J. *Lord Haw-Haw and W. Joyce*, London, Faber & Faber, 1964

Cookridge, E. *Inside SOE*, London, Arthur Baku, 1966

Crossman, R. 'Psychological Warfare', *RUSI Journal* (August 1952, August 1953, November 1953)

Cruickshank, C. *The Fourth Arm: Psychological Warfare 1934–45*, London, David-Poynter, 1977

——. *Deception in World War II*, London, OUP, 1981

Cunningham, C. Beaulieu: *The Finishing School for Secret Agents*, Barnsley, Leo Cooper, 1998

Cygański, M. *Z dziejów okupacji hitlerowskiej w Šodźi*, Šódź, Wydawnictwo Šódzkie, 1965

Dalton, H. *The Fateful Years*, London, Muller, 1957

——. *The World War II Diary*, London, Jonathan Cape, 1986
Daugherty and Janowitz. *A Psychological Warfare Casebook*, Baltimore, John Hopkins University, 1958
Davies, N. *Rising '44*, London, Macmillan, 2003
Deakin, W. et al. *British Political and Military Strategy in Central, Eastern and Southern Europe in 1944*, Basingstoke, Macmillan, 1988
Delmer, S. *Black Boomerang*, London, Secker & Warburg, 1962
Department of the Army. *Psychological Operations. US Army Doctrine*, Field Manual Fm. 33–1, 1971
——. *The Art and Science of Psychological Operations*, Washington, 1976
Dewar, M. *The Art of Deception in Warfare*, Newton Abbot, David & Charles, 1989
Dobroszycki, J. *Reptile Journalism*, New Haven and London, Yale University Press, 1994
Dorril, S. *MI6*, London, Fourth Estate, 2001
Dunan, E. 'La Propaganda – Abteilung de France', *Revue d'histoire de la deuxième Guerre Mondiale*, No. 4 (1951)
Dunin-Wasowicz, K. *Warszawa w latach 1939–45*, Warsaw, PWN, 1984
Evans, R. *The Coming of the Third Reich*, London, Penguin, 2004
Farago, L. *German Psychological Warfare*, New York, CNN, 1941
——. *War of Wits*, London, Hutchinson, 1956
——. *The Game of Foxes*, London, Hodder, 1972
Fellgiebel, E. *Aufklärung und Propaganda*, Militärwissenschaft Rundschau, 1938
Filar, A. *Nasz czšowiek w Abwehrze*, Kraków, Zw. Lit. Pol., 2000
Fischer, L. *Raporty 1939–44*, Warsaw, KIW, 1987
Fontane, T. *Der Krieg gegen Frankreich 1870–71*, Berlin, 1875
Foot, M.R.D. *SOE in France*, London, HMSO, 1966
——. *Resistance*, London, Granada, 1979
——. *SOE 1940–46*, London, BBC Books, 1984
——. 'What Use was SOE?', *RUSI Journal* (February 2003)
Ford, N. *Language in Uniform*, Indianapolis, Odyssey, 1967
Frank, H. *Okupacja i ruch oporu w dzienniku Hansa Franka*, Warsaw, KIW, 1972
Fraser, L. *Propaganda*, Oxford, OUP, 1957
Fritsche, H. *Es Sprach Hans Fritsche*, Stuttgart, Thiele, 1949
Garliński. J. *Poland, SOE and the Allies*, London, George Allen, 1969
Garnett, D. *The Secret History of PWE*, London, St Ermin's, 2002
Gehlen, R. *The Service*, New York, Popular Library, 1972
Geiss, I. *Deutsche Politik in Polen 1939–45*, Bonn, Opladen, 1988

Gellately, R. *Backing Hitler*, London, OUP, 2001
Gittig, H. *Illegale antifaschistische Tarnschriften 1933–1945*, Leipzig, VEB, 1972
Goebbels, J. *Diaries*, London, Hamish Hamilton, 1948
——. *Diaries*, Zürich, Lochner Doubleday, 1948
——. *Tagebücher*, Munich, KG Saur, 1996
Gourevitch, J.-P. *La Propagande dans tous ses Etats*, Paris, Flammarion, 1981
Grudziński, E. *N Drapacz*, Warsaw, Najnowsze Dzieje Polski, 1959, Vol. 2
Gunzenhaeuser, M. *Geschichte des Geheimen Nachrichtendienstes*, Frankfurt, Bernard & Graefe, 1968
Hadamowsky, E. *Propaganda und nationale Macht*, Oldenburg, 1933
Haldane, R.A. *The Hidden War*, London, Robert Hale, 1978
Handel, M. *Sun Tzu and Clausewitz*, Carlisle, Barracks, 1991
Hansi, W. *A Travers les Lignes Ennemies*, Paris, Payot, 1922
Harris, E. *The 'Un-American' Weapon*, New York, Lads, 1967
Herwig, D. and Rode, H. *Luftwaffe Secret Projects*, Hinckley, Midland Publishing, 2000
Herzog, L. and Radziwończyk, K. *Walka zbrojna Narodu Polskiego pod okupacją hitlerowską w świetle dokumentów Wehrmachtu*, Warsaw, Wojskowy Przeglad Historyczny, 1966, No. 4
Hertzstein, R. *The War that Hitler Won*, London, Hamish Hamilton, 1979
Hitler, A. *Mein Kampf*, London, Hurst & Blackett, 1938
HMSO. *Persuading the People*, London, HMSO, 1995
Hosang, J. *Gezahnte Kriegspropaganda*, Sollingen, the Author, 1954
Howe, E. *The Black Game*, London, Michael Joseph, 1982
Hundhausen, C. *Propaganda*, Essen, Girardet, 1975
Huxley, A. *Brave New World*, London, Chatto & Windus, 1987
Ishoven, A. *Willy Messerschmitt*, Vienna, Paul Neff, 1975
Jacobmeyer, W. *Die Polnische Wiederstandsbewegung in GG und ihre Beurteilung durch Deutsche Dienststellen*, Munich, Vierteljahrhefte Für Zeitgeschichte, 1977
Jones, R.V. *Most Secret War*, London, Coronet, 1978
Kawczyński, A. *Unternehmen N*, Munich, Vierteljahrhefte Für Zeitgeschichte, 1966
Keegan, J. *The Second World War*, London, Arrow, 1990
——. *A History of Warfare*, London, Hutchinson, 1993
Kirchner, K. *Wanted for Incitement to Murder*, Erlangen, Verlag D + C, 1972

——. *Achtung! Feind Propaganda!*, Erlangen, Verlag D + C, 1974
——. *Flugblätter, Psychologische Kriegsführung in 2 Weltkrieg*, Munich, Carl Hanser Verlag, 1974
——. *Krankheit rettet*, Erlangen, Verlag D + C, 1976
——. *Flugblatt Propaganda im 2 Weltkrieg*, XV+ Vols, Erlangen, Verlag D + C, 1978+
——. *Bayern und der Frieden*, Erlangen, Verlag D + C, 1983
——. *Handbook of Leaflets*, Erlangen, Verlag D + C, 2001
——. *Kriegsflugblätter – eine Waffe die jeden Traf*, Erlangen, Verlag D + C
Kitchen, M. *British Policy towards the S.U. during World War II*, London, Macmillan, 1986
Kochanowicz, T. *Na wojennej emigracji*, Warsaw, KIW, 1975
Korboński, S. *W Imieniu R.P.*, Paris, Instytut Literacki, 1954
Kozaczuk, W. *Wojna w eterze*, Warsaw, Radio i Telewizja, 1977
Koziej, S. *Teoria sztuki wojennej*, Warsaw, Bellona, 1993
Krause, G. *Die Britische Auslandspropaganda*, Berlin, Stubenrauch, 1940
Krausnick, H. and Wilhelm, H-H. *Die Truppe des Weltanschaungskrieges*, Stuttgart, DVA, 1981
Kwiatkowski, M. *Polskie Radio w konspiracji*, Warsaw, PIW, 1989
Laffin, J. *Links of Leadership*, London, Harrap, 1966
Lambert, R.S. *Propaganda*, London, T. Nelson, 1939
Lang, J. *Die Gestapo: Instrument des Terrors*, Hamburg, Rash & Roehring, 1990
Lasswell, H. *Propaganda Technique in World War I*, London, Kegan, 1927
Lenin, V. *Selected Works*, London, Lawrence & Wishart, 1921
Lerner, D. *Sykewar*, New York, GW Stewart, 1949
——. *Psychological Warfare against Nazi Germany*, USA, MIT Press, 1971
——. et al. *Propaganda in War and Crisis*, New York, GW Stewart, 1951
Lerski, J. *Emisariusz Jur*, London, PFK, 1984
Levy, C. 'L'Organisation de la propagande allemande en France', *Revue d'histoire de la deuxième Guerre Mondiale* (October 1966)
Lewandowska, S. *Akta Gestapo w Wiedniu*, Warszawa, Dzieje Najnowsze, 1980, No. 3
——. *Polska konspiracyjna prasa*, Warsaw, Czytelnik, 1982
Liddell Hart, B. *Defence of the West*, London, Cassell, 1950
Linebarger, P. *Psychological Warfare*, Washington, Infantry Journal Press, 1948
Lloyd, M. *The Art of Military Deception*, Barnsley, Leo Cooper, 1997
Luck, H. von. *Panzer Commander*, London, Cassell, 1989
Mackenzie, W. *The Secret History of SOE*, London, St Ermin's, 2000
Madajczyk, C. *Polityka III Rzeszy w Polsce*, Warsaw, PWN, 1970

Malczewski, F. *Z teorii i praktyki propagandy*, Warsaw, Czytelnik, 1967
Malinowski, K. *Zošnierze Šączności walczącej Warszawy*, Warsaw, PAX, 1983
Manderstam, L. *From the Red Army to SOE*, London, Kimber, 1985
Marks, L. *Between Silk and Cyanide*, London, HarperCollins, 1998
Matusak, P. *Front walki propagandowej*, Warsaw, Wojskowy Przegląd Historyczny, 1980, Nos 1/2
Mazur, G. *BIP*, Warsaw, PAX, 1987
——. *Akcja Dywersyjna N*, Wrocšaw, Ossolineum, 2000
Megret, M. *La Guerre Psychologique*, Paris, Universitaires, 1956
Muenzenberg, W. *Propaganda als Waffe*, Paris, Editions du Carrefour, 1937
Našęc, W. (Żenczykowski, T.). *Nowa broń*, Warsaw, TWZW, 1943
——. *Radio Jako środek Propagandy*, Warsaw, TWZW, 1943
Nobecourt, R. *Les secrets de la propagande en France Occupée*, Paris, Fayard, 1962
Nowak, J. *Kurier z Warszawy*, London, Odnowa, 1978
Paine, L. *German Military Intelligence in World War II*, London, Stein & Day, 1984
Pether, J. *Black Propaganda*, Bletchley Park, Bletchley Park Trust, 1998
Philby, K. *My Silent War*, London, Harrap, 1963
Pick, F.W. *The Art of Dr Goebbels*, London, Robert Hale, 1942
Pilcher, T. *War According to Clausewitz*, London, Cassell, 1918
Piotrowski, S. *Dziennik H Franka*, Warsaw, Wydawnictwo Prawnicze, 1956
Pollack, J. *Wywiad, sabotaż, dywersja*, Warsaw, Ludowa Spóšdzielnia Wydawnicza, 1991
Ponsonby, A. *Falsehood in War-Time*, London, Allen & Unwin, 1928
Prag, W. and Jacobmeyer, W. *Das Diensttagebuch des Deutschen GG in Polen 39–45*, Stuttgart, the Authors, 1975
Price, A. *The Last Year of the Luftwaffe*, London, Arms & Armour, 1993
Qualter, T. *Propaganda and Psychological Warfare*, New York, Random House, 1962
Radnitzki, S. *Die I-Waffen*, Munich, Herbig, 1982
Rhodes, A. *Propaganda in World War II*, New York, Chelsea, 1976
Riegel, O.W. *Mobilising for Chaos*, New Haven, Yale University Press, 1936
Riesch, E. *Das Flugblatt im Luftrecht*, Archiv Für Luftrecht, 1933, No. 3
Rigden, D. *SOE Syllabus*, London, PRO, 2001
Roetter, C. *Psychological Warfare*, London, Batsford, 1974
Rogerson, S. *Propaganda in the Next War*, London, Bless, 1938

Rossignol, D. *Histoire de la propagande en France 1940–1944*, Paris, Presses Universitaires, 1991

Rudziński, E. *Wojna i konspiracja*, Warsaw, PWN, 1987

Rzepecki, J. *Organizacja i działanie BIP*, Warsaw, Wojskowy Przeglad Historyczny, 1971, Nos 2–4

——. *O wydawnictwach Akcji N*, Warsaw, Wojskowy Przeglad Historyczny, 1972, No. 2

Scheel, K. *Krieg über Aetherwellen*, Berlin, V. der Wiss, 1970

Schmidt, H. *Kriegspropaganda und Propagandakrieg*, Zürich, Beer, 1947

Schnabel, R. *Misbrauchte Mikrophone*, Wien, Europa-Verlag, 1967

Schramm, W. *The Nature of Psychological War*, Washington, Department of the Army, 1953

——. *Der Geheimdienst in Europa 1937–45*, Munich, Heyne, 1980

Seth, R. *The Truth Benders*, London, Frewin, 1969

Shils, E. 'Cohesion and Disintegration in the Wehrmacht in World War II', *Public Opinion Quarterly* (summer 1948)

Shirer, W. *The Rise and Fall of the Third Reich*, London, Secker & Warburg, 1960

Ślaski, J. *Polska Walczaca*, Warsaw, PAX, 1985

Snyder, L. *Encyclopedia of the Third Reich*, London, McGraw-Hill, 1998

Stafford, D. *Wielka Brytania i ruch oporu w Europie*, Warsaw, PAX, 1980

——. *Secret Agent*, London, BBC, 2000

Steinert, M. *Hitler's War and the Germans*, Ohio, OUP, 1977

Stevenson, W. *A Man Called Intrepid*, London, Sphere, 1981

Stokes, L. *The SD of the Reichsführer SS and German Public Opinion*, USA, John Hopkins University Press, 1972

Stoliński, K. *Counterfeiting of Currency by Frederic II*, London, the Author, 2001

Stroech, J. *Die illegale Presse 1933–39*, Frankfurt, Rödergerg, 1979

Stuart, Sir Campbell Arthur, *Secrets of Crew House*, London, Hodder & Stoughton, 1920

Studium Polski Podziemnej. *AK w dokumentach*, VI Vols, London, SPP, 1970–89

Sun Tzu. *The Art of War*, Oxford, Clarendon, 1963

Taylor, P. *Munitions of the Mind*, London, P. Stephens, 1990

Tchakhotine, S. *Le viol des foules par la propagande politique*, Paris, Gallinnard, 1952

Tebinka, J. *Polityka Brytyjska wobec problemu granicy Polsko-Radzieckiej*, Warsaw, Neriton, 1998

Tennant, P. *Touchlines of War*, Hull, University of Hull Press, 1992

Thimme, H. *Weltkrieg ohne Waffen*, Stuttgart, Cotta, 1932
Volkoff, V. *La désinformation*, Paris, Julliard, 1986
Wedel, H. *Die Propagandatruppen der Deutschen Wehrmacht*, Neckargemuend, Scharnhorst, 1962
WIH. *Polski czyn zbrojny w 2 Wojnie Św., Polski Ruch Oporu*, Warsaw, MON, 1988
Wilkinson, P. and Atley, J. *Gubbins and SOE*, Barnsley, Leo Cooper, 1993
Winkler, A. *The Politics of Propaganda*, New Haven, Yale University Press, 1978
Wittek, B. *Der Britischer Aetherkrieg gegen das 3 Reich*, Münster, Fahle, 1962
Wojewódzki, M. *W tajnych drukarniach Warszawy 1939–44*, Warsaw, PIW, 1976
——. *Akcja Reichenau*, Warsaw, KAW, 1984
Wright, P. *Spy Catcher*, New York, Viking Penguin, 1987
Zagórski, W. *Wolność w niewoli*, London, the Author, 1971
Zawadzka, A. *Pešnić śšužbę*, Warsaw, PIW, 1987
Zawodny, J. *Powstanie Warszawskie w walce i dyplomacji*, Warsaw, PWN, 1994
Zazworka, G. *Psychologische Kriegsführung*, Militärverlag, 1962
Zeman, Z. *Nazi Propaganda*, London, OUP, 1964
Zenczykowski, T. *Wspomnienia z Akcji 'N'*, London, Orzeš Biašy, January 1980
Zióšek, Z. *Dywersyjna propaganda antyhitle rowska*, M/S WBBH 111/50/27
Zwiazek Šącznościowców. *Dziękuję wam Rodacy*, London, PFK, 1973

Main Primary Sources

Bundesarchiv, Berlin (BA)

NS 19: 1429, 2450
R 43: 11639
R 55: 20782
R 58: 209, 211, 218, 268, 953, 990

Bundesarchiv – Militärarchiv, Freiburg (BAMA)

RW4: 245, 249, 248 6

Instytut Pami¸eci Narodowej, Warsaw (IPN)

168/46, 168/47, 184/35.11.73

Instytut Pami¸eci Narodowej, Šódź (IPN LD)

1/110 8911 42, 1/115 19, 1/118

Liddell Hart Centre for Military Archives, London (LH)

Dobrski: 1/2, 1/3, 14

The National Archive, London (TNA)

PRO CAB 16 127
PRO CAB 21 1071
PRO CAB 23: 96 375, 99 325
PRO CAB 65 1 215
PRO CAB 66 2
PRO COS (40) 390
PRO DEFE 28 48
PRO FO 371 34556
PRO FO 898: 1, 6, 7, 8, 51, 52, 54, 61, 63, 64, 67, 70, 101, 178, 183, 224, 225, 426, 454, 501
PRO HS 4: 138, 165, 170, 302
PRO HS 6 696
PRO HS 149 11/11/40
PRO INF 1: 188, 265, 266

Polish Underground Movement (1939–45) Study Trust (SPP)

A1.4.1.42
A2: 3.1.1.3.3, 3.11.3.26, 3.11.3.75
A3: 1.1.4.88, 19.2/5
SK 15/10
2.3: 11.1.35, 11.3, 11.3.65
3.1.3/178
3.6.3.2/26
3.6.8.2

Index

Abetz, Otto 55
Amies, Hardy 30
Andorra 63
Andreas, Father 139
Ankara 65, 150
Antwerp 25
Arras 32, 52
Auschwitz 139

Baden-Powell, Sir Robert 8
Badoglio, Marshal Pietro 22, 24
Bapaume 52
Belgrade 63, 120
Bentivegni, General Egbert von 36
Berlin 49, 56, 65, 99, 104ff., 116, 119, 126, 200, 225, 227, 235, 255, 265, 287, 294ff., 305
Bern 112
Biašystok 234, 237
Bierkamp, Colonel 67, 258
Bismarck, Otto von 24, 272
Bletchley 17
Bletchley Park 267
Bock, Field Marshal Fedor von 212
Bologna 296
'Bór'-Komorowski, General Tadeusz 221, 236, 256ff., 264
Bowes-Lyon, David 118
Bracken, Viscount Brendan 76, 91
Braun, Max 114
Bremen 235
Brendt, Alfred 39
Bruce Lockhart, Sir Robert 12, 74, 91, 109, 123
Bruges 296
Brunswick 235
Bucharest 63, 65
Bülow, Freiherr Adam von 22

Casablanca 309ff., 313
Chamberlain, Neville 84
Cherbourg 296
Churchill, Winston 51, 58ff., 79, 87, 107, 115–6, 119, 135, 211, 217, 220, 263, 288, 309

Cicero 20
Cieszyn 187
Clausewitz, Carl von 22, 25, 46
Clayton, Brigadier I. 89
Cologne 111, 136, 217, 235
Cripps, Sir Stafford 109
Crossman, Richard 32, 274
Cunningham, Admiral 142

Dachau 215
Dakar 56
Dalton, Baron Hugh 37, 87ff., 91, 145
Danzig 54
Delmer, Sefton *passim*
Dietrich, Marlene 126
Dietrich, Otto 36, 55, 65
Dönitz, Grand Admiral Karl 72, 254
Dublin 59
Duff Cooper, Viscount Alfred 76, 79
Dunkirk 56, 277
Düsseldorf 288
Dziewanowski, Major 139, 248, 251ff.

Eden, Anthony 91
Eisenhower, General Dwight D. 135
Essen 228

Falklands 16
Fegelein, *Waffen-SS* Lieutenant General Hermann 140
Ferdonnet, Paul 41ff.
Fisher, Warsaw District Governor 222, 226
Flensburg 72
Florence 68, 120
Foot, M.R.D. 32, 75
Fort Stanwix 25
Franco, General Francisco 38, 47
Frank, Hans 232, 250ff.
Frankfurt 137
Frederick the Great 23
Freisler, Roland 284
Fritsche, Hans 13, 104, 109, 288
Fuller, J.F.C. 12

Gdańsk 221
Gdynia 221, 299
Geneva 65
Giraudoux, Jean 45
Goebbels, Joseph *passim*
Goering, Hermann 43, 73, 114, 155, 206, 216–7, 273
Grand, Major Laurence 85
Gregory XV 26
Grodno 237
'Grot'-Rowecki, General Stefan 30, 188, 189ff., 242ff., 250, 255
Gubbins, General Colin 74, 243
Gürtner, Franz 280
Gutenberg 23, 27

Hamburg 228, 235
Hannover 235
Harris, Marshal of the RAF Sir Arthur 79, 253
Hazell, Major Ronald 249
Helsinki 65
Hess, Rudolf 116ff., 208, 213
Himmler, Heinrich 70ff., 154, 163, 286, 307
Hindenburg, General Field Marshal Paul von 24
Hitler, Adolf *passim*
Howard, Sir Michael 33

Howe, Ellic 39, 58, 105, 138, 151, 163, 256
Huxley, Aldous 11

Istanbul 59, 65, 112

Johst 154ff.
Joyce, William (Lord Haw Haw) 59ff.

Kassel 235
Katyń 65
Kielce v, 15
Kirkpatrick, Sir Ivone 259
Komorowski *see* 'Bór'-Komorowski
Koppe, *SS* General Wilhelm 189, 222, 232, 268
Korboński, Stefan 261
Kot, Stanisšaw 246
Kraków 102, 188, 226, 228, 299, 304
Kurt Eggers 166, 307

Lahousen, General Erwin 16
Lammers, Hans 281
Lawrence of Arabia 87
Leeper, Sir Reginald 90, 117, 138, 278, 282
Leipzig 137, 235
Lenin 20
Ley, Robert 146
Lisbon 59, 65, 102, 111, 112, 150
Livorno 142
Lockhart *see* Bruce Lockhart
Lódź 197, 203, 229, 234, 267, 298–9, 302
London 65ff., 102ff.,105, 187, 242, 246, 260, 265, 293, 309
Lorient 132
Lublin 296
Luck, Hans von 312
Ludendorff, Erich 19
Lwów 120

McLaren, Moray 259, 263
Macmillan, Lord 76
Madrid 59, 65
Malta 142
Mander 130
Mannstein, Field Marshal Erich von 206, 211, 257
Matejka 216
Maurois, André 53
Mauthausen 140
Mers-el-Kebir 56
Metternich, Klemens Fürst von 26
Milan 189
Milton Bryan 124
Model, Field Marshal Walther 167
Mola, General Emilio 47
Mölders, General Werner 154
Mollwitz 23
Moltke, Field Marshal Helmuth von 17
Monte Carlo 63
Monte Cassino 307
Moscow 74ff., 262, 265, 293
Müller, Heinrich 198, 294, 299, 305
München-Gladbach 236
Munich 81, 84, 142, 209, 235
Münster 219
Mussolini, Benito 29, 142, 219, 306

Napoleon 22, 25
New York 63
Newsome, Noel 123
Northcliffe, Viscount Alfred 18, 28, 187
Nostradamus 47

Nowy Targ 188
Nuremberg 16, 73

Ohlenbusch 250
Ohlendorf, *SS* General Otto 290
Olbrecht, André 41
Oxford 99

Paris 27, 49, 52ff., 55, 187, 297
Pearl Harbor 144
Perkins, Colonel Harold 246–7
Philby, Kim 74, 90
Pontelier 238
Portal, Air Marshal Viscount Charles 30
Poznań 187, 213, 244, 264
Prague 265
Protasewicz, Colonel Michaš 247ff., 251, 256ff., 263
Prugar-Kettling, General Bronisšaw 237ff.

Radom 69, 300, 304ff.
'Rawa' *see* Protasewicz
Reichenau, Field Marshall Walther von 210ff.
Reiholz, Johannes 113
Reith, John 76
Ribbentrop, Joachim von 37, 44, 55, 62, 72, 146
Röhm, Ernst 36, 208
Roosevelt, Franklin D. 118, 144, 309ff.
Rosenberg, Alfred 36
Rowecki *see* Grot

St Nazaire 126
Schellenberg, *Waffen-SS* General Walther 64
Schleier, Rudolf 43
Schlieker, Willy 161
Schöngarth 304
Schweinfurt 46
Seckelmann, Peter 113, 114
Sedan 52
Selborne, Lord Roundell 91
Seyss-Inquart, Artur von 69, 72
Shanghai 63
Shirer, W.L. 52
Sikorski, General Wšadysšaw 59, 138, 211, 217, 246, 259, 261, 263ff.
Sinclair, Admiral Viscount Thurso 84
Skorzeny, *Waffen-SS* Colonel Otto 142
Sofia 65
Speer, Albert 161
Spiecker, 'Mr Turner' 105
Stalin 68, 71, 309ff., 314
Stalingrad 54, 217, 275, 287, 308
Stockholm 59, 65, 112, 126, 150
Stuart, Sir Campbell 80, 84, 85, 87, 89
Stuttgart 41, 42
Sun Tzu 19, 20, 33, 54, 163
Szczecin 221

Tallents, Sir Stephen 76, 83
Teheran 73
Thornhill, Colonel Cudbert 89
Thurston, Major 139, 247, 251, 254, 258
Todt, Fritz 211ff.
Toruń 298
Tours 49
Truszkowski, Major Richard 258

Udet, General Ernst 211, 214

Valencia 63
Valladolid 63

Vansitart, Baron Robert 77
Vatican 140
Versailles 310
Vichy 65
Vienna 119, 228, 289, 295
Vietinghoff, General Heinrich von 307

Warsaw 40, 52, 56, 68ff., 97, 102, 156, 186ff., 198, 204, 222, 226, 229, 234, 237, 242, 256, 258, 261, 302, 303, 314
Washington DC 119
Washington, George 25
Wedel, H. von 49
Wells, H.G. 18
Weygand, General Maxime 52
Wieliczka 233
Wiesenthal, Simon 250
Wilkinson, Colonel Peter 247, 251
Wilson, Horace 78, 83
Woburn 124, 134
Woburn Abbey 87
Wolff, *Waffen-SS* General Karl 286

Yalta 73

Zech-Nenntwich 140
Zeisel, Henry 125
Zeitzler, General Kurt 286
Żenczykowski, Tadeusz 190
Ziółek, Zygmunt 209
Zurich 59, 63